SEX AND SELF-RESPECT

SEX AND SELF-RESPECT

The Quest for Personal Fulfillment

PHILIP M. HELFAER

Westport, Connecticut
London

Library of Congress Cataloging-in-Publication Data

Helfaer, Philip M., 1933–
    Sex and self-respect : the quest for personal fulfillment / Philip
M. Helfaer.
        p. cm.
    Includes bibliographical references (p.) and index.
    ISBN 0-275-96185-0 (alk. paper)
    1. Sex (Psychology) I. Title.
BF692.H447 1998
155.3—dc21   98-4945

British Library Cataloguing in Publication Data is available.

Library of Congress Catalog Card Number: 98-4945
ISBN: 0-275-96185-0

First published in 1998

Praeger Publishers, 88 Post Road West, Westport, CT 06881
An imprint of Greenwood Publishing Group, Inc.

Printed in the United States of America

The paper used in this book complies with the
Permanent Paper Standard issued by the National
Information Standards Organization (Z39.48–1984).

10 9 8 7 6 5 4 3 2 1

Copyright Acknowledgments

The author and publisher gratefully acknowledge permission for use of the following material:

Excerpts from *Character Analysis* by Wilhelm Reich, translated by Vincent R. Carfagno. Copyright © 1945, 1949, 1972 by The Wilhelm Reich Infant Trust. Reprinted by permission of Farrar, Straus & Giroux, Inc.

Excerpts from *The Funciton of the Orgasm* by Wilhelm Reich, translated by Vincent R. Carfagno. Copyright © 1973 by The Wilhelm Reich Infant Trust. Reprinted by permission of Farrar, Straus & Giroux, Inc.

The poem, "The Abandoned Baby," by Kathleen Spivack, from *Swimmer in the Spreading Dawn*, published by Applewood Books, 1981. Reprinted by permission of the author.

Chapters (or parts thereof) 3, 5, 6, 8, 12, and 13 were adapted from material previously published in *Bioenergetic Analysis: The Clinical Journal of the International Institute for Bioenergetic Analysis*.

for Vellie

CONTENTS

ACKNOWLEDGMENTS

The emotional and intellectual sources of this book extend far back through my history, but here, following customary practice, I mention only the most immediate influences and supports. I am grateful for the gift of bioenergetic analysis which is the life work of Alexander Lowen, M.D. His writings, teaching, and therapy, and the opportunity to teach in the institute he founded allowed me to develop the tools for the work presented here.

I am grateful to four whose friendship goes back thirty years or more and whose presence in my life has buoyed and sustained my energy for this project. Over the years of our friendship Elliot Baker never flagged in his support and oft-spoken faith in me. Ildri L. B. Ginn, friend and colleague in many settings, has been an endless fount of loving faith and belief in my work. Kathleen Spivack—poet, novelist, teacher, encourager of creativity— generously gave wisdom and guidance in developing the book and in the ups and downs of seeking publication. Of only slightly more recent vintage, running buddy Frank Gallo helped me keep a lot of things in perspective.

Sarah Baker made available to me her excitement and knowledge of art history. Timely secretarial work by friend and good neighbor, Jody Burnham, with support from her husband, Pen, was big help just in time. I thank Nita Romer, acquisitions editor at Praeger Publishers, for her take on my project.

I am grateful to those who have entered with me into the profound process of learning about themselves—students and clients. The knowledge and understanding I have gained along with them is precious beyond words.

My indebtedness to my wife, Velma Helfaer, can hardly be expressed in a few words. The reader should know that this book is a joint project. She edited every page of every draft. More than that, however, the vision I have expressed here is one we arrived at together. We were there together every step of the way.

INTRODUCTION

In the enduring quest for sexual love, we seek our deepest fulfillment and find our deepest pain, and in this quest we find the most profound challenge to who we are and how we feel about ourselves. I arrive at this conclusion after more than twenty-five years as a psychologist listening to the painful stories of my clients. To learn to help others I found I needed to understand sexuality and the nature of the self in a depth, breadth, and manner that I could not have imagined when I undertook the study of clinical psychology as a young man. I needed theoretical knowledge about the biology of the human organism and the psychology of personality, and I needed to understand myself; so a lot of my learning was experiential. My own being and story became the laboratory and the book. I found this to be the toughest kind of learning. In this book, I try to put into words some of what I have learned so far.

Sexuality and selfhood are the broad themes. Human sexual behavior, like other animal sexuality, is the outcome of evolution, and sex is the medium through which evolution worked to create our present form. Human sexuality is unique, however, in being profoundly influenced by culture. Many versions of masculinity and femininity emerge when human biology—our sexuality—is lived in and through culture.

A profound aspect of our being emerges out of the confluence of our biology and our culture—the self. Each self—each of us—has cognizance of our own yearnings for fulfillment and, given fortuitous circumstances, will pursue fulfillment in one of multitudinous possible ways. This quest is necessarily, inevitably, and uniquely tied to the expression, fulfillment, and fate of our sexuality.

While the fulfillment of selfhood is ineluctably linked with the fulfillment of sexuality, the two are not always identical. I view them as two poles of personhood, two poles that stand in a dialectical relationship with one another. Sex is fundamentally the expression of one pole. I have chosen to use the term *self-respect* as the name for the expression of the other pole.

From these lines of thought I derived the title of this text: *Sex and Self-Respect: The Quest for Personal Fulfillment.* My aim is to explore the biology and psychology of sexuality and selfhood in order to understand how personal fulfillment is realized or frustrated.

Sex is considered by many to be one of the greatest joys and pleasures life provides. I offer no promise, however, that this book will enhance your joy or pleasure in sex, not that I might not wish that it would for any who so desire. While I do not believe in offering promises through a book, I do believe that deep *wanting*—wanting sexual love and sexual fulfillment—is a powerful force. If wanting is combined with honest, courageous exploration of the self, in all likelihood the effort will be rewarded. Portions of this book are about just such explorations and some of the kinds of terrain they are likely to traverse.

We can enhance the pleasure, delight, and joy of sex through a deeper respect and treasuring of it and its source. Sex is not a supplement to life. It is the essence of life. We do not command the sources of pleasure, delight, or joy any more than we command the forces of life itself. These are gifts of life. Sex is not just one drive among others, although it is that too. For most ordinary men and women a relationship in which sex and love are fused is the foundation of all happiness.

The complexity of human sexuality is captured in the distinction between sex and sexuality. What does this distinction mean? Sexuality is not defined simply in terms of sexual acts or their absence. Sexuality must be seen as nothing more nor less than a fundamental principle of organization of the organism. Sexuality is the way the human being is organized, as male or female. To say that it is a fundamental principle of organization implies that other organismic functions of the self are influenced by sexuality or can be looked at in relation to sexuality. The exploration of sexuality means looking into the organism at its deepest levels.

The significance of sex and sexuality for our lives is self-evident, I believe, and needs no justification as the subject for a book. What about the theme of self-respect? Why should this theme complement that of sex? Self-respect, as I use the term, represents a form of organismic self-regulation having the same biological and cultural roots as sex. Self-respect is a bodily matter, and it has a developmental sequence paralleling the development of sexuality, yet it is a separate function.

The significance of the concept of self-respect is grasped by considering guilt, shame, humiliation, and self-hate. Self-respect is their functional antithesis. Self-respect is the healthy alternative to unhealthy guilt, shame, and self-hate. Shame, guilt, and self-hate are commonly found entwined in the individual's sexuality in our society. Self-respect permits good feelings as well as mutual respect.

Ultimately, the self is the body. Self-respect means living a life based on the reality and truths of the body. The first truth of the body is that it is a male one or a female one. For the individual to have self-respect, he or she must respect the maleness or femaleness of the body—and the focus of that resides in the genital itself. Self-respect, then, is based on an identification with the genital itself: "This is me, and this is good." This is a development that, if unviolated, occurs in early childhood.

In using the term *self-respect* I do not intend to advance a moral agenda. The final chapter presents some thoughts about a sexual ethic, but these do not constitute moral prescriptions. As I use it, self-respect does not refer to holding one's self with dignity. I also differentiate self-respect from self-esteem. Self-esteem issues are always tinged with anxiety, and reflect the necessity to manage one's feelings about one's self. Self-respect implies a state underlying self-esteem. It is impossible to feel good about one's self without self-respect, yet having self-respect does not always imply feeling good. With self-respect, I can respect myself when I have failed, when all seems lost, when my dreams are dashed, when I'm not healthy and strong, or when I have not won favor in the eyes of others.

Self-respect is the basis of my ongoing relationship with myself at the deepest feeling level. It effects how all my experiences are integrated into my being, determining whether any given experience becomes a force for growth or a force for depression and destructiveness. Self-respect is the basis for self-acceptance, the antidote for nagging self-doubts and self-criticisms. It does not imply self-absorption, self-enhancement, or self-aggrandizement. It is "ongoing" in nature, calming and steadying, although "quiet," unlike shame or guilt which are "noisy" in their experiential effects.

Sexuality, self-respect, and personal fulfillment are deeply linked. Chapters 1 and 2 develop the relationships among sexuality and selfhood, sex and self-respect, and personal fulfillment. Viewing the self as the body is the cornerstone of bioenergetic analysis. This theory is outlined in Chapters 2 and 3. The first three chapters form the outline of what I consider an organismic theory of the self. This differs from a theory of the mind.

In Part II violations of sexuality are described and analyzed. Violations of sexuality are the result of traumatic experiences of childhood, of which overt sexual abuse is only one form. They all result in maladaptive personality functioning in adulthood. Basic violations of sexuality are explored in depth: sexual misery (Chapter 4); violations of the Oedipal period (Chapter 5); sexual craziness (Chapter 6); shock, genital injury, and dissociation (Chapter 7); the hated child (Chapter 8); and shame, humiliation, and guilt (Chapter 9). If this seems like a dreary list, each is nonetheless a common human condition, and each deserves respect and careful consideration.

In Part III I explore how the positive development of sex and self-respect can be fostered. Any study of sexuality contains or implies a view of childhood sexuality (Chapters 5, 10, and 11). I take a critique of the Oedipus complex (Chapter 5) as a starting point for a fresh look at some of the basic issues, including an exploration of the nature of the child's actual relationships, what I call the vital connection (Chapter 10). I approach child development with the basic question, What characteristics of the child's environment facilitate self-respect and sexual health (Chapter 11)?

The enduring partnership formed when a man and woman choose each other as sexual partners and remain together offers the deepest opportunity, in adulthood, for the further positive development of sexuality and selfhood, sex and self-respect (Chapter 12).[1] Since my investigations are directed toward understanding the realization of personal fulfillment, I address in the final chapter the meaning, as I see it, of living one's sexuality. This entails considerations of a sexual ethic.

Part I

TOWARD AN ORGANISMIC THEORY OF THE SELF

Part I presents the essential concepts of organismic functionalism. Pulsation, the ordinary rhythmic movement of living tissue, is the fundamental biological phenomenon of this view. Sex and self-respect are analyzed in terms of the principles of organismic functionalism. An individual's sexuality and selfhood are the outcomes of developmental adaptations of that person's biology to life in a given family and sociocultural world. An identification with the genital, or its disturbance, is the core of that adaptation, and will be reflected in the very being of the man or woman as he or she seeks fulfillment. The self's fulfillment originates more in the life of the cells of the body than in the ego's accomplishments.

SEX AND SELF-RESPECT IN PERSONAL FULFILLMENT

> The living *simply functions,* it has no "meaning."
> —Wilhelm Reich

SEXUALITY AND SELFHOOD

We humans are essentially sexual creatures. Our pursuit and fulfillment of a sexual life and reproduction are key elements of our personal fulfillment. Paradoxically, however, while they are key to personal fulfillment, they are not simply matters of personal choice: they are behavioral expressions of our biology. We do not choose to be or not be sexual beings.

Sex reaches into the deepest biological layers of the organism, and it extends into every aspect of the individual's social functioning. Consider a specific sexual act. Its bodily engagements—desire, genital sensations, the body's whole response in orgasm—are obvious; its social aspects, perhaps less so. Most usually, sex is experienced as a personal event apart from society. Its refreshment comes, in some measure, from just that aspect of the experience. In reality, however, meanings, feelings, roles, and relationships experienced in sex are also intrinsic to or derived from society and the individual's history and position in a society. We see here a polarity between organismic—bodily—aspects of sex and social aspects, both meeting in, and having a common root in, the individual person.

We see the same kind of polarity in the case of self-respect. Self-respect is an organismic, bodily matter, not simply a psychological one. It rests on the same biological functions as sex, and it arises from the same biological heritage as sex. At the same time, self-respect, a keenly personal matter, reflects our sensitivity to our position within our group, our tribe, our community. In fact, our sociality, itself, is given to us through our biological heritage at the same time it is indelibly colored by a unique, personal, sociopsychological history.

If biological, sociocultural, and psychological polarities characterize sex and self-respect, they must also characterize an understanding of the quest for personal fulfillment. In the light of these polarities, we can see that personal fulfillment is not something we either chose (egocentrically) to pursue, or chose (altruistically) to eschew in favor of some "higher" goal. Neither sex nor self-respect can be understood as simply "egocentric" or "altruistic," since each can be seen in the light of both these dimensions. I point this out because offering a discussion of "the quest for personal fulfillment" may evoke an equivocal response. For one thing, it might be taken to have a selfish ring, reflecting a discreditable self-centeredness. However, the nature of personal fulfillment, as I see it, is not such that it is amenable to glib manipulation, egocentric or otherwise, nor is it in our hands at all, in the most fundamental of ways.

Personal fulfillment, then, in all its positive or frustrated variants, is an experiential outgrowth of the inevitable and powerful movements in our lives driven by the forces of our biology and our adaptation to our social world. Sex and self-respect are twin aspects of that biologically rooted quest. In addition, personal fulfillment, in the terms in which I understand it, is not a condition in opposition to a meaningful sociality. On the contrary, they are both to be found along the same avenue—through sex and self-respect.

To understand these matters in the broadest perspective we need to think in terms of sexuality and selfhood. "Sex" refers to the sexual act, or to the fact of being male or female, whereas "sexuality" encompasses all that array of matters pertaining thereto, including the particular *way* in which one man or one woman *is* a man or woman in the world. "Selfhood" is a way of referring to the whole range of states—and estates—involved in being a person. Sexuality and selfhood can be viewed as two great principles of individual organization within whose terms we can find a comprehensive understanding of the person.

Sexuality and selfhood are intimately interrelated, two aspects of the same organism which are never separated. Their mutual development forms an integral whole, in the same way that the root and crown of a tree form a whole. If sexuality were the root, selfhood would be the crown; neither can be damaged without damaging the other. Sexuality and selfhood are also functions of the organism.

Sexuality and selfhood, by their very nature personal, are also expressions of the way in which the individual is embedded in his or her social world. Both personal and social aspects of these functions are expressions of the underlying biological life of the organism. This sequence of polarities can be nicely captured by a diagrammatic schema invented by Wilhelm Reich.[1] Figure 1 shows sexuality and selfhood as functions, or organizing principles, of the same biological organism. Their relationship is considered

Figure 1. Functional Polarities of the Organism

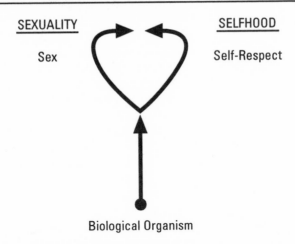

Source of diagram: Wilhelm Reich, *Function of the Orgasm,* Chapter 7.

a functional one because they arise from the same biological root, and whatever functions they represent must be coordinated for the organism's adaptation. Arising from the same biological root, sex and self-respect are initially identical. They then separate as distinct functions or principles of organization, and then they are juxtaposed as antithetical to each other. Reich termed this the identity and antithesis of biological functioning.[2]

It is not difficult to consider some of the surface possibilities suggested by the identity and antithesis of sex and self-respect. Sex in a situation that undermines the individual's self-respect has consequences, ones that inevitably cause distress. Sex in a situation in which self-respect is enhanced, enhances both, allowing for feeling good on many levels. Without sex, or its possibility, or capacity, self-respect may be undermined, leaving the person with a sense of impotence or emptiness. The sense of desiring and knowing one is capable of sex enhances self-respect, even without the actual experience or its possibility. In these ways, sex and self-respect function "identically."

Other examples indicate how they may function antithetically. The claims of self-respect may delay sexual activities, as when a person chooses to have sex only with a chosen partner. The claims of self-respect may help a person renounce an exciting but problematic sexual partner. The claims of self-respect may help one to free oneself from a burdensome sexual role, once assumed to be inherent in masculinity or femininity. Such "claims of self-respect," goading the individual to action, arise not simply from ideas about who one is or should be. They arise most fundamentally from real bodily distress and the need to be at home once again with oneself on a bodily level, with a better feeling in one's very

Figure 2. Functional Polarities of Sexuality

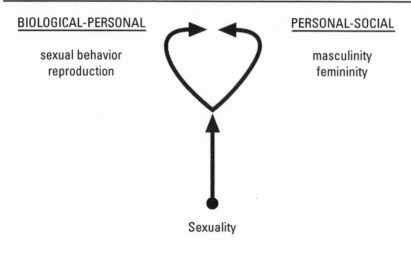

BIOLOGICAL-PERSONAL   PERSONAL-SOCIAL

sexual behavior   masculinity
reproduction   femininity

Sexuality

Source of diagram: Wilhelm Reich, *Function of the Orgasm,* Chapter 7.

Figure 3. Functional Polarities of Selfhood

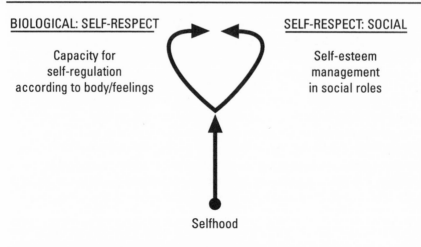

BIOLOGICAL: SELF-RESPECT   SELF-RESPECT: SOCIAL

Capacity for   Self-esteem
self-regulation   management
according to body/feelings   in social roles

Selfhood

Source of diagram: Wilhelm Reich, *Function of the Orgasm,* Chapter 7.

being. On the other hand, deep sexual longing may urge an individual to heroic efforts to overcome deficits of self-respect in order to be able to seek out sexual love, a situation more usual than otherwise when individuals seek psychotherapy.

Sexuality and selfhood, in themselves, can each be analyzed in terms of identical and antithetical polarities (Figures 2 and 3). The functioning of each of these organizing principles reaches into the organism, to the biological core, and extends out into the person's social functioning. In the case of sexuality (see Figure 2), being male or female is the biological given, with bodily responses to sexual possibilities and acts emerging from the biological core and ensuing in highly personal experiences. Such private sexual experiences are integrated, and their meanings, effects, and memories are carried within the person, changing him or her, and they effect who that person is in the social world. The masculinity and femininity of the individual find multiform expressions in the social world, in any case, and, indeed, such expressions are ultimately subject to a range of perceptions by others in the social world as well, perceptions which in turn effect the individual.

The biological basis for self-respect (see Figure 3), can be understood in light of the person's capacity for self-regulation according to his or her own actual feelings and body states. The man or woman with self-respect does not simply "take care of" his or her body as if it were a utilitarian object. On the contrary, his or her life is guided, over the short and long run, by the body and its realities, not by goals, programs, or images imposed on the body.

The social aspects of self-respect are reflected in the individual's self-esteem management in various social roles, including work role. Self-respectful management of social roles emerges out of bodily realities, a respectful way of attending to bodily feelings and states. The body offers moment to moment feedback through its continuous responses to the inner world and the external environment. Self-respect requires not only attention to this feedback; it requires the individual to be identified with his or her body, as if one were to say, "My body is me."

A criterion for healthy functioning is suggested by these diagrams. In each case some balanced confluence between the biological and social, mediated by the person, is necessary for health. When, for example, self-esteem is maintained by constant, exhausting overwork, self-respect is violated on the bodily level, and the organism will pay a price.

In the themes of sexuality and selfhood, as I have described them, there is a confluence of biological, social, and personal. For the individual, this confluence poses a series of ongoing life dilemmas. I focus on the personal—the story of the individual person—as it is lived out in this confluence. It is my belief that, in today's world, a deeper commitment to that which is most personal will lead to a fuller and more meaningful sociality. It is certainly the way to foster the biological health of the individual.

The sexual complexity of contemporary culture has increased continuously since the end of the Victorian era with no lessening of sexual anxiety. Each decade brings its own shifting, ambivalent perspective on sexuality, interpreting and reinterpreting a full menu of sexual issues. Some of these shifts represent real, positive changes in culture. Undoubtedly the most important of these, currently, is the changing and evolving roles for women, partly the outcome of feminism and women's movements, partly the outcome of economic change, and partly the outcome of other cultural factors, including psychoanalysis. Gay and lesbian activism have also forced reexamination of sexual issues, roles, and relationships. Other changes in the broader political and economic structures of society effect not only our views of sexuality but our practice of sex. The sexually transmitted human immunodeficiency virus (HIV) is a significant external factor. All these profoundly influence our understanding and our living of sexuality.

Yet, for all the many great external forces that impinge on the actual sexual expression of any given person, sexual fulfillment is an intensely personal matter. It is the individual man or woman who, as a person, seeks love, sexual gratification, and the desired partner. It is the individual man or woman who, in his or her own soul, makes the choice to join the chosen other for a moment or for a lifetime. It is the individual who must come to terms, on his or her own, personally, with whatever arises out of these quests and these choices—whatever of pleasure or pain, happiness or misery, excitement or conflict, years of accord or years of discord. Most personally, it is the two individuals who ultimately join in the genital embrace to realize their fulfillment. Through all this is the constantly flowing desire for sexual fulfillment.

THE BIOENERGETIC VIEW

A therapeutic experience of my own first brought my attention to the experience—not just the concept—of self-respect. I was in the presence of my therapist, and in this particular moment, something inside myself had caught my attention. At that moment I had identified an inner state which I, myself, wished to term "self-respect." It was a nice feeling. The experience was a quiet one, a calm one. There was an absence of shame, guilt, humiliation, self-criticism, or preoccupation with "self-esteem." The whole of the experience, its meaning and significance, were more than relief due to the absence of these negative states. A whole other *modus vivandi* was in operation and taking their place. It was a quiet process, but nonetheless real. It was a process which paved the way for self-acceptance, for attending to myself-as-body. It did not remove all pain, anxiety, sorrow, or anger. In fact, it permitted their presence, in a sense, more clearly. While shame or humiliation are "noisy" ongoing tumults within the self, this process was rather quiet, soft, no big uproar, even almost indiscernible, as if I had to listen quietly and carefully to be able to attend to it, and to allow it to offer me benefits which were nothing but momentous.

So began my explorations in self-respect. The therapist in whose presence this experience took place was Alexander Lowen, founder of bioenergetic analysis. With him I learned that self-respect is a matter of the body, not the ego. Much of what follows, in theory and clinical description, pertains to the body. Those who practice bioenergetic analysis have a particular way of observing the body, a particular way of looking and seeing, and that way can be taught and learned. This observational method and the data it provides establish the empirical foundation of our theory and clinical work.

As a distinctive approach to the understanding of the individual, bioenergetic analysis views both the mind and the expressive movements and form of the body as equivalent expressions. In approaching therapeutic treatment, it offers the avenue of direct bodily interventions. This therapeutic work throws light into the deeper functions and nature of sexuality and selfhood, revealing depths and facets that are less obvious or even obscured in the context of the verbal psychotherapies.

There are many valid ways in which the human body may be studied. Bioenergetic analysis, or bioenergetics, has a particular view of the body, and the depth of that view lies in its *organismic theory of the self*. Through distinctive analytic tools and forms of observation this theory opens fresh insights into sexuality and the self.

The terms *organism* and *bioenergetics* point to an underlying biological conception in bioenergetic analysis. This conception is based on the easily observed biological phenomena of pulsation. All living tissue, that is, all protoplasm, pulsates. The most basic forms of these pulsatory movements can be seen in one celled organisms, or in the living masses of multinucleated protoplasm called slime molds. Viewed at this level of organization, a variety of rhythmic and flowing movements can be seen in all protoplasm. In that movement is the mystery of life.

In the bioenergetic or organismic theory of the self, the higher levels of human functioning rest on the foundation of this primal quality of protoplasm. To someone who is not accustomed to observing this rhythmic, moving, living aspect of the organism, it may sound odd to say that higher levels of human functioning are based on it. After all, this is the age of the brain and neuroscience. An image of the nearly infinitely complex networks of neuronal pathways of the brain, linked in computerlike, information processing operations, offers a contemporary myth of human behavior. However, the brain, itself, is a pulsating organ, made up of the same kind of living, pulsatory, protoplasmic matter as an ameba. I observed such movements with fascination from the time I was quite young, both in single celled organisms, and in such remarkable creatures as the foot-long sea hare, large sluglike animals, soft, living forms of pulsatory matter populating warm, shallow Florida tidal waters.

There is a biological elegance to viewing the human organism and human functioning in the light of pulsation. It brings all human functioning into the natural realm. Sexuality and selfhood are tied in not only to evolution but to the underlying qualities of the natural movements of life itself. In understanding these simple but basic life processes we can learn the ways in which they can be influenced to promote health and heal illness. Adding this dimension to our understanding and knowledge of the body deepens respect for the bodily self.

The bioenergetic approach keeps a focus on the centrality of sexuality, and allows the passions to retain their bodily realities. In the focus on the body it reveals the biological basis of identity, belief, and faith. In working with the body it brings into the therapeutic work the real, bodily source of healing and fostering health, and it offers a healthful approach to life generally. Through the bodily, biological approach of bioenergetic analysis I, myself, came full circle back to the awe and delight I first felt as a young boy in the beauty and wonders of the natural world.

THE STUDY OF SEXUALITY

While the studies in this book were motivated by compelling forces and conflicts I experienced in my own life, my understanding emerged in the course of my work as a bioenergetic therapist. The therapeutic setting offers the opportunity to explore individual sexuality in a depth and detail possible virtually nowhere else. I consider the people I see to be relatively healthy, to the extent that, generally, they have managed to acquire an education, employment, and a place in the social world. Since I take them as a cross section of what could be called middle-class society, I have drawn some conclusions about the society and the times in which we live. In seeing into the depths of one life, we see into the depths of one class and station of the society.[3]

The inability, in some form, to find fulfillment in sexual love underlies the suffering, discontent, and painful yearning that brings many to therapy. I find this to be virtually universal. An inevitable accompaniment is a disturbance in self-respect whose roots lie entwined with the roots of the disturbance of sexual love. We have, then, every bit as much reason to study sexuality today as did Sigmund Freud and Wilhelm Reich in their time,[4] and their works remain good starting points.

The therapeutic study of sexuality inevitably involves painful, disturbing matters. Is it necessary or desirable to disturb ourselves by going into such matters? I can only say that I have recorded here what I have seen and experienced. Perhaps I would be more accurate if I say that I have found a way to see, and I have found words to describe, what I have experienced in myself and others. For the study of sexuality has a peculiarity. The observer can see only what his or her eyes are open to see, and his or her ears are open to hear. The preparation is not simply mental. It is bodily and emotional.

Here, in brief, is what I have found. In recent years, I have found a sexual misery in almost all those who seek therapy. Sexual misery seems to be very widespread. It is closely associated with disturbances in identity and the self. In sexual misery, there is, first of all, the repeated experience of misery in sexual relationships from sexual frustration, lack of love, lack of understanding, conflict, repeated losses and disappointments, and an overall inability to find fulfillment. There is a weakened sense of self; and there are feelings of not being sure of or grounded in who one is, of not knowing how to find one's self, and a sense of inadequacy for the quest to establish a loving relationship; often there is a sense of shame and not being right in the depths of one's sexual being.

I repeatedly and consistently find a violation of some sort in sexual development. This includes, but is not limited to, sexual abuse. For another thing, it is more usual than unusual to find the experience of having been hated in childhood, and I mean in a significant way, by one or both parents, something that seems, and is, unnatural. Both the violations of sexuality and the hate are actual trauma in childhood, and they are a significant cause of the misery I see. The effects of the violation of sexuality persist in the adult in the forms of sexual craziness, shock and dissociation, genital injury, the self-hate system, and shame and guilt.

I do not see shame and guilt as necessary or inherent aspects of development, as necessities for controlling and containing the "primitive impulses," as necessary vehicles for becoming "civilized." I see them for what they are, lingering results of violations of natural movement and feeling.

The violations of sexuality and their aftereffects are impediments to fulfillment. For the individual, the discovery and exploration of the effects of violations of sexuality is the way to begin the path of healing and fulfillment.

What I see in the clinical setting has influenced my perception of sexual matters in the society at large. Disrespect toward sex and sexuality commonly pervades social attitudes, values, and behaviors. This disrespect is more confusing, ambiguous, and some ways more undermining that outright hatred or negativity toward sexuality, although here and there the latter attitudes are also still present.

Sexual matters of every kind are aired publicly in all kinds of ways and in every communications medium. The functions of all these displays of sexuality are commercial. Sex is used to sell, stimulate, make "news," and so on and on, an erotic flood of imagery running through the great commercial rivers of our times.

Contemporary populations are constantly bombarded with sexual imagery which is absorbed by youth whose young minds do not have the capacity to sort out reality from fantasy. The result is they may have a terrible time finding or even never know the realities of love, tenderness, beauty, and sexual fulfillment in a relationship with another actual person.

An occasional voice in this wilderness is heard and then squelched. A recent nominee for the American governmental post of Surgeon General, an African-American woman physician, spoke up to say that young men and women should have access to birth control and protection from sexually transmitted diseases. This common sense threatened to paralyze the U.S. Senate. Later she was forced to resign her post because she spoke openly about masturbation. Politicians put on a show of outrage at the mention of adolescent masturbation. This display covers over a very real underlying current of sex-negativity in the American culture. This episode is only one sign, out of many, that the real, painful, and troubling matters of sexuality, are, for the most part, still hidden, glossed over, lost in a vast conspiracy of denial and silence.[5]

Intermittently in recent years the denial and silence have been breaking down. The common sexual abuse of children has been brought into the open and, at least here and there, it is being addressed. However, the diminution of women continues to be the most obvious evidence of the antisexual attitudes of the culture. More slowly and secretively, perhaps, a recognition is dawning of men's sexual injury and their pervasive confusion about sex and masculinity. Hatred of and ambivalence toward sex and sexuality is, I believe, the source, as well as the manner of continuing, both the oppression of women and men's confusion.

SEX AND SELF-RESPECT AS GIVENS

The drive to find fulfillment in sexual love was matched in my own person with the need to find self-respect. For much of my life this need goaded me on in an illusory quest, like a mirage in the desert glimpsed by the parched traveler, but always over the next dry mountain. From my earliest years, self-respect seems to have been understood as the reward for some kind of monumental achievement. All the while, of course, no real achievement ever proved to be adequate to winning it. Later I discovered that self-respect is exactly that: nothing more nor less than a respectful attitude toward my own self. Of course this had nothing to do with achievements; it had only to do with being.

What I discovered, above all, is that self-respect is a matter of the body, not of the ego. Respect for one's bodily realities is the basis of self-respect. I also saw that it is a developmental matter. Self-respect develops in a child who is treated respectfully. Where the child is treated with disrespect, there will develop a disrespectful attitude toward the self. Permissiveness versus strictness is not the dimension being addressed here. The issue is respect versus disrespect. Education, for example, can be conducted respectfully, and it can be conducted disrespectfully. Similarly, discipline of various kinds can be learned under respectful conditions or disrespectful. Very different things are learned by a child under the different conditions, and the effects on him or her physically, emotionally, and mentally are very different. The developmental environment fosters either self-respect or its various alternative forms of self-hate.

The basis for respecting the child is the respect for his or her sexuality. This is the most fundamental and essential way in which children must be respected. This means different things, of course, at different stages of development. However, there is no stage of development where it does not have a bearing.

Self-respect is a simple matter. For my own part I would prefer to see any child with a carriage that reveals a simple attitude of self-respect, rather than any other imaginable attribute—including those that are meant to guarantee "success" in the social world. A self-respecting person is a person who is capable of responding realistically. I believe self-respect is the basis for the ability to live in a respectful way with others and in relation to the environment generally.

Self-respect, like sexuality, develops in children in the matrix of relations with others, and both are lived out fully only in relation to others. This I believe to be true from birth through the whole life cycle. In the sexual love relationship, the two, as ongoing life issues, are joined in the most intense possible way. The sexual love relationship thus offers a unique opportunity, a kind of experiential laboratory or workshop, for the evolution of the individual and of his or her fulfillment.

Throughout I write as if sex and self-respect were good universally, that is, desired attributes of the good life for any man or woman. I do believe this to be the case; as far as I can tell, many others believe this too. Making attributions about the good life verges into the domain of ethics. An ethical argument in fact may be seen to underlie the main themes of this text.

Sex and self-respect are both inherent functions of the human organism. Impediments to optimal expression of these functions are commonly found, and these impediments operate at the biological and psychological levels of the organism. Studying the impediments will help us learn either to get freer of them or to live with them, and it can help us learn more about preventing their development in children.

KRISTIN'S STORY

Consider Kristin's story. It is rich in revelations of the themes of sexuality and selfhood.

The summer of her sixteenth year, Kristin had been living and working on a farm neighboring her own in the rural, mountainous region where she had been born and raised. One beautiful day that was to prove fateful for her, she and her companions had gone up into the mountains to enjoy themselves. Kristin was thrilled and exalted by the glorious day and the mountains. She returned by herself, and, as it happened, she was given a ride down the mountain by a young man whom she found to be exceptionally beautiful. In that moment, as she rode down the mountain with him, she felt a passionate love for him. She had never made love with a man, but she both hoped and feared that her young man would respond to her passion, pull over to the side of the road, and take her by her hand into the forest and there make love to her. Despite her passionate desire, she did not communicate in any way, and he silently continued his sober drive down the mountain to her farm.

A couple of days later, as she and her friend came into the farmyard, they saw his truck. Inside herself Kristin instantaneously had the knowledge that if her friend teased her—even the least bit—she would feel mortified. When the young man appeared, Kristin blushed deeply, and her friend did tease her, just a tiny bit, and Kristin was indeed mortified to her core.

So far, Kristin's story is an ordinary experience of adolescence—"normal." But, as perhaps with every story, there is more, and the memory of this experience became an epiphany in Kristin's life as an older woman.

To her dismay, in the days that followed her young man's appearance in the farmyard, Kristin's bowels stopped functioning. This went on for so long that she became ill, but she was too ashamed to say anything to anyone. In a couple of weeks she was so ill that she required hospitalization. There, her doctors apparently were at a loss—these were not psychological times or places—and diagnosed her as having diphtheria or some such thing. In the meantime, she began to contemplate throwing herself down a nearby cliff and into the river. At wit's end, she finally confessed her dilemma to her sister, who told their mother.

Kristin's mother had a solution that freed her bowels but multiplied her sexual distress tenfold. A masseur had at one time been of help to her mother, and Kristin was sent to him. Each treatment ended with the masseur masturbating her. Kristin tried to keep her orgasm secret, but to this day she remembers the masseur's heavy breathing behind her. She felt dirty and shamed. To compound matters, Kristin felt betrayed when her mother explained her problems to the neighbors where she had been working.

She began the fall school term in a bad state: depressed, confused, feeling dirty and ashamed, and in shock. It was her bad luck that term to have a male physics teacher whose disrespectful, authoritarian pedagogy included doses of sadistic shaming and punishment, supposedly because Kristin was not performing well enough at her lessons. Kristin ended up sitting looking at the page by the hour, unable to learn a thing. Kristin's life did not get better for a long time, and then only for short periods.

Years later Kristin asked her mother about the masseur. Had she known about his masturbating her daughter? Had he done the same with her? "Oh," the mother said, "I thought that was just part of the treatment." Kristin was dumbfounded. This was the same mother who had always been extremely strict regarding sexual matters. She had made a point of repeating to Kristin her own sentiment that if she, the mother, had ever become pregnant out of wedlock, she would have "thrown herself into the waterfall."

OUR BODIES, OUR SEXUALITY

This story reveals one young woman's sexuality. The story also reveals for us clearly enough the obvious scope and meaning of the concept of sexuality. The story has everything to do with who Kristin was as a young woman at that time. We see the strength of her desire for the sexual love of a man, her vulnerabilities to the frustration of those desires, and her profound vulnerability to shame. We see her trapped in herself in such an intensely conflicted way that her bowels stop functioning. At the same time, there are no sexual acts in the story—until the perverted masseur appears on the scene. Then the story of her sexuality is complicated and confounded by the effects of an undesired, shame-inducing, abusive sexual experience inflicted on her under desperate, confusing circumstances. That experience, occurring even before she herself had yet to actively give or receive sexual love, becomes a further element in the story of her sexuality and of her sexual fate.

There is a clear continuity to the story, and it is in the nature of sexuality that there is such continuity. From unfulfilled passion, to shame, to a crippling bodily dysfunction, to an unfortunate compounding of sexual abuse and parental ignorance, to academic stalemate, her story's continuity has its own inherent logic and meaning. In addition, the story of Kristin's sexuality can be extended back in time to her childhood, and forward in time to her mature years, maintaining the sense of continuity and the sense of an inherent logic. Her sexuality is a stream that runs through different landscapes, climates, and different moments of time. We could follow the flow of that strong stream through the years; and we will have the opportunity to do so, at least briefly.

The story of her sexuality extends itself into matters that on the surface are not sexual: her academic stalemate, her inability to do her physics lessons. In Kristin's state of confusion and trauma, the line between the sexual and that which is not sexual became confused. An authoritarian, punitive pedagogue added to her sexual confusion and her misapprehensions about men.

In following Kristin's story, I feel it urgently important to say that I am not offering an explanation of her life; I am telling its story. To put it in another way, I do not want to answer the question "Why?" I want to describe what—what happens to us and what we are.

As to the question, What are we? I offer a brief answer. We are our sexuality. The story of our sexuality is the story of our life.

The history of our sexuality makes up a large and important part of what happens to us in our lifetime. Sexuality happens to us. Actions taken out of choice and will can be contrasted with experiences that happen to us.[6] In viewing the accrued outcomes of events which have happened to us, it is appropriate also to speak of fate; and, as it turns out, actions that were initially conceived as choices—acts of will—in the end often appear fated. Much of our life is fate, and surely much of the story of our sexuality is. (Of course, not all that is our fate has to do with sexuality; the historical, economic, political, racial, and social world that one is born into are also aspects of our fate.)

The story of actions chosen and guided by will—all the works, successes, failures—is the story of the person's *ego*, one aspect of an individual's personality. The story of the rivers and streams of the passions of a life would be more about what happened to the person, their fate, the story of their sexuality. Falling in love, is something that happens to us. The story of these experiences is the story of the self. Sexuality is an expression of the self and the self is an expression of sexuality.

The body *happens*. From insemination to death, it is life emerging, unfolding, ceasing. As it is and becomes our body, it is and becomes our fate. We tend to have a vast unease and outright anxiety about our bodies, our fates, our sexualities—our *selves*. Our bodily self is not something we control. There are many aspects to this, but the fundamental and first one is that we are born either male or female. "I am a man" or "I am a woman" is the first statement of our beings in every life situation. The story of our sexuality, of this deep part of our fate, is the story of the development and history of our masculinity or femininity. Our bodily self is the sexual self, our sexuality is our fate, and our sexuality is our maleness or femaleness. Selfhood and sexuality are intertwined expressions of one biological organism, described from slightly different perspectives.

The stream of sexuality, its many currents, its sources, and the ocean it flows into—these are not just a set of images. In Kristin's story, for example, the first flush of adolescent sexual passion was the full-bodied movement of a healthy and very sturdy young woman. It literally flooded through her whole body as well as her genital. A few days after her first encounter with her young man, shame flushed through her body. The flush of the shame was an expression of the same stream as the sexual passion, but forced into a countering direction. Two streams met in a conflictful encounter, and the one stopped the other, causing a real bodily stoppage. After that, with death's shadow cast over them, the flows were often stopped, often turgid, confused, conflicted.

These are real movements, pulsatory biological waves of excitation flowing through the fluid medium of the body's tissues. We experience such movements as emotions, passions, or excitation. We speak of being moved by deep feeling, and we are. The word *emotion* itself signifies movement, movement outward toward the world. Kristin's movement toward death was also a bodily movement, inward on the self, contracting, as the fires of passion were quenched, leaving ashes of despair and helplessness.

It was Wilhelm Reich[7] who had the vision to see the movements underlying these passions and who described and named them. The flush of love is an example of an expansion of the whole organism, and the opposing flush of shame is a contraction of the organism. Reich saw that in their opposition there was an underlying unity. His descriptions of the biological nature of these movements reaches into the depths of the organism. In his analysis of these phenomena he explored the pulsation of life. He has received little credit for his work; and this is extraordinarily unfortunate, since his work on the human organism and sexuality sheds enormous light on our lives and our ills.

HER STORY CONTINUED

Two questions, at least, are begged by Kristin's story. What made Kristin's response to her first disappointment in love a matter of life or death—first with a bowel stoppage and then with suicidal thoughts? Then, what happened and what's the resolution? Every story begs for its proper completion. The first question means that we have to look more deeply into the event itself, and it means that we will have to look back in time to her younger years. The second question, of course, takes the story into her later years. We look into the now, the then, and the afterward. I do not want to call this kind of exploration an explanation or a search for causes. It is true that such an exploration often leads one to say, as in the therapeutic situation, "Now I understand!" Understanding is a desired and a healing experience in its own right; but it is different from explanation and finding causes. It is the idea of an exploration, however, that applies here. In looking into the now, the then, and the afterward, it is possible to discover who and what we are, to reveal the nature of sexuality and the self.

It was my good fortune to have the opportunity to explore her story with Kristin in later years. As we looked together at the episodes just described, they seemed to reveal the essence of her very being, and at the same time, they seemed mysterious and to hide their meanings. A lovely young woman, flowering and full of life, and then—relatively suddenly, because of emotional events—close to death! We came back to the memory of that day on the mountain a number of times.

On one occasion, it occurred to me that the deep shame she felt in the subsequent brief encounter must have been present even in the first moments she began to feel her passionate love for the man. When I shared that thought with her, it struck Kristin that way too, perhaps for the first time.

We were led, then, to take a second look at her memory of the young man. He drove on with seeming indifference, unmoved by Kristin's sexual arousal. How could he do this? A beautiful young woman is ready to offer herself to him out of sheer sexual excitement, and he calmly goes about his mundane business. It is the first time this young woman has had such full-blown feelings in a situation where their realization was possible and appropriate. What does the man's apparent indifference communicate to her about the value and meaning of her feelings? Whether he had made love to her or not, for the sake of her feelings and her youth, some positive acknowledgment of her excitement and its desirability to him would have meant a great deal to her. Just as it was clear enough to Kristin that her passion was not necessarily his concern, that made it even more necessary to understand why mortification filled the abyss formed in the absence of his response.

With this clarification of the memory of the truck man, Kristin remembered her own father's seeming indifference to her first love and excitement for him. The passion that Kristin experienced that day on the mountain had been ignited many years before, and had been in waiting to be reignited, and the shame too had lain in wait—for a cold appearing man who would reawaken Kristin's bad feelings about her sexual desire.

We might recall Kristin's feelings about her mother's role in the story of those weeks: that she had felt betrayed when her mother revealed her secret to those neighbors where the crucial scene took place. Kristin has an earlier memory of an encounter with her mother. "I shot my little fist up into the air," she said, "and I said, 'There must be *something* right about me!'" Such insistence, of course, implies that, between her and her mother, Kristin was prone to feeling that not much at all was right about her. Her mother, too, had a role in the development of a sense of not-rightness, of shame, or of guilt.

The themes of this story reverberate deeply throughout Kristin's life. Even in later years, as we explored these and related themes, one day Kristin felt again a bottomless chasm in herself, a feeling of terrible badness, of guilt and shame—that same feeling that had followed her through the years. In the earlier days of her youth, she had more than once feared falling into that chasm and falling to her death, whereas now, in her imagination, she could leap across it, since the chasm was perhaps as deep but nowhere near as wide. Kristin had found fulfillment in her loves and work as the years had gone on, but that bad feeling had remained in some measure, emerging from time to time. As to that fist shooting into the air, it remains a fitting symbol of a fighting spirit.

THE SELF

In the unhappiness that leads us to seek psychotherapy, we are usually unable to accept ourselves for who we are. This difficulty is usually accompanied by constant self-criticism and a chronic sense of not being of sufficient value in ourselves—especially not of sufficient value to be loved. When there are relationship difficulties, they are often the result of an interpersonal style whose function is to protect a damaged sense of self. What can be said about the nature of the self?

In ordinary discourse, the sense of self is commonly expressed through the use of the words *I, me, myself,* and an attentive listener will readily gather thereby an understanding of at least some aspects or expressions of the self of the speaker. Similarly, an attentive observer will gather as much, or even more, about the self of another by observing their demeanor, manner, and characteristic ways of expression. It might be thought, therefore, that a definition of the self and a discussion concerning its nature would be simple and self-evident. Such is not the case. Even while from every syllable and movement a listener or observer makes assumptions and gathers information about the nature of the self of another, a psychological writer embarks on a risky business as soon as a definition of the self is undertaken.[8]

It will be useful enough to take a relatively simplified approach to understanding the nature of the self. The view taken here is that the self must be comprehended as an organismic, bodily function, similar in that regard to other bodily functions. In this sense the self and the body are equivalent. In simplest terms, the self is the body. This formulation reveals the basic and most important meaning of self-respect. Self-respect on the most basic level is obviously respect for one's own body. This implies respect, not just for the body as an object, but for the life of the body. The life of the body is literally our soul and spirit. The life of the body is revealed and expressed in movement—from the movement of the breath in and out to the deep movements experienced as feelings and passions. Ultimately, self-respect means basing one's life on the reality of the life of the body.

Each body has its own particular life, of course, with unique features as well as elements in common with all human bodies. In presenting Kristin's story, we described some aspects of the reality of the life of her body. In doing so we described her experience, but we also described more than that. We described how her story unfolded, that is, her fate, and we described some elements of the inherent logic or structure of that fate, and this we might call her character. Shame was an inherent element in that structure, we saw, as was a fighting and determined spirit, as was a healthy interest in sexual love. These elements all compose the "reality of the body," for Kristin, and this becomes her reality as a person—who she is, who she was, who she became. Her reality as a person encompasses mind, spirit, and soul, as well as body. If these terms have a real meaning in a person's life, and I believe they do, they too must be understood as expressions of organismic function, not as realities lying outside of that function.

Kristin's experiences and the episodes of her story were appropriately presented as expressions of her sexuality. Sexuality is a main principle in terms of which many elements of her story can be organized and understood. The elements of her story can also be seen and understood as expressions of the self. This is no coincidence, since, selfhood and sexuality as the two great organizing principles of the organism are functionally equivalent (although not identical) expressions of the organism.

Three categories can be utilized in psychological theory for the exploration of the self: (1) the strength of the self; (2) the self in relation to the self, or "self-relations";[9] (3) the relations between self and others. To some extent these categories correspond to three of the "psychologies" of psychoanalytic theory: ego psychology, self psychology, and object relations.[10] The functioning of self-respect may be seen in each of these categories.

Strength of Self

Lowen has explored the nature and dimensions of the strength of self in terms of other self words, such as self-assertion, self-acceptance, self-awareness, self-expression, and self-possession.[11] These phrases all capture important dimensions of the strength of the self and of the sense of the self. Self-respect can be seen to function through each of these dimensions as well. I would add that the fundamental strength of the self can be said to reside in the strength of the person's sexuality, and the strength of a person's sexuality can also be analyzed along more than one dimension.

As a sixteen-year-old, Kristin is very strong in herself in some ways. She felt a deep passion for her young man, and between that and the whole dark depth and storm of her conflicts we can sense a primal strength. The weakness of self and sexuality at this point in her life is reflected both in the way in which her passion is deeply held in, quietly and secretively, and in the unfortunate susceptibility of passion to be conflicted and eroded by shame. The functions of self-respect, to all appearances, failed her in the crunch.

Self-Relations

White[12] uses the term *self-relations* to refer to a complex developmental line involving conscious and unconscious processes having to do with establishing the self as an object more or less positively valued by its own ego.

[W]e can recognize that self-relations are just as important an ego function as object relations. . . . [I]n terms of an evenly distributed libidinal cathexis between self- and object representations . . . normally we should love ourselves as much as we love others. . . . [This] represents a departure from Freud's economics of love.

Just as object constancy requires acceptance of the object's needs, despite the frustrations this may impose, so we might think of the necessity of self-constancy as involving increased tolerance of our shortcomings and a self-love or appreciation subsuming our disappointments in ourselves. (160, 162)

White's psychological concept is functionally equivalent to the organismic concept of self-respect I am developing. Self-esteem, according to another psychoanalytic investigation of these concepts,[13] is a related but different concept. It can be thought of as a conscious ego state, positive or negative in affective tone, that is an outcome of self-relations and other ego processes.

At one point, Kristin's relations to herself are almost as bad as they could get. She was not only feeling terrible about herself, she was also considering the option of throwing herself away—down the cliff, into the river, just as her mother had long ago promised she would if she had been shamed. She was not able to continue to love herself in the face of the frustration of the love for the other and her friend's teasing. Her state at this point was the unhappy outcome of her whole life up until then. The experience of shame and her bowel stoppage reflected who she had become—especially who she had become *for herself*—when, for the first time, the full force of her sexuality was thrust out into the world. Self-relations are here strongly entwined with sexuality.

Self and Others

Psychological theorists have considered the self's standing in relation to other selves.[14] Looking at Kristin's story, we see that somehow she lost herself in relation to the other members of her family and in relation to her neighbors with whom she worked. She acted as though she had no standing with anyone. She kept her secret even as her bodily health deteriorated. Desperation finally enabled her to give a signal of her dire straits. Here too, the ground on which she was not able to stand before the others was the ground of her own sexuality. It was as if for her to stand in the farmyard and declare for all the world to know "I wanted to go into the forest and make love with him" were the worst thing in the world, rather than the best. The dysfunctioning of self-respect led her to self-abnegation rather than self-assertion, as if to hide and suffer were, for her, necessary in relation to others.

Each of these three categories for analyzing the nature of the self are related to sexuality, and they thus also represent expressions of bodily states or movements. We have already looked at passion and shame in terms of bodily movements, and that analysis can be related to the first category, the strength of the self and sexuality. Shame, a phenomenon very important for understanding self-relations (the second category), represents, as we have seen, the flow of a movement in the opposite direction to sexual passion. The terrible experience of feeling bad about oneself pervades the body, the person, as a whole, an experience not adequately captured by a psychological concept of self-esteem.

Similar considerations apply to the third category, "self and others." Kristin's standing before others, her ability or inability to claim a place in the attention and sympathies of those near her, and her ability to stand up for herself—all come to our attention in her story. All are based on the actual physical ability to stand before others and to show and express oneself in one's emotional and bodily being. For Kristin, this would have meant the ability to stand in the farmyard and let all the world know, as she looked at her young man, that she would have liked nothing better than for him to be her lover. Such a capacity is a bodily capacity, just as surely as it is a bodily capacity to run a mile.

The "reality of the body," then, is a complex flow of processes whose reflection can be seen in the story of our sexuality, the various qualities of our sexuality, the strength of our self, our relations to our self, our relations to others.

SELF-RESPECT

Self-respect is the capacity to base every-day functioning in a healthy, pleasurable way on the reality of the body. The functioning of self-respect and its disturbances are observable in the behaviors falling into the above three categories.

At the most obvious, surface level, in considering Kristin's experiences, the concept of self-respect implies that each quality in her experiences is to be respected in their turn. The strength of her passion and the reality of her feeling of shame, her intense excitement, the dreams and hopes we might guess at, the terrible chasm of her despair, the stoppage of her bowels, her tendency to secretly hold in her feelings, her terrible feelings about herself, her nearly fatal inability to communicate her situation and her ability to signal—all of this is to be respected.

Self-respect, however, as I use the term, means something deeper than a deliberately or consciously respectful attitude toward experience, although this conscious attitude would grow out of it. Self-respect is an ongoing condition of the person which finds its expression in a whole way of living and being based on intimate communication with bodily realities, feelings, and inner being. Similarly the various failures and distortions of self-respect are based in deep disturbances in the organism and its history. Self-acceptance, self-expression, and self-esteem and their disturbances are all expressions of the function of self-respect and its disturbances.

Consider the shame that was part of Kristin's story. As biological processes, shame and sexuality form a polarity, and each pole has a functional equivalence and a functional antithesis with the other. In Kristin's story, these functional relationships between her shame and her sexual arousal are perfectly evident. The former is a direct function of the latter, while being its opposite. Shame (a contraction), flushed through her body in just the same way, but in the opposite direction, as had her passionate arousal (an expansion). Both emotions are real bodily movements.

How can we understand the workings of self-respect in her situation? We can understand it by looking at what is not there, by imagining the scene and the story as it might have been if—if the story had unfolded more favorably for Kristin. An ideal situation would have been one in which Kristin knew and valued her sexual passion, believed in it, and saw it as something of the best of herself, something that might be expressed by the words "This is me, and this is good." These words describe an important and specific condition, one for which I use a specific term. In this condition I say that she is "identified with" her sexual passion. This would be strong self-respect.

Yet another ideal possibility would be one in which she could acknowledge, accept, and even identify with her shame, accepting it as a difficult, painful part of herself. This might be expressed in the words "Yes, this is me too. I am passionate and conflicted, ashamed I have strong sexual desires. This makes it difficult for me, and I will come to terms with my difficulty." This would also be an action of self-respect. This too acknowledges, accepts, and acts on the body as it is and as it functions.

Yet a third possible movement of self-respect, one we would wish to see in a sixteen-year-old, could be expressed perhaps in the words, "All that is happening to me is too much for me to bear. I don't know what it all is or what it means. Who is this person—this me—to whom this is happening? I need guidance from an older person to help me sort it all out." This too would be a movement of self-respect.

Shame heightens a painful self-consciousness, a sense of self as seen by others, or oneself, in a negative light; it is a movement toward the self. *Desire* yields to a blissful state of the self in which self-consciousness is diminished; it leads to a movement toward the other and fulfillment. For the self to be freed from the painful self-consciousness of shame, the shame has to be respectfully experienced to its fullest as a bodily experience, a movement toward the self. This movement toward the self then allows for the building of the capacity for movement toward the other. In this movement, shame shifts toward desire, and a fulfillment of the self in sexuality becomes possible. Each movement is allowed and based upon self-respect, the bodily capacity of the organism to follow and experience its own movement.

If we imagine Kristin as she might have been, had she not been prone to such devastating shame about her sexual desire, we will see other workings of self-respect. She might have held her ground with her excitement with a degree of pride, knowledge, and surefooted purpose. She might have done so, not in an egoistic or exhibitionistic way, but simply as an expression of the reality of her being. Her sexual life could then have been simply lived out through her, and she might have been able to surrender to its joys and passions and taken its difficulties more in stride. In this condition, she is identified with her sexuality, that is, with her genital movement. In this state, her body would not have turned against itself in either shame or bowel dysfunction; nor, later, would her brain have been in such a state of shock that she was unable to do her schoolwork. That healthy state would demonstrate strong, positive functioning of self-respect, and it would indicate a strong sexuality.

Suicide was nearly an issue, for Kristin. If we were to imagine the young Kristin as our parental or therapeutic charge, the question would be, How do we respect—should she respect—her own suicidal feeling? We would want to protect her from the act, while respecting her feelings and her perception of her situation giving rise to her considerations of the act. An important part of that protection is provided by just that respect for her, her perceptions, feelings, and experiences. To be respected are her despair, her sense of being hopelessly trapped in a situation where her self-respect can never be reestablished, her belief that throwing herself over the cliff is the only solution, and, if present, her wish to die. This was her reality for a time. This reflected her bodily state. Finding self-respect here can be dangerous and frightening. Sometimes a genuine self-respect for that terrible state can be found only in later years, and, even then, it can foster a movement for the better.

IDENTIFICATION WITH THE GENITAL

And the man and his wife were naked, and were not ashamed.

—Genesis 2:24

THE DEVELOPMENT OF WILHELM REICH'S CONCEPTION OF SEXUALITY

All the evidence I have seen suggests that, like Kristin, the sexual lives of people throughout the history of the modern western world have been commonly burdened, to a greater or lesser degree, by guilt, shame, and conflict. To this list must be added humiliation, ambivalence, anxiety, confusion, and outright hatred of sex. This burdensome atmosphere of "sex-negativity," as Wilhelm Reich termed it,[1] has precluded what should be the universal acknowledgment of a simple reality. The sense of self for men and women is based on an identification with the genital.[2] The whole organization of the person is fundamentally grounded in the genital and its function and the feelings and movements that become focused in the genital. In this chapter I discuss the theoretical developments that lead up to and support the perceptions I have summarized in the phrase *identification with the genital*.

The self as an aspect of the human organism must have an evolutionary significance, and the capability of the individual human to be organized in this way must serve biologically adaptive purposes. Such purposes are not difficult to infer. It is through the feelings, perceptions, and experiences we understand as constituting the self that we discern with exquisite sensitivity our relationships with the other people in any group of which we are a part. The emotions, perceptions, thoughts, and experiences we have in relation to others obviously serve to help us monitor our situation in the social group, ensuring that both our needs and the goals of the group are furthered according to priorities, schedules, times, places, and appropriate

An Exercise

This exercise offers a simple experiential exploration of the idea of "identification with the genital." Stand with the feet more than shoulder width apart, maybe two and a half to three feet apart. The feet should be toed in somewhat. Place the hands on the hips, and slowly allow the knees to bend. Stop if there is any pain to the knees. They need only be slightly bent. Pay attention to how you hold your pelvis. See if you can allow it to sway forward and back easily and gently. Now attend to your breathing. Allow the breathing to go as low into the abdomen as you can. There need be no strain in this exercise. In this position, the floor of the pelvis is able to relax. Press into the outer edges of the feet, and you may see that the floor of the pelvis can let go more. Now bring your awareness to the genital and imagine that you can allow your breath to go all the way to the root of your genital. As you do this, say to yourself, "This is me."

---

persons. The self is actually formed and emerges out of this complex monitoring. As societal life emerged and evolved in human populations, so too the sense of self would develop, as well as the awareness of the self as separate from and poised against the group.

We have seen how self and sexuality are equivalent and antithetical, and we could also say that there is a sense in which self and group are equivalent and antithetical. At times the individual's needs or purposes and that of the group's are identical, say in collective efforts in the acquisition of food or establishing protection; at other times, they may be entirely antithetical. Sexuality in the service of reproduction serves the necessity of the continuation of group life; at the same time, the individual's pursuit of his or her own sexual needs can prove disruptive to group life. Sexuality is a constant irritant in the life of the individual and the life of the group, pressing on the individual for discharge, pressing on the society to establish boundaries, controls, and accepted modes of expression.

Over the millennia, people evolved sociocultural structures to accommodate their intensely sexual nature. My understanding of the fundamentally sexual nature of the human organism is based on the work of Wilhelm Reich. Reich profoundly deepened and extended Freud's conception of sexuality through a lifetime of clinical, theoretical, and experimental explorations. I will discuss four aspects of Reich's work, and then I will discuss the new form of therapy Reich developed. Each aspect supports, gives content to, and helps define the concept of identification with the genital.

Orgasm Theory

Reich entered a career as a psychoanalyst in 1920; he was armed with Freud's conception of the sexual etiology of neurosis and a personal conviction of the importance of sexuality.[3] The sexual meaning of neurotic symptoms is hidden in the contemporary life of the patient, and its roots are hidden in his or her childhood past. The task of the analyst was to unearth those meanings and the memories and feelings that lie buried with them. Reich was well aware of his own sexual misery as a young man. He was also aware of his own childhood tragedy and sexual trauma.[4] Like anyone else, he was not entirely aware of their effects on him.

In his effort to understand the many instances of analytic failure, Reich undertook a more careful scrutiny of genitality, the patient's actual sexual functioning. For Reich, this meant getting detailed answers to very specific questions about specific sexual experiences. What was it like to have sex with so and so last night? What did you feel when you took your clothes off? What did you do? What was the nature of the foreplay? Was it brief or prolonged? What did you experience when you entered or were entered? What were the movements like? What was the experience during different phases of the intercourse? What was the orgasm like? Did you have one? What did you feel after intercourse? What did you feel for your partner before and after? What fantasies intruded or accompanied? Were you able to have eye contact? Was the experience fulfilling or frustrating? Then there would be a lot of questions about masturbation. How? When? What fantasies? What movements? It was Reich who showed us that all such questions mattered, and just how much they mattered. He brought the sexual issue into the here and now. It is not just a matter of childhood history.

Orgasm theory[5] emerged from this line of clinical investigation. The primary observation on which orgasm theory rests is that at the core of every analysis lies a disturbance in sexual functioning. Reich made it clear that ordinary kinds of unsatisfactory experiences were *disturbances*, and he was convinced that they were the core of the problem. Reich termed all such disturbances "orgastic impotence."

The disturbance of genitality is not, as was previously assumed, *one* symptom among others, *but it is the symptom of the neurosis.* . . . [T]he neurosis is not merely the result of a *sexual* disturbance in the broader sense of Freud; it is rather, the result of a *genital* disturbance, in the strict sense of *orgastic impotence.*[6]

Orgastic potency is the capacity to surrender fully to orgasm with a loved partner. To be free of neurosis, that is, to be healthy, means to be orgastically potent. "Complete involuntary vegetative surrender . . . constitutes the primal biological function that man has in common with all living creatures."[7]

Reich's fundamental conception of sexual health and his description of the full orgasm remain valid. The complete orgasm will feel full and gratifying. It will involve a relatively complete discharge of sexual tension from the whole body, a degree of loss of ego awareness, and a surrender to the deep involuntary movements of the body. There may be a sense of merging not only with the partner but with the cosmos as well. The aftereffect is one of pleasure, relaxation, fulfillment, and love for the partner.

In reality, it can be said that orgastic impotence characterizes a good deal of everyday sexual experience. This includes, besides actual impotence and frigidity, intercourse in which there is little genital feeling, premature ejaculation, a cold attitude toward the partner, any form of exploitation of the partner, an orgasm that is partial, leaving one frustrated, dissatisfied, and unfulfilled; it includes sexual intercourse in which fantasy, negativity, and sadomasochistic behavior enter; it includes experiences of sex which are followed by painful, empty, cold, depressive, or angry feelings; and it includes sexual experiences followed by disappointment, fear, or distaste for the partner; it includes a cold, asexual relationship or lifestyle, or a sexually driven and sexually preoccupied lifestyle.

Orgastic potency is, perhaps, a male formulation. A woman might not have chosen the word *potency*, as it usually implies a male version of sexual strength. The term does suggest a certain anxiety about its opposite, "impotence," a male preoccupation, reflected in Reich's other term, "orgastic impotence." An examination of sexual experience and of these terms from a woman's point of view is needed. Reich intended the concept to apply equally to the woman's experience of full and strong sexual feeling and a convulsive, orgastic discharge centering in and spreading out from the woman's genital.

Reich's conception of the orgasm has entered both popular and professional culture in a variety of ways, some potentially useful, others not so useful. In the hands of some of his followers, it became a tyrannical ideal and a criterion for criticism; in others it aroused a kind of hopeless longing or became a rationalization or illusion about sex growing out of unconscious erotic fantasies. From others it received a certain amount of humorous derision; and others incorporated his ideas without crediting him.[8]

Orgasm theory remains a powerful conception of sexuality and its place in human life. It opened the way to a deeper conception of organismic as well as sexual functioning. It basically supports the view that the individual is organized around his or her genitality.

Character and Character Analysis

As Reich was formulating orgasm theory he was also seeking to discover the underlying conditions that created orgastic impotence and how they could be changed. His work on these problems led to a clearer formulation of the nature of neurosis, a new approach to psychoanalytic therapy, and eventually to a new kind of therapy. It led from the mind to the body, from the talking cure—the verbal—to a treatment focused on the body itself—the nonverbal. It led from a psychology of desire to the bioenergetics of involuntary movement, from a theory of the mind to an organismic theory of the self.

Out of a persistent and systematic study of patients' hidden resistances, Reich formulated a concept of character and character armor. His observation is fundamental, precise, simple, brilliant, and to the point. The basic resistance to change is the individual's characteristic way of being.

"In the vernacular, we speak of hard and soft, noble and base, proud and servile, cold and warm people."[9] The type of behavior Reich was observing here has nothing to do with the content or meaning of what the patient said, conscious or unconscious. It has to do with the characteristic manner in which it was said or not said. As long as the patient kept on being that way, and relating to the analyst that way, not much changed.

The woman suffering from hysteria, for example, will be *apprehensively* silent and behave timidly; the woman having a compulsive neurosis will be *obstinately* silent or behave in a cold, haughty way toward the analyst. . . . We would say that in both cases the id conveyed the same wish, which the ego warded off differently.[10]

These ways of being are typically not experienced as symptoms. We are often totally unaware of these characteristic ways of being, even though they are what everyone else identifies about us. Reich called this aspect of the individual the "character" and said that it represented a "hardening of the ego" or, in other words, an "armor." Armor guards against pain and the stimulation both from the outside and from within that might evoke that pain.[11]

Therapy can be seen as treatment for a symptom, impotence or anxiety, for example. Symptoms are consciously experienced as disturbances, as something that is not-me, as "ego dystonic." We go to therapy for treatment of our symptoms. Being cured means the symptom goes away.

An understanding of character reveals the symptom to be an outgrowth of the total organization of the self, an organization which we do not differentiate from our self. Now what is to be treated? The whole organization of the self is in some way "sick," maladaptive, or just not right.[12]

Changing character is difficult. It means that going on about our business as usual is out of the question, because our usual way of being in the world is what is creating the symptom. In actual practice, what all this comes down to is that, if a person wants to "get better"—whatever that might mean to him or her—he or she has to change. When confronted with character, changing can seem overwhelmingly difficult.

Following Freud, Reich saw the resolution of the basic "infantile sexual conflict" of childhood, that is, the Oedipus complex, as the core of character formation. This means that the very essence of the way a person is in the world is a living expression of the resolution of that early sexual conflict. It is a here-and-now matter. Each person's sexuality is expressed through and as the character. Character is the specific form of a man's or a woman's sexuality.[13] Reich's emphasis on the genital aspect of the resolution of the Oedipus complex, discussed in detail in a later chapter, contributes to the validity of the concept of identification with the genital.

Seeing the Body

In his effort to understand character resistances, Reich moved his chair from behind the couch to where he could look at, as well as listen to, his patients—a small change that made a world of difference. Now he had the opportunity to observe a characteristic way of lying on the couch, composing the body, and a myriad involuntary expressive movements. The whole person was now on the couch. The way was open to bring the body into the therapeutic process.

Examples of the kinds of observations Reich was making at this time are:

(a) toneless, languid, or high-pitched voice; speaking with a tight upper lip; a masklike or immobile facial expression; even slight suggestions of a so-called baby face; an inconspicuous wrinkle of the forehead; drooping of the eyelids; tensions in the scalp; a concealed, undetected hypersensitivity in the larynx; a hurried, abrupt, constrained manner of speech; faulty respiration; noises or movements in the act of speaking which appear to be merely incidental; a certain way of hanging one's head, of shaking it, of lowering it when looking, etc.[14]

Reich said that contained in such phenomena are "the most important secrets of pathological displacements and the binding of vegetative energy."[15] He is identifying these body movements as functionally equivalent to expressions of the character armor of the ego, the psychological concept described earlier.

Reich always had a certain penchant for looking at things in bodily terms. In this regard, he seems different from Freud, who thought in terms of a model of the mind. One cannot imagine Reich in a study like Freud's, surrounded by a collection of archeological artifacts, books, and manuscripts. Freud's is the study of the professor, a bourgeois, Victorian doctor,[16] a study where one wears a suit. Photographs of Reich most often show him in an open-necked shirt in the out of doors or in a lab, close to some hands-on situation. While he was gifted with the mind of a genius, he did not have the quiet temperament of the scholar.

If we look at the person, we see the body. Looking at the individual as a biological organism immediately brings into focus the fact of their gender—male or female. As humans, however, we cannot see that gender without seeing the quality of masculinity or femininity, the qualities of sexuality. We see the person as the man or woman they are, and that has to do with the way in which their genital being informs their whole being.

Pulsation

Even in his early years as a psychoanalyst Reich's clinical observations were often biologically oriented and encompassed the bodily reality of the patient and the therapy process. Out of a number of brilliant clinical observations from his early years, one in particular reveals this predilection. It also became the seminal observation of an understanding of pulsation and a major new theoretical orientation.

In the cases of two women patients who had cardiac symptoms (symptoms of anxiety), their symptoms disappeared when they experienced genital feeling and pleasure. "In 1924, I treated two women with cardiac neurosis in the psychoanalytic clinic. With them, whenever genital excitation appeared, cardiac anxiety subsided. . . . Every inhibition of vaginal excitation would immediately result in oppression and anxiety 'in the region of the heart.'"[17] I find this a remarkable observation. It was new. Reich was prepared for it, and he saw its extraordinary significance.

He saw that genital feeling and anxiety must have some form of biological equivalence, but at the same time they are obviously antithetical. They are equivalents in the sense that the patient can and will have one or the other, each one in the same measure as the other, and they are antithetical in the sense that having the one precludes the other.

Based on these observations, Reich advanced a new and more profound understanding of sex and anxiety.

Freud's original formulation thus underwent the following correction. *There is no conversion of sexual excitation into anxiety. The same excitation which appears in the genital as pleasure, manifests itself as anxiety if it stimulates the cardiovascular system.* . . . The vasovegetative system will function at one time in the direction of sexual excitation, and again, when the latter is inhibited, in the direction of anxiety. . . . *[S]exuality and anxiety present two opposite directions of vegetative excitation.*[18]

It made sense to conclude that a common underlying excitatory process unifies both. Reich's formulation carries understanding of sex and anxiety into deeper biological territory. His formulation has an elegant simplicity characteristic of the best science, and it has a naturalistic sense of the depths of the organism, giving the formulation the ring of truth.

Underlying and unifying anxiety and genital feeling is a common excitatory process and a set of opposing directional movements. This is the basic bioenergetic model unifying antithetical affective experiences. Since excitation means movement, anxiety and genital feeling each can be understood as movements and movements in opposite directions. More specifically, genital feeling can be seen as an excitatory movement from the core of the organism to its periphery, that is, toward the world. Anxiety can be seen as a movement from the periphery toward the core away from the world, into the organism.

Bringing in the autonomic nervous system allows a final elegant, unifying step. Pleasurable movement outward toward the periphery is mediated by the parasympathetic branch of the autonomic nervous system. The anxious, unpleasurable movement inward to the core is mediated by the sympathetic system. Outward and inward movements themselves form a unity. They form a pulsatory expansion (outward) and contraction (inward).

The parasympathetic (sexual) effect is essentially the function of *expansion* and peripheral tension, and the sympathetic (anxiety) effect is essentially the function of contraction and central tension, if we do not consider the individual organs, but rather the *overall function* of the organism. There is an antagonistic functional relationship between periphery and center. *Expansion and contraction are the basic functions which govern the total innervation of the organism.*[19]

The genital is a significant focus of peripheral excitation, and the heart is a significant focus of excitation of the core. A movement outward toward the periphery (the genital) would be experienced as pleasure and genital excitement; such a movement would also be considered an expansion of the organism. A movement in toward the core of the organism (the heart, other inner organs, and the solar plexus) would be experienced as unpleasure or anxiety; such a movement is a contraction of the organism.

Why isn't energy moving in to the core a source of another kind of pleasure? Energy retreats into the core, away from the environment, in a situation of danger. In contrast, when the heart fills with love, it fills with love (energy) for another person, being, or object. The energy is expanding, moving out toward the world. When movement toward the world is blocked, the excitation (or energy) moves toward the core, creating a state of anxiety or "unpleasure." This movement creates symptoms (anxiety, organ symptoms), as opposed to pleasure.

Reich established that anxiety and sexual excitement are functionally identical *and* antithetical. The "and" is important. They are not *just* identical, nor are they *just* antithetical.

Anxiety as a psychic affect is not an "expression," or a "consequence," or even an "accompanying phenomenon" of the sympathetic retreat into oneself; it is the direct inner perception of the process and is *functionally identical* to it. Likewise, sexual pleasure in the broadest and narrowest sense—namely, any sensation ranging from the simplest state of relaxed well-being to the sensual tension of excitation—is the inner perception of the parasympathetic function of expansion, which goes together with the increase in surface tension. . . . It is the inner perception of melting, merging with the world, emerging completely from oneself, and it is functionally identical with the physiological process.[20]

Here is a truly functional formulation of the unity in identity and antithesis of mind and body, of affective experience and bodily movement.

Reich tied expansion/contraction to the functions of the autonomic nervous system.[21] Because the term *vegetative nervous system* was also in use at the time, Reich used terms such as "vegetative energy." For a time, he called his new form of therapy "vegetotherapy," a term still used in Europe.

Living tissue does not just expand, nor does it just contract. It expands and contracts; that is, it pulsates. The life, health, and sexuality of the organism can be understood in greater depth in light of pulsation.

Biological pulsation is readily observed in all living tissue and in any living organism. The pulse felt beneath the finger tips and visible in the throat is the beat of life. The heartbeat, respiratory wave, and peristalsis are fundamental pulsations of the body. Orgasm is another. These are pulsations of the organism as a whole or of large organ systems. Every cell pulsates, and cellular pulsation can be readily observed when living tissue is viewed under a microscope. One-celled organisms, like paramecia and amoebas, which are easily cultured, are excellent subjects for observing pulsatory phenomena. Slime molds, multinucleated masses of undifferentiated protoplasm, easily cultured, are excellent specimens to observe. Pulsation is life itself, and it holds life's secret; dead tissue does not pulsate.

Protoplasm is in continuous motion. Much of the motion looks like streaming. The fluid protoplasm streams first in one direction, then another. The flowing and streaming are pulsatory phenomena. A remarkable range of these movements has been demonstrated.[22] One might say that those movements are the result of the organism being alive, but one could also say that those movements are life.

The Function of the Orgasm

Including the principles of pulsation in orgasm theory led to further developments, deepening the biological picture. In Freud's theory, libido is the mental representation of the sexual instinct. With Reich, the energetic concept became embodied, and the economic viewpoint assumed very different aspects. When Reich spoke of quantities of energy being released he did so in relation to real bodily movements and reactions. An energetic concept is essential to the understanding of the phenomena Reich was observing and working with clinically.

In 1933 Reich wrote the first paper on what was to be a new form of therapy, "Psychic Contact and Vegetative Current."[23] In this paper he has a foot in each of two worlds, using psychoanalytic language and also referring to vegetative current. He specifies a new therapeutic goal: "to reestablish the capacity for vegetative streaming."[24] In referring to "currents" and "streamings," he is referring to sensations arising from autonomic, involuntary movement, such as sexual feeling or anxiety. Libido is first embodied here.

Reich's development of his concepts was always tied to direct observation and to basic theoretical positions previously established. As an investigator, he constantly asked himself remarkably good questions. In a paper shortly following the one on psychic contact, there is a fascinating section titled "Some Peculiar Features of Sexuality."[25] The "peculiar features" under consideration are really questions deriving from the prevailing view in psychoanalysis that sexual pleasure is the result of tension reduction. Reich asked a series of questions which demonstrate that the relaxation of mechanical tension cannot explain the phenomenology of sexual experience. One observation is of special interest.

To start with, it might seem as if *mechanical relaxation* is restricted to men only and is not a valid explanation in the case of women. It is this mechanical view of events which led to the idea, predominant in sexology, that it is 'natural' for women not to experience orgasm. . . .

Orgastic phenomena in the healthy woman, which fully resemble those of the man, thus require explanation. Women are able to experience the same kind of rhythmic-clonic convulsions of the involuntary muscles; they experience peripheral concentration of excitation before climax and centripetal draining and ebbing away of excitation after climax, exactly the way men do.[26]

Reich asked other questions. For example, in *coitus interruptus*, there is a mechanical discharge and relaxation (for the man) and a lingering dissatisfaction. What is the source of the dissatisfaction? How can a man have erection, intercourse, and discharge with little feeling? Why do gentle, slow movements create more feeling than fast, hard, thrusting ones? What is the source of sexual compatibility? What is the explanation for some of the specific sensations of good sexual intercourse, such as the wish to penetrate, the desire to take in? And so on.

From these questions, which are based in observation, Reich drew the conclusion that "besides mechanical relaxation, a *bioelectrical discharge* occurs during orgasm."[27] He seriously tried to study biolectrical charge experimentally. Later, his understanding of the nature of this charge changed. He felt there must be a specific biological energy—bioenergy. Electricity, after all, does not promote pulsatory phenomena in living tissue; it stops it.

Having established that only a bioelectrical charge can make understandable, the exact phenomenology of sex and orgasm, he took the next theoretical step. The previous understanding of sexual pleasure could be expressed in the simple formula mechanical tension–mechanical relaxation. Now, Reich saw the formula as mechanical tension–charge–discharge–mechanical relaxation; he called this the orgasm formula.

Grasping the significance of this formula is not easy because it requires a grasp, first, of the whole line of reasoning and clinical evidence leading up to it. Second, and even more demanding, it requires us to look at living substance or tissue in a new way. It requires that we see its movement as the essential feature of life itself and then asks that we seek ways to comprehend that movement without, as most biological science does, breaking down the living tissue into component materials in such a way that it is seen to be made up only of nonliving chemicals. Third, and not least of the difficulties, the "royal road" taken to this formula is through the study of orgasm, "the Cinderella of the sciences," as Reich says. In contrast with later sex research, in studying orgasm, Reich has omitted none of the passionate feelings and experiences that go with it, and these very feelings and reactions are the essence of the investigation.

The tension-charge formula must apply "to all involuntary functions of living substance." The reason is that all living substance pulsates, and it is all made up of a specific and peculiar combination of mechanical and electrical "functions."

[T]he *particular combination of mechanical and electrical functions was the specific characteristic of living functioning. . . .* in living matter, *the functions of mechanics* (tension-relaxation) *and those of electricity* (charge-discharge) *are combined in a specific manner which does not occur in non-living matter.*[28]

It is important to note Reich's use of the term *functions*. It indicates that he is staying within the realm of the mechanisms of the living organism pertaining to what the person actually experiences. When he talks about charge and discharge, it is always in the context of bodily movements, the kind of inner movements whose perception is the actual experience of feeling, especially feelings of sex, anxiety, or anger. The same pertains to his reference to relaxation. What is involved is an organismic mechanism which accounts for and is an aspect of the biology underlying experience. The perception of the reduction of tension is experienced as relaxation; an example is the experience of falling asleep in a relaxed state after satisfying sexual intercourse.

The claim of the tension-charge formula is that it describes an inherent aspect of the functioning of living tissue. Hence, the healthful functioning of any organism, or person, can be assessed in terms of its capacity to maintain the expressions of that formula in its own bodily being. We can begin to appreciate how Reich understood the function of the orgasm itself.

Orgasm, of course, is the prime representative of the orgasm formula: "*Orgastic gratification is a Bio-electrical discharge, followed by a mechanical relaxation (detumescence).*"[29] An overriding implication of this for human life is that sexual pleasure is not an ancillary to life, it is the essence of life. "Thus, the process of sexual pleasure is the life process per se. This is not just a manner of speaking, but an experimentally proven fact."[30]

In light of this series of observations, orgasm can be seen as the regulator of the person's bioenergies. Reich used the term *sex-economy* to refer to the individual's own

manner of regulation of bio-electrical energy, or, what is the same thing, of the economy of the sexual energies of the individual. "Sex-economy" means the manner in which an individual handles his bio-electrical energy; how much of it he dams up and how much of it he discharges orgastically.[31]

These observations apply to the daily life of the individual, that is, they are functional. Pulsation is the very life of the individual. The stronger, fuller, and more energetic the pulsation, the more alive and healthier the person. Orgasm is pulsatory, and it follows the formula tension-charge-discharge-relaxation. Orgasm is the fundamental expression of the individual's life. Its strength and pleasure depend on the expressive aliveness of the partners. The specific function of orgasm is the regulation of the individual's energetic economy.

In a healthy adult person, there is a buildup of a certain amount of free energy that will be experienced as an increase in tension and then as a longing for sexual release and gratification. A fulfilling sexual experience with a loved partner discharges the surplus of energy and releases the tension. Mature, healthy men and women are in need of regular orgastic sex. Where gratifying orgasm is blocked, an energetic stasis results, effecting the individual physically and emotionally. Stasis can throw him or her back into the sexual conflicts of childhood.[32] This is a bodily, bioenergetic process, not one that can be explained in psychological terms.

In sexual foreplay and in intercourse, there is a buildup of charge or excitation in the genital apparatus, and in orgasm, there is a convulsive release of that charge. Subjectively, the stronger the charge that can be built up, and the more completely it can be released, the greater the pleasure and gratification. In orgasm there is a release of energy, like a dam bursting, allowing a release of energy from a pool concentrated in the genital apparatus to flow back into the whole pelvis and throughout the rest of the body. The effects of the flux of energy buildup, release, and flow in orgasm can be compared with water flow in and out of an ocean tidal pool. Waters rest in the pool until the next wave or tide comes flowing in and through the pool, flushing out the old water and refreshing the creatures living there with fresh, oxygenated, nutrient-bearing water. If the water stayed too long without changing, it would become stagnant and would cease to support life.

A healthy person has the biological capacity for each of these stages of sexual response:

- the capacity for generating a certain amount of free energy
- the capacity for allowing that energy to become focused in sexual feelings, for yearnings for a loved partner, and for allowing the buildup of tension
- the capacity to build the genital, sexual charge in love-making with another
- the capacity for genital intercourse in which the genitals join and move together, further building the charge toward orgasm
- the capacity to surrender fully to the feelings, experience, and involuntary movements of orgasm, which includes
  - the capacity to be overwhelmed by orgasm
  - the capacity for allowing the refreshment and relaxation that is the aftermath

These capacities are inherent aspects of orgastic potency. They are the necessary conditions of the full and free function of the orgasm. They are bodily, organismic capacities or functions. They underlie our "psychology." They are its biological basis, as much as any neuron or brain circuit. They determine our capacity for love, for pleasure, for being functional, contributing members of society. The function of orgasm underlies each individual human being's capability to be a member of society.

Reich had a profound sense of the depth of the function of the orgasm and its expression or evolution from life itself. "*In the orgasm, the living*

organism is nothing but a part of pulsating nature."[33] I see this as a profoundly respectful view of sex, and it provides the basis for self-respect and
a self-respecting sexuality. The developmental realization of these capacities is based on the identification with the genital.

THE NEW THERAPY

Reich's comprehension of the function of orgasm and individual sex-economy permits a comprehension of health and neurosis in energetic terms. It
establishes a solid theoretical basis for a new approach to therapy. The
spectrum from health to neurosis is a function of how much of the individual's bioenergy is dammed up and how much is discharged orgastically.
Neurosis is not merely a psychological phenomena, caused by psychic conflicts or fixations. The conflicts and fixations are somatically anchored, and
neurosis is the expression of disturbance in the individual's sexual energy
economy.[34]

In his first groundbreaking paper[35] on the new therapy, Reich gave a new
clinical description of a major effect of the damming up of bioenergy. He
called it contactlessness. Contactlessness is experienced subjectively as apathy, deadness, inwardly dying, isolation, a feeling of being unreal, uncon-
nected, alienated, feelingless, frozen, and so on. Contactlessness in another
person is experienced as artificial, mannered behavior, as behaviors generating a lack of interest in another, as overly expressive or inexpressive, as
unreal, not genuine, and so on. Contactlessness is a result of the withdrawal of energy from the surface of the organism, the anxious withdrawal
into the self. Since the individual must compensate for contactlessness, it is
often not experienced until uncovered in therapy.

In describing contactlessness, Reich wrote one of the many poignant
utterances that seem to come from his very soul: "The road between vital
experiencing and inwardly dying is paved with disappointments in love."
While able to look into his soul and acknowledge his own anguish, he was
also able to follow his very active curiosity and find the good questions to
ask. "This," he continues, "bitter as it is, still does not explain the mechanism involved in the process."[36] For many psychological investigators, it
would have been enough to show that disappointments in love result in an
inward dying. This is not enough for Reich. He needed to know how it
worked. What was the mechanism?

If the result is an inward dying, the mechanism must go to the heart of
life itself, and at the energetic heart of life is the orgasm. "[T]he fear of
orgastic contact constitutes the core of the fear of genuine, direct, psychic
contact with persons and with the processes of reality."[37]

The contemporary focus in the therapeutic world on sexual abuse, for
just one thing, brings Reich's work on orgasm anxiety and his way of
working with it directly into today's world. Orgasm anxiety refers to a
deep fear of the experience of surrendering to the feelings and experience

of orgasm and to the soft feelings of love that bring one to orgasm with a loved partner. It is a fear that becomes attached to the feeling of pleasurable expansion itself. It reflects a childhood history in which early sexual feelings and feelings of love were met with punishment or some other traumatic response. Orgasm anxiety puts a block between the individual and his or her world as a whole.

Out of the conditions that cause contactlessness arise further characterological developments in the form of "substitute contact." Substitute contact represents the compromise between the actual energetic withdrawal from the world and the necessity of social adaptation. From the beginning of his work as a therapist, Reich had a keen nose for any hint of artificial, ungenuine substitute contact, and his descriptions of such behaviors are masterful. For example, he contrasts

the difference between living sexual rhythm and calculated sex appeal; between natural, unaffected dignity and put-on dignity; between genuine and sham modesty; between the direct and the pretentious expression of life; between vegetative muscular rhythm and the swaying of hips and squaring of shoulders in imitation of it.[38]

This is a significant concept for the clinical understanding of human behavior, and Reich achieved a masterful description of it. In addition, the conception is anchored in a profound view of the human organism, and it is usefully embedded in a consistent form of character analytic therapy. Like other of his concepts, Reich's views on genuine and artificial behavior, contactfulness and substitute contact, entered the professional and popular culture, with barely a nod or a wink in his direction. Anchoring the conception of contactfulness in the foundation of orgasm theory provides a solid basis for distinguishing between superficial social engraftments and the confrontation with the depths of organismic life in sex and deep emotion.

The goal of therapy becomes overcoming orgasm anxiety and establishing genuine contact. The new therapy is based on the discovery of the functional identity of character armor and muscular armor. "When a character inhibition would fail to respond to psychic influencing, I would work at the corresponding somatic attitude. Conversely, when a disturbing muscular attitude proved difficult of access, I would work on its characterological expression, and thus loosen it up."[39]

In the simplest terms, the approach could now be through the mind or through the body. Reich might talk with the patient, or he might intervene in a muscular pattern. "A typical friendly smile, e.g., which impeded the work, could be eliminated by describing the expression as well as by disturbing the muscular attitude."[40]

Reich deepened the conception of sexuality through the way in which he learned to "read" the muscular armor. Initially Reich described "the formation of a muscular armor around the person's biological core." The armor is made up of muscular tensions and muscular attitudes, particular ways of composing the body or manner of holding it. The muscular armor's function is to bring about "the inhibition of the life functions (libido, anxiety, aggression)."[41] The muscular armor is equivalent to the ego's character armor or character attitudes. Reading muscular attitudes has the same significance it does in ordinary life. Facial expressions and body language usually carry unmistakable meanings. We know an angry look or a frightened one; we know an "official" bearing or a beggarly one. In the therapeutic setting such expressions, on the characterological level, can be subtle, and Reich was a master at picking them up: the "typical friendly smile;" the foxy look; the slight, subtle expressions through which the patient's contactlessness found expression, revealing a disengagement from the therapist and the therapeutic endeavor.

In the course of several years of working with the muscular armor, Reich discovered a completely new level of phenomena. He discovered that the armor was arranged in functional segmental rings running around the body perpendicularly to the longitudinal axis of the body. He had discovered the worm in the human being.[42] Each segment is capable of its own expression, independently of the ring above or below it. The expression and movements of the segments are functional, that is not correlated with anatomical structure.

Therapy works by breaking down, softening, or loosening armor. When armor is loosened, there may be various kinds of "peculiar somatic sensations,"[43] and sooner or later emotions will be released and expressed—anxiety, rage, crying out of grief and sorrow, and pleasure. This is a primary purpose of working with the armor—to release the accompanying emotion. Emotion is the expression of "the motility of the body plasma . . . the pulsation function of all the organs."[44] The pulsation of the body, its inner movement, is its very life, so the body's life is being restored as armor breaks down and emotion is freed. Pulsatory movement is the free movement of the body's energy.

Reich uses the word *organ* here in an interesting way. He is not simply talking about stomachs and livers. He is talking about expressive organs. The heart can be an expressive organ, and so can the mouth, the eyes, or the throat. The chest is an expressive organ, and so is the pelvis, the belly, and the thoracic diaphragm. These, in the language of expression, are all "organs."

Reich described seven segments: ocular, the band around the eyes; oral, around the mouth; the cervical, around the throat; the thoracic, around the chest; the diaphragmatic, the narrow band around the middle of the torso; the abdominal, around the stomach; and the pelvic which includes the lower back, sacrum, and genital. The arms are considered a functional part of the thoracic segment, and the legs are considered a functional part of the pelvic segment. Each segment circles the whole body, so some of a segment is in the back, some in the front. When there is armoring in a segment, there will be muscular tensions front and back.

When Reich worked as a therapist, he sat by the couch in such a way as to be able to observe the patient's whole body and close enough to touch the patient. The patient will now lie on the couch in reduced clothing, so that it is possible to see the expression of each segment. What does Reich see? Breathing is the first and most important movement to be observed. Reich soon discovered that every manifestation of armor was accompanied by a disturbance in breathing, and even more specifically, respiratory inhibition is "*the basic mechanism of the neurosis* in general."[45] The reason is simple and profound. Emotion can be suppressed through the inhibition of respiration. Repression is based on chronic inhibition of respiration.

Useful therapy, then, depends on the restoration of natural respiration. If the person can breathe he or she can feel and move. Armoring is the mechanism for maintaining respiratory inhibition, a kind of chronic holding of the breath. Restoring natural respiration is not a mechanical process. The person cannot achieve it by mechanically doing breathing exercises. It is an emotional process, depending on the functional relationship between the muscular tension of the armor and the held emotion. The tension must be released and the emotion freed for the capacity for full respiration and feeling to be restored.

Reich made another discovery while working with segmental armor. As the segments are sequentially freed and natural respiration restored, he repeatedly observed a characteristic involuntary movement in the body. As respiration became fuller and deeper and the excitatory wave stronger, the shoulders tend to lift slightly, the head drop back, and the pelvis reach up. The dropping back of the head expresses surrender, and for the movement to occur the person does have to surrender to the respiration and to the body's feelings. As the pelvis reaches upward, the expression is of yearning, as of yearning for fulfillment or gratification. Reich called this movement the orgasm reflex.

The movement is undoubtedly orgastic, and in orgasm, very similar movements occur; however, the orgasm reflex, as it occurs in therapy, is not an orgasm. The occurrence of the orgasm reflex was, for Reich, the criterion of a successful therapy. It signifies that "the motility of the body plasma" has been restored.[46] Both orgasm and orgasm reflex involve surrender to bodily ("organ") sensations and involuntary pulsations. Reich felt that establishing the orgasm reflex in therapy would ensure the capacity for orgastic potency in sex.

In discovering the orgasm reflex, Reich had discovered a deeper layer of sexual meaning in the pulsatory involuntary movements which underlie human life. In addition, where he had found the segmented worm in the human being in the segmental arrangement of the armor, he found an even earlier phylogenetic model for the orgasm reflex, the jelly fish. In the mollusks, there is no anatomical segmentation, and the two ends of the jelly fish come together as it pulsates itself through the water.[47]

Reich captured the dramatic paradigmatic shift of the new therapy. "[The new therapy] attempts to influence the organism not through the use of human language but by getting the patient to express himself biologically."[48]

The orgasm reflex is a biological expression of the organism. The person who surrenders to it is expressing him or herself in a biologically profound way. The organism "expresses itself through movements; we therefore speak of expressive movements."[49] The word *emotion* itself refers to movement; emotions are "plasmatic movement."[50] Felt or experienced emotion is therefore the perception of movement. The autonomically anchored expansion (pleasure) and contraction (anxiety, unpleasure) of the organism are the fundamental movements upon which all emotions are built.

The expressive language of the body and its inhibition in another person can be "read" because my body, in this regard, is the same as yours. My body senses the other's movements and can understand it, often being able to translate the expression into words. This does not mean that the words reveal the "real" meaning of the movement. On the contrary, the *real* meaning is the movement. The movement is the expression of the organism, and it needs no translation. More significantly, Reich observed that in orgasm, as in the orgasm reflex, there were movements which are expressive but which are not translatable into language. Here, the expression must, in some sense, be "suprapersonal." The expression goes beyond the realm of the living, and must in some way reflect the meeting of the living and the nonliving. For this reason, Reich felt that the energetic, expressive movement of orgasm met a cosmic energy, an energy of the universe. He related this possibility to universal human religious and cosmic yearnings.

At a late point in Freud's development, the concept of the death instinct emerged in his theoretical vision, the tendency of the living to return to the nonliving out of which it emerged. The death instinct is a suprapersonal principle, one that is outside of or beyond the functioning of the individual organism. Reich too, at a somewhat similar stage in his development, found a suprapersonal principle, not of death, but of an actual energy which he called orgone energy. While it is an energy existing apart from the biological organism, it is an energy at the heart of life, taking a specific form in the biological organism, and the freeing of which in the living organism enhances life.

A final implication of segmental armor and orgasm theory pertains to psychosomatic disease. Since armoring permanently structures into the body conflictual and traumatic childhood developments, it is a permanent stress. It requires energy to maintain, limits the expression and motility of the body, and creates energetic stasis. Associated with armor is a respiratory disturbance or inhibition. These conditions describe a state of chronic contraction. Since contraction is anchored in the sympathetic nervous system, armor is a state of chronic sympathetic hyperactivity. Reich called it chronic sympatheticotonia. Depending on the organs and muscle groups involved, various parts of the body and organs are effected. They are under long-term stress which can lead to chronic disease.[51] This formulation of chronic stress is totally compatible with contemporary formulations of the physiology of stress and disease.[52] Reich's functional formulations go beyond many of these, however, in their holistic unification of mind and body, of self, sexuality, and emotion.

IDENTIFICATION WITH THE GENITAL AND SELF-RESPECT IN THE LIGHT OF ORGASM THEORY

Through orgasm theory, Reich defined a profound level of discourse about the human organism, about the body. He did it in a way no one had before or has done since. I will sometimes use a phrase such as "on the body level" as a shorthand reference to this level of discourse. Reich, himself, gave the simplest definition of this level of discourse when he said, "deep feeling is identical with having contact with the living organism *beyond the limitations of language.*"[53] While this poetic apothegm captures the essence of this mode of discourse, the whole array of description, clinical observation, and theory which has been reviewed in this chapter stands behind it.

Self-respect means to be in touch with this level of deep feeling in one's self and to respectfully base one's life on it. The need to respect the potential for others to do the same is inherent in this form of self-respect. Deep feeling is the perception of the fundamental pulsatory movements of the body, the various manifestations of expansion-contraction and of charge-discharge. This is the expressive life of the body, of the living, as Reich aptly put it, and hence of the self. The effect of characterological and muscular armor is to break the contact with this fundamental organic movement, separating the person from deep feeling and leaving him or her contactless to some degree. The substitute contact which compensates the individual for the loss of organic function is a social engraftment of some kind, a work role, for example, a more or less artificial behavior mode that accommodates social adaptation. Substitute contact results in the individual being deeply divided between biological being and social being. The structures that maintain this division, the armor, are a form of chronic stress and autonomic hyper- or hypo-activity which can eventually lead to disease.

Of the organic movements underlying deep feeling, respiration and orgasm are the most fundamental. Both are purely biological, and in fact, an argument can be made, as Reich did, that they are supra-biological, that they are not evolutionary but a more fundamental expression of a life energy. In any case they are the basic pulsations of the organism. They may be full and free, or, when characterological armor is present, they will be bound, inhibited, and constricted. For both to be free and full, that is for a state of health, the body must be relatively free of negative characterological attitudes and muscular armor, muscular attitudes, and chronic tensions.

Identification with the genital can be simply understood in light of these considerations. The genital apparatus is the mechanism through which the function of orgasm, of charge and discharge, is achieved. This is the fundamental expression of the organism, and at the core, the organism must be identified with it, as if to say, "This is me."

Each human being is faced with dilemmas resulting from the inevitable conflicts between biology and society. While it is also true that each can and does support the other, there is enormous clinical and historical evidence that even where outright neurotic dysfunction is not the upshot, civilized people tend to be anxious, stressed, and widely diseased.[54]

Consider again the functional relationship between sex and self-respect. In states of stress, both functions are effected, whether the stress is temporary or chronic. To take a simple example, a person with a bad cold who doesn't feel well will wish to be home in bed, if possible, away from the demands of family, work, and colleagues. If the person is self-respectful, rest will soon restore health. When long-term stress is based in characterological armor, the individual may have the same wish, but feel compelled to slog on, an unpleasant state of affairs often leaving little energy for sex, pleasure, or for feeling good about one's self. Both the sexual function and the self-respect function are disrupted. There will be less energy and capacity for sexual love. What happens to the function of self-respect is complex.

Ongoing efforts driven by the need to sustain self-esteem may not permit the man with a cold to take time off, in which case it will take longer to restore vitality. The function of self-respect can be dominated by the chronic effort to sustain self-esteem (as contrasted with self-respect), in a social setting. Similarly, ambition in the service of building self-esteem, and the need to be special or outstanding, may drive a person. These needs, arising as they do from an armored state, are distortions of the more organic, self-regulating functions of self-respect. Here is the split between biology and society. In the effort to gain a reputable standing in society, the individual may appear to be self-respecting. The appearance is deceiving if the effort is made at the expense of the self and through the suppression or actual break from self-respect.

It can appear that the functions of sex and self-respect are actually split, with the individual pouring all his or her energies into social adaptation at the expense of his organic, bodily self, and sometimes falling ill in the effort. In reality, both functions are suffering in equal degree. The energies of the individual are absorbed primarily by a distorted sociality in the form of the struggle to maintain self-esteem. Underlying these distortions are fear, guilt, shame, and humiliation.

Guilt and shame are disturbances of sex and self-respect. Characterologically, they function to channel the individual's energies into a societal adaptation, always to some degree at the expense of biological expression. The demands of self-respect, a biological function, and those of self-esteem, a societal function, may well be at odds with one another, and this can be a confusing and difficult state of affairs. A child, for example, may know perfectly well that masturbation feels good and therefore is good, while knowing at the same time that a parent may be disturbed by it or consider it bad. The child's self-respect and self-regulation require the pleasure and release of masturbation, the child's self-esteem, how he or she stands in the eyes of the parent, requires that masturbation be hidden or relinquished. What will happen, of course, within the being of the child, is a painful compromise. Such compromise, whether it be hiding or suppressing the masturbation, usurps the child's biological energies. The child's relationship with the outer world, including the parent, is changed for good, as are its sex and self-respect functions. It will have replaced the latter, to some extent, with the guilty, shameful need to reestablish self-esteem, a need which will undoubtedly carry over into every aspect of its life.

REFLECTIONS ON REICH AND HIS WORK

The releasing or softening of blocks leads to a gentle pulsatory movement, but the process of getting there can be anything but soft and gentle.

My interpretation of this defense immediately released great excitation, intensified the tic and the self-consciousness, and led, to my surprise, to violent convulsions of the pelvic musculature. . . . The patient's immediate reaction . . . was kicking of the feet, followed by violent pelvic movements with masturbation and orgasm during the session.[55]

We can assume that this quote gives a fair indication of the emotional and energetic climate of Reich's consulting room. It takes a lot to deal with situations of this sort under any circumstances, let alone to be the one whose therapeutic innovations lead to them.

Perhaps the most important aspect of Freud's innovative work is the pioneering exploration of a new kind of interpersonal, dyadic relationship. New and revealing emotional realities emerged, and so did new forms of exploring emotional and relational boundaries, and it was found that all of this could be turned toward healing.

Reich, in turn, forged into new territory in the interpersonal domain. By observing, commenting on, and intervening in actual bodily movement, profound emotions were released and reenactments from the patient's traumatic past emerged. The patient's experiences to which Reich became witness had an intense and sometimes terrible here-and-now reality. Such experiences can have a frightening prospect, and this is as true today as in Reich's time.

I find it remarkable that Reich had the courage to voyage into these realms of emotional experience. I believe he was able to do so because he had already faced, in a very lonely way, issues of life and death.[56] From painful crises of his own, he must have found the courage and understanding to permit his patients to enter the darkest depths and offer them illumination, understanding, and guidance.

Reich's personal voyage and his intellectual explorations are both remarkable. He also combined them in a remarkable way when he asked the poignant question, *"What is the origin of the extraordinary role of the genital drive?"*[57] Here, as he often was, he was ahead of his time. The evolutionary theorist suggests it derives from "[t]he obligation to engage in sex to reproduce."[58] In fact, this does not entirely answer the question. Evolutionary theory, for example, is hard pressed to offer much of an explanation for female orgasm.[59] If, however, the genital drive is itself the expression of the very nature of the "specific biological energy," the "extraordinary role of the genital drive" finds an explanation.

Sex and sexuality are inherently difficult topics to deal with. From Freud on, each researcher carries to the topic his or her own deep vulnerability. This applies as much to Reich as to anyone. However, to Reich, we owe an understanding of sex as "natural." He described sex as a natural, inherent quality of life, an aspect of pulsation, the soft spontaneous movement of the organism. He described a level of sexual surrender and fulfillment that in most people could only awaken longing, or perhaps outrage. He said that a kind of pathology he had newly discovered, armoring, made humans antagonistic toward that movement and that kind of sex. He propounded the idea that armoring, as a particular form of developmental distortion or pathology, would make humans antagonistic to what was best in themselves. He was, in my own view, entirely correct in all this. Thus, if Reich's intellectual, scientific, and therapeutic formulations helped lay the foundation for the sexual revolution of the mid-twentieth century, they also laid bare the reasons it would go awry.

The capacity to make the kind of observations Reich learned to make about pulsatory phenomena is very important. This capacity gives a further meaning to Reich's concept of orgone energy. It represents, in these egoistic times, our contact with the earth, nature, and the cosmos. It represents and calls for a humble acceptance of, and respect for, our bodies, our sexuality, our emotional experience as humans. It calls for a gentle surrender to the human realities that are closest to us, the realities and truth of our own bodies and the bodies of those closest to us. It gives comprehension to the possibility of pleasure, of melting, of giving in, letting down.

Reich showed that to experience and observe pulsatory phenomena, we have to be in an unarmored state. We have to be open bodily and emotionally. We will not be able to see what he saw if we maintain attitudes that are stiff, mechanistic, pedantic ("scientific" or otherwise), competitive, compliant, or frozen. It was Reich who helped us to understand these attitudes in their bodily and mental manifestations, and it was Reich who made it clear that as long as we are stiff and frozen in our bodies, we couldn't really see or feel life or have love.

Life and love are lived through the body; and there is nothing on earth or in the heavens that substitutes for love. Being able to observe pulsation means softening the body, clearing the eyes and the mind; it means to breath fully, to give in, to allow life to be lived through us. It means to acknowledge the deep yearning for sexual surrender with a loved partner, and the honesty and self-awareness to feel when there is the inhibition to such surrender in our own body. It is to Wilhelm Reich that we owe our deepest understanding of these attitudes. The world is a better place as these attitudes are more widespread.

SEEING THE PERSON: BIOENERGETIC ANALYSIS

> Therapy aims to increase sexual feeling not only in the genitals
> but throughout the body. This translates into a sense of one's manhood or
> womanhood. It is reflected in the way an individual holds himself and moves.
>
> —Alexander Lowen

THE DEVELOPMENT OF BIOENERGETIC ANALYSIS

Wilhelm Reich arrived in the United States in 1939. Among his first pupils was Alexander Lowen, a young man of thirty at the time. Lowen was attracted to the theme of the first course Reich taught in America—the relationship between body and mind. Lowen became Reich's student and then a practitioner of the new therapy. His therapeutic innovations, his enthusiastic espousal of the work, and his own forceful personality led to the establishment of a separate school of therapy which he called bioenergetics or bioenergetic analysis.

Lowen brought a fresh perspective to Reich's new therapy that was simple, realistic, down to earth, and honest. His personal experience showed him that achieving the orgasm reflex in the course of his intensive three-year therapy with Reich by no means meant that all his problems were resolved. He was very aware that his own body was full of very deep tensions.[1] With a close colleague he began to work out techniques to help soften the tensions. The same techniques would prove useful in therapy with others.

One innovation Lowen introduced represents a symbolic break with the whole European analytic tradition. He got people off the couch and onto their feet. Just as Reich had significantly changed the Freudian paradigm when he swung his chair around from behind the couch to where he could look at his patients, Lowen shifted the clinical paradigm by working with people in a standing position. He developed exercises and movements that help to get more feeling into the whole lower half of the body and the legs, and he emphasized the sense of having the feet firmly planted on the ground. He called this "grounding." The couch remained as one alternative.

Lowen has a genius for developing physical techniques and exercises, and he added numerous others that aid the release of tensions and foster a deepened respiration and the release of emotion. Another of his innovations, universally used by his students, is the "bioenergetic breathing stool," used in working with respiration. It is a stool about two feet high with a rolled-up blanket strapped to its top. One can lie back over it, and it stretches open the chest and throat and softens the back, allowing a deepened respiration to occur. Lowen said he got the idea for the stool from the inclination to stretch against the top of a chair as one sits, in order to get a good stretch and take a full breath, using the top of the chair as a fulcrum.[2]

A new vision of therapy emerged for Lowen out of his own experience. Just as he recognized that achieving the orgasm reflex in therapy was not a sure sign of health, he also concluded that it is unrealistic to make orgastic potency the goal of therapy. He was still convinced that problems of sexuality are at the heart of neurosis. He also recognized the theoretical validity of the concept of orgastic potency, and he kept it as a yardstick for health. However, he feels that the kind of sexual health that Reich envisioned is intrinsically incompatible with modern culture.[3]

In his effort to come to terms with the theoretical validity and practical unreality of orgastic potency as a therapeutic goal, Lowen sought and found practical, useful approaches, theoretically and clinically. The theoretical keystone for his approach is the actual, overall functioning of the adult in his or her world. What is at question is a form of maturation, which "ends up being a life-time task."[4] "The goal of therapy has to be the development of a healthy, mature personality."[5]

This brings the focus to the ego, its strength and functioning, in contrast with the more narrow focus of sexual functioning. The issue is to integrate the ego with sexuality. "The ego exists as a powerful force in Western man that cannot be dismissed or denied. The therapeutic goal is to integrate the ego with the body and its striving for pleasure and sexual fulfillment."[6]

Lowen shifted the focus of therapy from sexual functioning to ego functioning. This gives the appearance, initially, of shifting the focus away from biology, in Reich's terms, and back to psychology in psychoanalytic terms. The term *ego*, of course, comes from psychoanalysis. What happens, in this shift, to the world of pulsation, the deep level of biological discourse about the organism that Reich had discovered and articulated so beautifully? Lowen, in fact, bent the concept of the ego, as he did other concepts, to encompass both worlds. Ego functioning, he said, is based entirely in self-expression, and the criteria for health are now understood in terms of self-expression. "In bioenergetic analysis, as opposed to Reichian therapy, the main criterion of health is the fullness of one's self-expression. A healthy person would be characterized by the free flow of excitation through the body."[7]

Lowen's understanding of ego functioning is entirely related to Reich's organismic theory of the self and by no means omits the central importance of sexuality. Lowen's concept of self-expression here derives directly from Reich's. Self-expression is another way of talking about the expressive language of the body, and the strength of self-expression depends upon "the free flow of excitation through the body," just as Reich demonstrated. In fact, in the therapy situation, such a free flow of excitation may indeed elicit the orgasm reflex. The requirement of the free flow of excitation for health and the potential for the orgasm reflex indicate that the functioning of the ego rests on the foundation of the person's sexuality. Ego and sexuality, in Lowen's terms, are functionally related.

However, self-expression must be understood in the actual world of adult functioning, not merely as a biological expression observed in the therapeutic office. In this way Lowen brings in the psychological aspect of ego functioning, familiar from psychoanalysis. Lowen thus manages to use concepts which in themselves already contain the functional unity of ego and body, psychology and biology.

Adult, mature functioning requires not only expression but containment and control, self-possession, in Lowen's terms. Similarly, these both require self-awareness, a deep awareness of one's own feelings. In addition to self-expression, the capacities for self-awareness and self-possession are also criteria of healthy, mature ego functioning. Without these two capacities, self-expression could be egoistic, impulsive, immature, and destructive. Both self-awareness and self-possession have bioenergetic and psychological aspects. Both require the free flow of excitation, and both require, in different ways, the energetic capacities of managing and differentiating excitation in the presence of others. These capacities are also functional expressions of being grounded.

Armor, muscular tension, or chronic sympatheticotonia, are the basic inhibitions to the free flow of excitation. Therapy is oriented to releasing muscular tensions and the restoration of basic movements, including sexual, respiratory, emotional, movement itself, feeling, and self-expression.[8] Therapy builds ego strength as well as developing the capacity for sexual surrender. To be grounded in reality is a primary ego function. To have the capability of sustaining a strong charge; choosing when, where, and with whom to surrender sexually; and to be capable of aggression when appropriate are all aspects of a healthy, mature ego.

In these descriptions of ego functioning, we see the ego in support of the body and what can be called the values and truth of the body. This is the ego functioning in the service of self-respect. The essential truth and the essential value of the body is pleasure, not only sexual pleasure, but the pleasure of daily, healthy functioning with "good feelings."[9] "Bioenergetics aims to help a person open his heart to life and love."[10]

Ruefully, Lowen says, "This is no easy task," because the ego can function in opposition to the body. This powerful aspect of the ego—its essential opposition to the body—is, Lowen feels, inevitably inculcated into modern humans. The values of the ego in this aspect of its functioning are essentially those of the society, especially power in all its manifestations— success, fame, money, achievement, control, and domination. Here is (patriarchal) man in opposition to nature, the ego functioning contrary to self-respect. Throughout his life, Lowen has wrestled with the opposition between body and ego. The dilemma, and indeed, his ambivalence, come through in such statements as: "The villain in the scenario is always the ego, with its need to control life. Of course, the ego is also a creative force, but it can become destructive when it is not grounded in the body, supported by faith in the body and in nature."[11]

The dilemmas of this struggle have been Lowen's major preoccupation. His many books, over the years, have all addressed various aspects of this opposition, always searching for the way to enlist the ego in the service of respect of the body, its truth, and its values.

In the effort to come to terms with this basic dilemma, bioenergetics became the applied art of seeing the whole person. Mind, spirit, soul, faith, grace, and graciousness—over the course of the years of his writings, Lowen introduced all these into his view of the person in therapy. Lowen always related these aspects of a person's humanity to their biological functioning. Thus, for example, graciousness, emerges from grace, the ability to move from a grounded position.[12]

Therapy must still focus on character, and character itself "must be understood in sexual terms." The issues of character are sexual issues.[13] What is referred to by "sexual issues" has to do with how the individual man or woman functions in the world. Consider an example of a sexual issue.

FROM A BIOENERGETIC WORKSHOP

Maria was a participant in a three-day workshop, where I met her for the first time. She wore a two-piece swimsuit to work in so we could observe her body. Maria was a young woman in her late twenties, very intelligent and clever, and presented herself to me in a way that was coquettish and challenging at the same time. I shared my initial impressions with the group by saying that while Maria was clearly a grown woman, she had the body of a twelve- or thirteen-year-old girl, and her head, on a rather long neck, went off to one side.

The observation about the girlishness of her body reveals the sexual issue. It tells us who Maria is, *as a woman,* her character. There is a certain immaturity about her as a woman for which her keen intellect could not compensate. She had in fact told me that she did not feel like the woman she could be, and that she had recently fled a loving relationship with a man. So her subjective feeling about herself was a true reflection of her bodily reality. This indicated a good grasp of reality. As the perceptually given reality, the body is the yardstick of truth.

Following my comments, she informed me that at the age of twelve or thirteen, her father had begun beating her and being abusive to her. Her father seemed to have been unable to tolerate his daughter's sexuality. His abuse conveys the hidden message, "If I can't have you, no one can," so in the abuse there is a sadistic and confusing seduction. Maria had been thrown into a terrible conflict between wanting his love while remaining loyal to him and her excitement about relationships with young men outside her home. Her conflict made it almost impossible for her to reach out into the world for her fulfillment. Her development had been arrested in a large measure in that conflict.

Just as it was essential to take seriously the immaturity of her body to understand Maria, I felt it was essential to understand the way her head was held in relation to her body. After all, there is the expression "having your head on straight," and Maria's head definitely went off to the side. As Maria's head was not "on straight," I had to take that as indicating the severity of the trauma she suffered. It was severe enough to force a degree of dissociation; that is, she was partially dissociated from her body, her feelings, and her sexuality. The work we proceeded to do was a beginning step in healing that dissociation.

Initially, I asked Maria to stand so that she was aware of both her feet on the floor, with her weight resting evenly on her feet, and her feet parallel or slightly toed in. As she talked about herself, I reminded her to "let down" into her legs and feet and to be aware of her breathing. The phrase *let down* captures a bodily feeling that results when giving in to the breath, relaxing the shoulders and belly, and becoming aware of the legs and feet. It is a letting down toward the earth, a giving in to gravity, and a surrendering to the breathing and the body's natural position in gravity. Letting down contrasts with "holding up," literally a bracing of the body against the force of gravity, and against the relaxation of the body in a standing position. The military position of "attention" is a common version of holding up; and, in fact, many people look like "good soldiers" when they stand.

Maria and I established a nice rapport during this initial contact as we identified the crucial conflict of her adolescent years. The fact that this problem might have begun before then, in her Oedipal years, was in the back of my mind, but I felt that we could begin with her more recent adolescent experience. The subsequent steps in working with her had the purpose of deepening her contact with the emotional realities of her sexual trauma. This deepened contact with herself would permit the initiation of a healing of the dissociation and a freeing of her energy, allowing her to move forward in her life. Much, of course, would remain to do after this initial step.

With this in mind, the work focused first on breathing, then on the expression of anger. An obvious tightness in her chest restricted her breathing, and this prevented her from feeling the sadness, grief, and despair she might feel from being trapped for so long in an intense conflict. To help free her respiration, I invited her to use the bioenergetic stool. This allowed her to cry, and she felt some relief. To help her protest her situation, I then asked her to lie on a mattress and kick and scream "No" as loud and long as she could for a number of times. As she did so, the depth of her feeling and the pain of her suffering were experienced by all the members of the group.

If we shift our attention to the atmosphere of the group, we will find that it illuminates Maria's experience and the nature of the process in which she is involved. Each person in the group was moved when exposed to the deepest emotional expression of Maria's pain and to the heroic proportions of her life's struggle. Uniquely communal and accepting feelings developed amongst the members of the group, and there was even an atmosphere of awe and reverence as Maria touched into her depths. There is a feeling of being privileged to participate in a deeper, more real, and saner aspect of life than is usually possible in everyday life. Bioenergetic work is a route to the human depths that inspire awe and reverence.

It is also interesting that a group of professional people never before exposed to bioenergetics, as was the case with most of Maria's group, will understand the basic assumptions of this work quite quickly after seeing a working session of the sort I just described. Once exposed to the work, its assumptions seem intuitively correct and natural. The work has an excitement, aliveness, and life-giving quality, so it generates genuine and intense excitement. Again and again, I have observed and participated in these reactions in bioenergetic groups and workshops.

BASIC ASSUMPTIONS

Bioenergetics rests on the foundation provided by Reich's organismic theory of the self. In bioenergetics some of its assumptions underwent a degree of evolution. I will discuss those basic assumptions as they operate in bioenergetics.

Seeing the Person

The theoretical framework that Reich inherited from Freud was based on a theory of the mind. When Reich began to look at the bodily composure and the bodily reactions of his patients, he needed a framework with which to integrate those observations with the theory of the mind.[14] Reich's formulations brilliantly overcame the problem of mind-body duality, but the problem remained embedded in his writing. Each actual moment of bioenergetic therapy demonstrates that the idea of the duality of mind and body is an artifact of philosophizing. There is always and only simply the person in different modes or aspects of expression.

A person is not "made up" of a body, a mind, a spirit, and a self. When I looked at Maria as she stood there, I looked at the person. When I see her, I see the person, the woman, Maria. The sense of "seeing" that matters in this context is the sense in which to see is to know and understand the person.[15] As our work proceeded, my attention shifted from one to another aspect of the person. In listening to her talk about herself, her past, her difficulties, I do not *listen* to a self different from the one I *see* when I see the immaturity of her body. My understanding of her deepens. I get to know her. As I *listen* to Maria speak her mind while I *observe* her body, I am still in the process of getting to know and understand *her*. I see her more deeply and clearly as a person. It would be ludicrous to speak of encountering two different entities—even two entities with such a distinguished philosophical history as mind and body—and then wonder how to put them back together to make up a person. Similarly, when I focus on, and work with, Maria's respiration, I am still working with Maria, herself. I have condensed these realities in the phrase *seeing the person*.

A phrase that I used previously, "The self is the body," is also problematic and is vulnerable to the same irrelevant philosophical dilemma. When I looked at Maria, I did not look at a body, I looked at a person, and when I saw her, I didn't see a body, I saw her. For this reason, I have headed this section (and this chapter) "seeing the person." In bioenergetics, we work with and get to know persons. We listen to what they say, and we work with other functional expressions of the person—breathing, kicking, and so on—that most other therapies do not. Since these are all functional, biological expressions—breathing, moving, talking—of the person, the best phrase to capture this theoretical framework is "organismic functionalism."

While the formulation of identity and antithesis involved the problem of mind-body duality, it is still a significant and useful formulation. There are, indeed, organismic functions whose relationship is one of identity and antithesis. Self and sexuality is one such pair that has already been discussed. Sexual feeling and anxiety is another. Others are ego and impulse, reality principle and pleasure principle, expansion and contraction, pleasure and pain; these are all opposites with an underlying organismic unity. The principle of identity and antithesis makes sense here as long as each of the pair is a specific biological function. That means that they represent real ways in which, at any given moment, the organism—the person—is organized. We have, for example, Maria in a state of anxiety or excitement, Maria contracted or expanding, Maria talking or expressing feeling, Maria kicking and breathing or immobilized, and so on. The shorthand phrase "The self is the body," can be used to capture these realities. It means there is an identity and antithesis between states psychologically conceived (e.g., anxiety) and bodily states (contraction).

After all, when I looked at Maria, I did look at her body, too. While this means, of course, that "looking at the body" means the same thing as "looking at the person," there is a little more to it. We are really talking about a particular way of looking. If Maria had gone for a medical examination because of a stomach ache, the physician would also look at her body, but it would be a different way of looking. I am talking about looking at the body to see functional expressions of the person, the way Maria holds her head, for example.

Seeing the body as the self has further implications. First, the person's therapeutic problems and history are expressed and reveal themselves in the body. Of course, it is necessary to know how to look at the body to see these things. In bioenergetic analysis, this artful discipline is called "reading the body." The vignette above gives a fairly clear example. I have found that acquiring this clinical art requires years of practice and personal experience.

The second implication of this view is that therapeutic change means change on a bodily level. The body itself has to change as the basis for significant personal change. There are a few categories of bodily change to be considered. Chronic patterns of muscular tension need to be released. The individual has to sustain the emotions that go with such release and also sustain a greater capacity for energy buildup and release. Chronic patterns of hyperactivation have to calm down (as in "driven" individuals). Conversely, a person with chronic patterns of energetic depression has to change bodily to an increased capacity for energetic movement. These body characteristics are visually discernible to those trained to see them.

In Maria's case we would look for a maturing of her body to underlie a maturing capacity for relationship. We would look for a deeper connection with her own body. This would be revealed in a stronger subjective sense of herself and in less reliance on her cleverness and more on her emotional reality. A change in her dissociation would be indicated by a capacity for deeper emotions and a capacity for experiencing an energetic wave moving through her body. This would in turn depend on the release of her overall bodily tension, and the development of more capacity for feeling in her lower body—her feet, legs, pelvis, and abdomen. As she was able to be more in the present, with her feet on the ground, I expect her head would come back into line with her body.

These changes go into the very tissues of the body. It is the tissue itself that has a greater capacity for energetic excitation, charge, and discharge. This brings us to the energetic principle and its meaning.

The Energetic Principle

An energetic process underlies all organismic functions. It is the basis of the unity and equivalence of the various pairs of antithetical functions, such as anxiety and sexuality. The energy is the biological energy of the organism, bioenergy. The source of energy for the organism is the cellular metabolism of food, using oxygen. Lowen points out that our energy comes from a kind of slow fire in a watery medium.[16] The biological organism creates its own kind of energy and energetic process which cannot be reduced to either a chemical or electrical process, although both exist within the body.

We do not observe the energy itself, but energetic processes are manifested in pulsatory phenomena and excitatory phenomena, and we observe these. Furthermore, Reich described fundamental laws of these phenomena when he described expansion-contraction and the charge-discharge (orgasm) formula. Expansion-contraction and charge-discharge are qualities of the organism that can be directly worked with in therapy. They are addressed when we work with breathing and when we work with the chronic muscular tensions which sustain contraction and suppress breathing. Furthermore, both emotion and aggression are direct expressions of pulsatory, that is, energetic, processes. These are fundamental qualities of the organism.

The deepest level of pulsation in any organism is the cellular. The pulsatory movement inherent in living protoplasm can be observed in every cell of the body. This movement could also be called excitation, representing the excitatory capacity of the cell. In complex living organisms, pulsation is organized on the various systemic levels. Groups of cells act as units which are integrated into larger masses of tissue, organs and organ systems. The excitatory wave or pulsatory movement is organized on these corresponding levels of increasing complexity. It also makes sense to conceive of pulsatory waves effecting unitary integration of the overall functioning of the whole organism. Grounding, discussed later, is an example. The respiratory wave and the heartbeat have already been mentioned as two of the fundamental pulsations of the organism as a whole. Self-respect has to do with the organism's management of its own pulsation and excitement in relation to the world, and it hence requires a unifying pulsatory sense of the self.

When the newborn enters the world, its first breath is the first movement of its own in relation to the external world. That first breath is the first aggressive act the newborn makes: the gasp of life. "Aggressive," here, has a specific meaning. It means "moving toward"; it does not mean "hostile." The first breath is a movement toward the world in the service of meeting the first survival need. If that breath is never taken, the organism dies. Breath, very simply, fuels the fires of life, and a stronger breath is literally a stronger, hotter life.

There is a direct relationship between respiration and emotion. In emotional experience, one breathes more deeply and fully, whatever the emotion is. In deep crying or sobbing, the breathing is full. After a deep cry one usually feels refreshed and whole. The crying releases tension, relieving the pain or sorrow which made us cry, while the full breathing energizes the body. This is a process of charging and discharging, releasing tension, and deepening breathing. Crying is a very important mechanism of relief and healing. It is the basic way in which infants and young children release tension which they have not been able to release through movement. Those grown-ups who cannot cry, whom we often meet in therapy, are unable to relieve their tension, and unable to heal. Crying is an innate and necessary mechanism for keeping our breathing free and full.

The suppression of crying or other emotions is effected by suppressing breathing. This may occur consciously, as when one "doesn't dare breath," or it may occur unconsciously and chronically as a learned or conditioned response from childhood. Chronic suppression is dealt with in bioenergetic therapy by working with the muscular tensions and constrictions relating to the breathing apparatus. In doing so, suppressed emotion is usually released as well. This is not an easy or simple process, and requires practiced and patient therapeutic intervention.

To breathe fully, then, we must be able to feel fully; and to be able to feel, we must be able to breath. A freedom and fullness of emotional life is thus a fundamental requisite for a healthy organism; it is not a secondary matter. To suppress emotion, or to learn to live a life with diminished emotion, is literally to suppress life itself, and create a degree of ill health. A man who cannot cry or a woman who cannot be angry is to that degree less of a man or a woman and one suffering an unhealthy bodily state. Feeling and emotion are not supplements to life, they are the essence and expression of life.

Daily life has a certain emotional flow to it. It waxes and wanes, there are floods of feeling and deserts, storms and periods of calm, periods of high excitation and lower, sometimes lethargy or fatigue. Emotional life does not stop entirely in sleep, as our dreams reveal. The organism's capacity to sustain an emotional flow reflects its underlying energetic capacity and hence its degree of health. The capacity for pleasure and good feeling rests on this energetic process.

I am not presenting arguments here for the freedom of feeling or emotional expression, or to reform society in that direction. While I think this might be good, my argument here goes far deeper than that. I am talking about the essential pulsatory nature of the human organism. For it to be fully alive and healthy, it has to breath; to breath, it must feel. The very excitatory nature of protoplasm requires that we feel. Our well-being and life are only an organized expression of the same pulsation we see in an amoeba. This is our life. This is the nature of the organism.

Some functional aspects of pulsation are more directly apparent when looked at in terms of excitation. An emotion is a state of excitement, and an excitatory state underlies chronic tensions. The same kind of biological excitement underlies what we experience as sexual excitement. Humans have a need for a suitable level of excitement. Perhaps the healthiest expression of this general need is the need to have a pleasurable, exciting engagement with one's own environment in a fairly continuous and ongoing way. The level of excitement that can sustain different individuals varies, but it is expressed in a feeling tone of enjoyment and being interested. Boredom represents a decreased level of excitation that becomes painful because it is brought on by an inability or lack of opportunity to sustain excitement and novelty in relation to the world.[17]

The need for excitement can take a pathological turn, and this is seen everywhere in today's world. Seeking constant intense stimulation or activity often signifies the effort to counter an underlying deadness, boredom, or apathy. People are constantly being bombarded with noise and stimulation everywhere in cities, and often in homes, too, with television or radio. Self-respect requires enough quiet for the individual to be able to tune in to his or her own being. In the person who is deadened on an organismic level, there can also be an attraction to violence and even war, since there may be no other way to bring excitement into life. Evolution has left us with the adaptive problem of how to deal with our need and capacity for excitation and, most fundamentally, the sexual organization of that excitement.

Sexuality

At the core of the bioenergetic study of the individual is the study of his or her sexuality. Orgasm theory is the basis for understanding sex and sexuality in bioenergetics. In his clinical application of orgasm theory, Lowen shifted the emphasis from sexuality to the ego and "sexual issues." Sexual issues need to be understood in the context of character, the topic to which we will soon turn.

Before doing so, I will review, briefly, some of the essential aspects of orgasm theory which are retained in bioenergetics. In the sexual act and in sexual life the charging and discharging characteristic of pulsatory phenomena are clearly manifested. When healthy, reasonably energetic men and women are living in normal circumstances, without undue duress, they will, over the course of time experience the buildup of sexual energy and desire and then a yearning for contact with a sexual partner and the opportunity for orgastic discharge. In the presence of the partner and in foreplay, the excitement builds, and as the sexual act is initiated, the excitation builds further and becomes focused in the genitals. In the initial phases of intercourse, excitement builds still further to the point of orgasm, at which point there is a convulsive discharge of energy. The energy focused in the genital apparatus is discharged and a pulsatory wave spreads out from the genital flooding through the whole body and the mind, a wave that, if it is full enough, leaves the body refreshed and relaxed. Excitation drops quickly back to a base line after orgasm.

The capacity for this kind of periodic sexual charging and orgastic discharging is a basic criterion for the bioenergetic health of the individual. Underlying the varieties of misery and unhappiness individuals bring to therapy, there will always be, at core, a disturbance in this very capacity to build, sustain, and discharge sexual excitation with a beloved partner.

Orgasm functions as the regulator of the energetic economy of the organism. In normal life the human organism tends to generate more energy than required for its daily survival. In children most of the surplus of energy goes to growth. In adults some of this surplus of energy is available for sex and sexual excitation. When we are unwell or under severe stress, there is less energy for sex.

Referring to the energy available for sex as "surplus" might make it sound as if sex were a kind of extra, one of life's side dishes we could do without, or as if we had the choice of channeling the energy into some other activity. This is not at all the case. The point is, the healthy functioning of the organism requires that surplus of energy and further requires that it be regulated in the regular charge and discharge of orgasm in the genital embrace with a loved partner. That is the ebb and flow of the organism, as much as the tides are the ebb and flow of the oceans. Just as the life in tidal pools needs the tides, so does the human organism need orgasm. It is just that surplus of excitation and energy and its orgastic regulation that allows for the pleasure, fulfillment, joy—and health—of life. When we "get along" without sex, it is usually just that—getting along, surviving. Inevitably there is a decline in health and fulfillment. In such periods of a life, there are many who pray for love and the opportunity to once again allow the body to live in joy and the full splendor of its sexual capacity.

Disturbances in sexual functioning, at least of the sort that are generally explored in the psychotherapeutic setting, occur in the context of character structure.

Character

A thorough discussion of character and its bioenergetic analysis would require a lengthy treatise in its own right. This limited and brief discussion of character will build on the organismic theory of the self and establish the relation of the concept with sexuality, the self, and self-respect. To help simplify the matter, I will discuss character under four headings: (1) further description, (2) the Oedipal origins of character development, (3) the organismic or bioenergetic changes which make up characterological adaptation, and (4) character and self-respect.

Further Description. "Character" is the term for the ongoing process of a dynamic boundary where the individual's biology contacts society and the biology is permanently modified. In this process the individual's pulsatory capacity is changed; the individual's excitatory movements of all kinds are limited, stopped, or distorted; there is a kind of hardening. From the individual's point of view, excitatory movements refer to aggression, reaching out and moving into the world, pleasure, self-expression, expression of feeling, and the daily sense of well-being associated with the buildup and discharge of sexual excitement.

From the observer's point of view, character refers to an individual's way of being in the world, literally, what is characteristic, the surface of the person's behavior. Psychotherapists say that the character is "ego-syntonic." It is entirely compatible with the ego, that is with the individual's perception of himself or herself. It is so much the basis for usual operations that it feels natural and familiar, a kind of given and in the nature of things. For example, a characterologically shy person might be familiar with his or her discomfort in social situations, but the problem is that he or she is all too familiar with it, and it would never occur to such a one to act boldly; he or she "wouldn't know how." The uneasiness engendered by a directive to act boldly would be, if not more discomforting, at least of such a qualitatively different kind of discomfort, that acting shyly might be preferred, given a choice, even when it leads to a repetition of symptomatic behavior (e.g., sitting out this dance like all the others).

Character is thus a limiting constraint on spontaneous, desired, and desirable movements, and this indeed is its function. Originally this constraint was a way of protecting the person from what otherwise might be dangerous or painful. Reich first identified it as a hardening of the ego; later he recognized its functionally identical somatic counterpart in organized chronic muscular tensions, or "muscular attitudes." Character is a structure within the core of the self blocking, forming, and modifying the capacity for love, the expression of emotion, the capacity for work, freedom, creativity, and pleasure. It is the kind of limitation about which, in the end, we have to say, "I can't help it." It is a kind of fate.

The functions of character are antithetical to the regulatory function of orgasm. Orgasm is the culmination of the buildup of excess energy focused into a contactful genital embrace, a discharge, and a refreshing of the organism's energetic state. Its fullness and depth of gratification depend on the overall pulsatory aliveness of the organism and is an expression of, and regulator of, that state, guaranteeing its continuation. Character functions in the opposite direction. It diminishes the potential for orgastic fulfillment, dampens excitation, limits the expression of feeling, pleasure, and sexuality. The bioenergetic function of character is to limit pulsation, to limit pulsatory aliveness in its core expressions, and character consists of bioenergetic changes having these effects.

The Oedipal Origins of Character Development. The formation of character begins in the first years of childhood. The development and modification of incipient character structures continue through childhood and into adolescence, when the form and function of the character is largely coalesced. Development can continue, however, through early adulthood, and even into later adulthood, as life experience adds layers, as it were, to the character organization. Fortuitous experiences—health, love, or good fortune in life—can sometimes soften character as well.

The origin of the specific structural form of any person's character, however, lies in the Oedipal period of development, between the ages of forty-two months and maybe six years. At this point, the child has matured enough physically, sexually, and cognitively for character structure to assume a shape. Reich's original statement about the oedipal origins of character is specific, to the point, and veridical.

"At the core of the armor's *definitive* formation, we regularly find, in the course of analysis, the conflict between genital incest desires and the actual frustration of their gratification. *The formation of the character commences as a definite form of the overcoming of the Oedipus complex.*"[18] This is a powerful statement and in some ways a remarkable one. Let's consider some of what it means. It builds, of course, on Freud's basic discovery of the Oedipus complex as the heart of neurosis. Reich's formulation—"the conflict between genital incest desires and the actual frustration of their gratification"—has a here-and-now real-life drama rarely found in Freud's deftly subtle characterizations. Reich is not referring to fantasy! He is talking about desire, and he is talking about real, "actual," frustration. Both the desire and the frustration are real bodily states. Reich is thus talking about a state of arousal—excitement—and conflict. The child is in a state of excitatory conflict.

The Oedipal child's excitement includes the genital. The child's loving excitement for its parent now is directly informed by erotic, genital feeling. Identification with the genital is initiated, so to love has a genital meaning. And to love is to desire; thus "genital incest desires." In talking about desire and frustration, Reich is not implying that the child's desires should be "fulfilled," that there should be no frustration. He is acknowledging the universality of the frustration. He is also implying the universality of conflict for the child in its new developmental situation, and conflict leads inevitably to frustration.

These first experiences of excitatory conflict inevitably occur within the family—the child's family dramas. Excitatory conflict was clearly in evidence in the stories of Kristin and Maria. In both their cases we encountered their intense conflicts as it irrupted in their adolescence. This is not atypical. An adolescent has the capability of expressing and experiencing the turmoil whose foundation is laid down in earlier years. With some investigation, the roots of Kristin's Oedipal conflict was revealed. In Maria's case, too, I had good reason to suspect the earlier roots of her conflict.

Every child must in some way come to terms with these situations, and this is what Reich means by "the overcoming of the Oedipus complex." What is implied in Reich's statement is that the effects of the first conflicts of love and sexuality leave a life-long imprint. The imprint in question is not a matter of memories and fantasies. It is a matter of actual changes in the body. "[T]he armor itself is the form in which the infantile experience continues to exist as a harmful agent."[19]

Bioenergetic Changes and Adaptation.   It is not surprising, really, that the childhood situation that Freud termed the Oedipus complex should have a marked effect on the individual's lifelong development. In question, after all, is the child's first love or loves—as a male or female person. From Freud we learned that this stage of development establishes the person's conditions for loving and determines fateful dynamics of love relationships—psychodynamics and interpersonal dynamics. Reich added a new and deeper dimension. From him we learned that this stage of development actually shapes the core of the organism. The pulsatory functioning of the body itself is effected, and the very self is shaped. To understand this further, we need to appreciate character as an adaptive function.

Character is the result of the child's adaptation to its early developmental environment, from the beginning of life on through adolescence. Specifically what is adapted is the core biological function of expansion and contraction. This includes the child's pulsatory state, its capacity for excitation, and its capacity for self-regulated charge and discharge. Within evolutionary theory, the issue of adaptation is related to the survival of the species: adaptation implies survival. That implication applies in the case of character as well. Character is a matter of the biological survival of the self. In character formation, the child adapts by using its own biological resources to modify itself. Only the pressures of survival could account for the kinds of biological, bodily changes observed in individual character formation.

Human adaptation can be observed on three levels: evolutionary, culturally, and individual familial. Evolutionary adaptation refers to the survival of the species on earth. Cultural adaptation signifies that each human being is born into a particular culture occurring at a given time and place. Character formation is the result of an individual's developmental adaptation to his or her familial environment. Character development takes advantage of an evolutionary quality of the human organism. Human's display an extreme plasticity in their capacity to develop and live under a range of sociocultural and environmental conditions, a capacity that far exceeds that of any other species. Human sexual life, as well, is characterized by great plasticity.[20] This by no means implies that anything is acceptable, biologically, to the human organism. Specifically, there are very definite limits for healthy development within our own society, for example.

Character formation is the result of familial stresses placing survival demands on the child that are far beyond cultural necessity. While these demands call on the plasticity of human adaptive capacity, they push that capacity to the point of ongoing chronic stress, where the child must draw on its own biological resources to modify itself for the sake of survival. Such stresses are in themselves traumatic, and such stresses regularly occur within the context of, or in relation to, the child's Oedipal situation.

The Oedipus complex is typically considered to involve the child not only in a situation of intensified, genitally involved love for one parent, but also a threatening rivalry with the other. This threat, usually thought of as castration anxiety, could easily be considered the source of the survival threat. If this threat were experienced universally or nearly universally in some degree, castration anxiety would be the source of the threat to survival.

Castration might not mean literal death, but it is surely deathlike in terms of limiting the expression of life, and may indeed be experienced as a threat of death by a child. While this analysis is valid, the bioenergetic issues still need to be directly addressed. There are actual bodily changes that occur in character formation.

Character involves biological modification of three layers of the organism. On the surface of the organism are muscular tensions. These can go into the deeper layers of muscle and the organs. The second layer modified is the autonomic nervous system in both central and peripheral aspects, chronic sympatheticotonia. The third layer of the organism effected consists of the hormonal and neurotransmitter systems. These layers, of course, do not act separately; they are interrelated, although their mechanisms of modification differ. Research evidence suggests that the autonomic nervous system is conditioned, in the classical sense, by aversive stimulation.[21] Research evidence also suggests that the hormonal and neurotransmitter systems are conditioned, acclimated, depleted, or otherwise modified through exposure to chronically stressful experiences.[22]

Dissociation, suppression, denial, repression, and other of the so-called defense mechanisms have all become familiar terms, some of them household words. However, the significance of these words can be fully appreciated only when it is understood that they are processes based on real biological changes in a person's body. Consider some commonly observed examples of bodily changes set in motion in childhood adaptation.

Suppression and repression are carried out by the physical suppression of respiration, that is, tensing the musculature of the respiratory apparatus. When there is not time, place, and relational opportunity for the child's expression of feeling, the feelings are held in the body, as are states of upsetness. Overalertness, overcontrol, and the child's solicitous preoccupation with the parent all require a complex pattern of tension and activation of the neuromusculature of the head, neck, and eyes. Suppressed demands, anger, rage, and hate require tension of the large musculature of the back, shoulders, stomach, buttocks, and thighs. Chronic anxiety and fear result in a sucked in gut, tension in the pelvis, pelvic floor, legs, and feet. In a family where the release of tension and self-expression on the part of the child are poorly tolerated, inconsistently responded to or not at all, or pose an outright danger, the tension pervades the whole musculature and even the organs. All these tensions impinge, some directly, some indirectly, on the genital apparatus. They also effect perception and cognitive functioning.

In the face of adaptive necessity, the child's energies go to sustaining the activation and tension of these states. There is autonomic nervous system involvement and the hormonal and neurotransmitter systems are eventually affected. This results commonly in depression, anxiety, and panic attacks, and eventually various illnesses.

These examples illustrate some of the kinds of biological changes involved in armoring and character formation. They also illustrate the severity and depth of the stresses initiating such changes—changes that per-manently alter the form and functioning of the self. How common are such severe stresses in childhood? I believe they are more the rule than the excep-tion. Have I offered extreme and rare examples? I believe not. The clinical illustrations in the following chapters will bring home the commonness of what is being described here.

Do these severe stresses constitute challenges to the actual survival of the child? And, in what way do the stresses of "overcoming" the conflict between "incestuous genital desires and their actual frustration" constitute a threat to survival? These two questions remain to be considered in light of the claim that character is an adaptation to a survival issue.

The energetic significance of the Oedipal phase must be focused on more clearly. The significance of this period of development has to do with bod-ily maturation, including emotional, cognitive, and physical maturation. As this maturation occurs, the organism also develops energetically. The organism has taken another crucial step toward its adult form in which there is a capacity for orgasm, and for self-regulation of energetic charge and discharge generally. Specifically, the genital apparatus has been inte-grated energetically. The child has identified with his or her genital. With a newly developed aspect of sexual identity, the child, always a person, is now a more fully formed self.

What all this means is simple, clear, and straightforward. In his or her primary love relationships, the child is now putting his or her whole being on the line. In loving a parent, for the first time its whole pulsatory appa-ratus, from head to genital, is involved. Its basic life function of expansion and contraction enters the world as a formed self in these relationships. How that life function is met determines its fate. Since that function *is* the child's life, and since that function is expressed in love and excitement for and in relation to the parent, if it is stopped, life itself is stopped. In this way, survival is always an issue at this stage of development.

This new level and organization of excitation is sexual, and as it emerges in his or her familial setting, the child begins to participate, to some mea-sure, in the more complex world of adult sexuality. Along with the excita-tion, there is conflict and frustration. Often enough, there is also fear and exposure to elements of adult sexuality that are beyond the child's self-reg-ulatory capacity. There can be a level of excitation, conflict, fear, and arousal that the child is not equipped to handle. When this happens, sur-vival is an issue. The child's adaptive capacity is pushed to a limit where the organism must begin to use its own resources against itself to adapt. There are many ways in which these first expressions of love and excitement can be stopped, frustrated, and overwhelmed; the resulting characterological developments usually lead to painful life experience and often painful lives.

Character structure and armoring contain and bind that level of excita-tion, frustration, fear, and arousal from conflict that the child has not been able to discharge and integrate within the family relationships. The infantile experience, as Reich said, continues to exist in the biological changes required for this to be accomplished, and through these changes acts "as a harmful agent" in the long term.

Anchoring childhood experience in the character or armor makes it an agent in the ongoing, functioning life of the individual; it is no longer simply a matter of the past. It is now, just as all body functioning is now—each heartbeat is now, each feeling, each breath. While it is true that human beings are creatures of memory, there is more to memory than a mental image of the past. On a bodily, bioenergetic level, we are the past. The past lives in us, because the form we have taken is based on childhood experience. What is significant is that current functioning is formed by—and takes the form of!—past experience.

Characterological conditioning freezes the organism in time. The conditioned mechanisms become part of an ongoing adaptation. The adaptation is meant to hold off a dread experience, guaranteeing survival of the self, but the conditioning at the same time preserves the conditions under which the trauma was created in the first place. A body state is created in this way in which the dread trauma is constantly being relived. The individual goes through life as if, for example, the rejection and judgment of the needed parent were still imminent.

If the person is effective in their adaptation, they may develop a socially successful persona, but it may turn out to be just that—a mask, a superficial layer of the person which is maintained at great expense by exerting an ongoing effort utilizing an enormous amount of energy. Sometimes this aspect of the person is called a false self, and sometimes the individual becomes aware of its emptiness and seeks therapy.

The dictates and maintenance of the character structure can absorb an enormous amount of the individual's energy, even to the extent of gradually exhausting the person. The character structure also tends to harden as the individual gets older if there are no propitious circumstances for resolving the underlying sources and origins of the character. The absorption of energy in the character structure and its rigidification make it increasingly difficult for the individual to find movements in life allowing for a healthy renewal, new developments, new approaches to life, and refreshment.[23] All of this means that the character formation becomes, as life proceeds, a greater and greater stress on the organism, a stress that operates at the level of the tissues, as well as in the diminution of feelings and of emotional and physical well-being.

As these developments proceed the individual may not have the energy and resilience needed to deal with the stresses and distresses that everyone's life will inevitably provide. Various kinds of breakdowns in function, either in the form of illnesses or a gamut of emotional disabilities, are inevitable. Many of the difficulties, disabilities, personal dysfunctions, minor breakdowns, and so on that occur in very many people from their middle thirties onward are the result of these accumulated, characterologically driven stresses. Without the fresh energy of youth, with the adversity of life, with the depletion of the energy by the character, the individual no longer has sufficient energy to overcome the limitations imposed by the character structure, and a degree of breakdown in functioning ensues.

Character and Self-Respect. There is a direct relationship between character and self-respect. To the extent that an individual's character structure limits or modifies his or her self-expression, that is pulsatory functioning, to that extent, it is impossible for the individual to operate on the basis of self-respect. Secondary formations such as inhibitions, shame, guilt, and egoistic and narcissistic motives replace the body's life, needs, and values as the basis for choice and action. These developments are not within control of the individual, nor are they conscious choices; they are the mechanisms through which fate operates. Furthermore, to the extent that a character formation carries within it a destructive and traumatizing childhood experience, the individual's efforts at self-respectful self-regulation will be warped in an eternal effort to avoid the past trauma. In this manner, too, the here-and-now reality of bodily needs, feelings, and values will be overshadowed by misrepresentations deriving from the past. The longed-for love, for example, might not even be recognized, and fear might prevent the longed for sexual partner from ever being chosen.

At the same time, self-respect can be the guide used to free one's self from the past. If this is to be the case, the individual must painstakingly make the effort to relearn self-respect based on the truth of his or her body, relinquishing long held ideals, fantasies, beliefs, and memories, and experiencing, or reexperiencing, painful past events, allowing them to be seen in a new light.

GROUNDING

The common underlying theme of the previous four sections has been biological pulsation as it can be observed and understood in the human organism. The section titled "Seeing the Person" discussed looking at and seeing a person in the light of organismic functionalism. The person is seen as an alive, pulsating organism. This includes observation of the modifications of that organism which occurred in the course of development. The sections "The Energetic Principle" and "Sexuality" clearly addressed different aspects of pulsatory phenomena in the human organism. Similarly, "Character" provided a description of that peculiarly human way in which energetic aliveness, especially sexual aliveness, is developmentally modified under adaptive pressures. In the light of the range of these topics, the study of pulsation can be seen to be of the first significance for an organismic theory of the self.

Grounding touches on another facet of understanding the complexities of pulsation in the human organism. Grounding is a way of describing and conceptualizing a pulsatory wave that is the energetic foundation for the integration of the upright human organism standing in its environment. Grounding describes the organism's energetic relation to the ground, that is, to the stress of gravity.

The concept was introduced by Lowen, and it is one of his most important contributions to the development of Reich's work. Lowen tells a story about how he began to think of this concept. He noticed that some male athletes, like fighters, whom he admired because he wanted to feel as manly as they did, looked as if they were close to the ground as they moved. Timid people and "heady" people may look like they are "up in the air," "have their heads in the clouds," or "don't have their feet on the ground." These perceptions must reveal something real about the energetic states or movements of these people. In any case, Lowen felt it would be good if he could feel closer to the ground, with his feet more on the ground, and with more sensation in his feet and the lower half of his body generally. In such ways do the personalities of all innovators enter into their visions, and out of personal experience come valid universal principles. This section is an elucidation of Lowen's concept and some of its implications.[24]

As a person stands on the ground, an excitatory wave can be said to pulsate between the two ends of the organism, and this pulsation creates an energetic relation with the ground; we can call this the pulsatory grounding wave. Lowen called this movement a "pendular swing,"[25] because the wave swings from one end of the organism to the other, although the person would have to be lying down for the swing to be in the plane of a pendulum. With that rotation in mind, we can see that the pendular swing Lowen is describing must be the same energetic wave as the one that Reich described for the orgasm reflex.

When standing, however, the individual is under the stress of gravity, so the pulsatory grounding wave occurs under very different conditions from those of the orgasm reflex. Standing is a position of mobilization, not one of surrender. In organizing itself under the stress of gravity, the body must inevitably mobilize whatever chronic character tensions are present. The body has no other way of mobilizing itself. Thus as soon as we look at a person standing, we can immediately see aspects of their carriage and movement that reflect characterological disturbances in grounding.

Many people, for example, actually look "up" in a variety of ways. Not only is the inclination of the body to move downward in gravity countered by the natural mobilization to remain upright; it is as if extra energy is put into countering gravity so that the whole body, especially the upper body, seems to want to rise *up*. Others seem to hold themselves rigidly in a variety of ways, as if extra energy is needed to keep them stiff to guard against falling or flowing. Others seem to be making extra effort to hold themselves up against imminent collapse. Others immediately give the appearance of being split at various levels of their bodies, so that extra energy goes to maintaining an integration, as if to keep pieces from falling apart. Sometimes a head seems to be separated from its neck or shoulders and the rest of its body. Other people seem compacted, as if their energies were compressed and under pressure, as if gravity were denser for them than for others. As I mentioned at first, there are many variations on being "up in the air," having one's "head in the clouds," being "spacey," and so on. All these are depictions of real differences in the way people appear, and they all represent variations on disturbances in grounding. There are as many subtle variations as there are individuals. I have indicated that each of these disturbances involves an expenditure of energy over and above that which would naturally be required to maintain an upright stance on the ground. This extra expenditure of energy is one source of the energy drain of character structure. Further, since distortions of grounding alter the person's relation to the ground, they alter the person's relation to reality. What the world is and how it appears for each person depends on this relation to the ground.

When a person is looked at in this light, it quickly becomes apparent that there is a complex system of energetic relationships which can be observed and studied in the standing individual. The analysis of these relationships offers important insights into human functioning and the organismic theory of the self. The relationship between the two "ends" of the organism can serve as a basic starting point for this analysis.

The pulsatory wave swings between the two ends of the body, the head (cephalic end) and the tail (caudal end), so there is an energetic relationship between the two ends. Ordinary language captures the perception of that energetic relationship in the phrase "bright-eyed and bushy-tailed,"[26] a phrase that captures a real energetic quality that we sometimes ascribe to people. The underlying connotations of the phrase reflect not only the sense of a perceived relationship between the two ends of the body, but it also indicates the desirability of having liveliness at each end. In fact, it is not possible to be lively in a real way at one end and not the other.

It is also interesting to compare the human form with the four-legged animals. For example, at our home, we have many squirrels visiting our deck to take advantage of the seed we put out for birds. These little animals are definitely bright-eyed and bushy-tailed. On this matter humans and four-legged animals can be similar. The obvious difference of the human body from that of the four-legged animals puts the two ends of the human organism in a very different relationship with each other. With our upright, bipedal organization, standing in gravity, the head is lined up above the pelvis. With one above the other, the two ends are both in a different kind of relationship with the ground. As Lowen points out, it is as if the whole front end of the organism were lifted off the ground.[27] Upright, the two feet and legs support the whole structure and give it its energetic, functional connection with the ground it stands on.

If the pulsation is to swing between both ends, the organization of the structure must permit an equal charge to reach both ends. This consideration suggests important implications for the energetic relationships between legs and pelvis, and head and tail. For the tail end to be capable of receiving and participating in the pendular swing of energy, the pelvis must be capable of movement and feeling. That is, it must be alive and free of tensions, a state usually called "motile," or having "motility." The pelvis can be seen as the keystone forming an arch with the legs. This arch supports the whole body, and if motility is to be maintained, it cannot be held tightly, stiffly, and rigidly, nor can it be deadened. A necessary condition for this freedom of movement in the pelvis is a strong, lively energetic connection of the feet with the ground. The legs must be alive, free of tensions, and have feeling. If the feet are tight, collapsed, or too tense, the energetic connection with the ground is broken, and similarly, when the legs are tight and contracted, or held and deadened, the motility of the pelvis is restricted. With tight legs, the musculature of the pelvis must compensate by tightening and contracting, as if to supply the energetic support that has been lost in the legs and feet. The relationship is reciprocal. When the pelvis is contracted and held because of unresolved sexual tensions, the motility of the legs will always be compromised. Grounding and sexuality are clearly reciprocal functions.

This is a sketch of some of the basic conditions that permit a strong pulsatory movement to reach and move through the pelvis, through the legs, to the feet, and to return. When this happens, the individual is "grounded," and it is a quality that can be observed in that individual. However, this is only half the story. Conditions in the upper part of the body also affect this movement. For now, I will discuss only the head.

The head has a crucial bearing on the pulsatory grounding wave. The head is generally considered to be the seat of the intellectual functions and the functions of control. While this is an oversimplification, there is some truth to it. Many people complain that they "can't stop thinking," "can't let go," "can't give up my control," and so on. Their intellect has in a sense become an organ of control. Associated with this condition is a difficulty about giving in to feelings, especially softer, more vulnerable ones, including love. The overuse of the intellect in the service of control represents a restriction in the motility of the head end of the body, and since the pulsatory grounding wave is a unitary phenomena, it also represents a diminution of grounding and sexuality. It should be noted that I have used the words *intellect* and *thinking*; I did not use the word *mind*. The free, creative, and pleasurable use of the mind is an expression of the free motility of the head.[28]

With these further relationships in mind, we can take the analysis a step further. I have been referring to the "head end" and the "tail end" of the person, but for better or worse, we have lost our tails, and "head" is a gross anatomical designation for a large piece of the body. Lowen has defined more specific functional points on the body which correspond to the two ends of the pulsatory grounding wave, and my own and others' observations support his. The point at the head end is the glabella, the point described in some eastern philosophies as the region of the third eye, and the lower end is in the perineum, at the root of the genital.[29] The two pendular end points of the pulsatory grounding wave, then, are essentially the genitals and the face.

This analysis supports the analysis of the functional equivalence of sexuality and self. Since they are the end points of a unifying pulsation, the face and genitals must then have a functional equivalence, and this corresponds with the functional equivalence of sexuality and selfhood. The functional root of sexuality is the genital. Similarly, we can say that the face is the location of the functional expression of selfhood. There are many expressions in ordinary language and ordinary life that reflect these principles. The obvious mark of great portraits is that they capture the essence of the subject—the character, being, and self of the person. In some bawdy expressions of sexual intimacy, the genital is often referred to as "he" or "she" and given pet names, and the face and the genital are equated.

There are further implications of this analysis which Lowen illuminated in a brilliant insight into energetic functioning. With the differentiation of the forelimbs (arms) and hind limbs (legs), and with the reorganization into a vertical plain, the two ends of our bodies have evolved a functional differentiation specific to our species. As the pendular wave swings up into the upper body it moves through all those functions that have primarily to do with charging the body: breathing, food intake, the senses, heartbeat. As it moves downward through the body, it sweeps through the lower half of the body where the functions of discharge reside: sex, locomotion, and excretion. In the head, the senses, the organs of speech, and the brain are the basis for ego functions, whereas the genital is cupped atop the pelvic floor, near the tail.

This heightened differentiation of the function of the two ends of the organism also heightens the differentiation and energetic capacity of the functions of charge and discharge, and this allows the human organism an enormous increment in control and differentiation of impulse formation and in the discharge of impulse in action. These capabilities—of differentiation and control of impulse and action—are the very ones which are the basis of what is usually called the individual's reality function, or the ego's reality principle. The reality function refers to the individual's ability to act with good judgment and with adequate effectiveness in his or her environment. This capacity is based on the ability to delay action, impulse, and gratification; the capacity for delay is based on self-possession along with the capacities for self-expression and self-awareness. These capacities are made possible by the head and the pelvis acting as energetic reservoirs, "condensers," as Lowen says, containers of large amounts of energy which can be held until the right time and place for action and discharge.

The differentiation of the two ends of the organism and their unification through the pulsatory grounding wave is the underlying energetic or functional basis of the reality principle, and the ego's reality functions.[30] For this reason, Lowen says, "This swing (the pendular swing of the pulsatory grounding wave) as the basis of the reality principle is the cornerstone of all bioenergetic principles and therapy."[31]

From this discussion, grounding can be seen as another criterion of health. To say people are grounded is to say that they are capable of living in and mastering their complex environment to a degree sufficient, not simply for survival but in addition for finding some measure of fulfillment, pleasure, and the realization of valued aspects of the self. Health depends on the body's capacity to sustain and enliven the pulsatory grounding wave, the functional and energetic relationship between the two poles of the body and the ground. In bioenergetic therapy, there are ways to directly enhance that capacity, and ways to restore it in some measure when it has been distorted or interfered with.

Grounding, sexuality, and selfhood are functionally interrelated concepts, or ways of viewing the organism. Each has its own developmental sequence in childhood. For a person to develop healthfully, he or she has to develop with feet contactfully on the ground; for the feet to be on the ground, the development of the sexual function cannot be interfered with; when sexuality is allowed to blossom, a defined self will also develop; and, finally, the person who is grounded in the world and who sustains the sexual function, will, from childhood through old age, continue an evolution as a person out of a realistic sense of contact with the self and the world. These are bodily realities, and they emerge in a developmental sequence and in a developmental environment.

Grounding also sheds light on self-respect. Each is a requisite for the other. One aspect of maintaining self-respect is to maintain a sense of the feet on the ground and a feelingful presence in ongoing reality. Bringing one's self back to a sense of the feet on the ground, allows one to bring oneself back to an ongoing sense of self-regulation and self-respect. Similarly, the self-respecting response to the energetic sense of the body in both ego and sexual aspects allows one to maintain one's grounding. Grounding is based on a complex set of energetic, pulsatory interrelationships between upper and lower body, head and pelvis, and pelvis and legs. Changing or charging of any one of these relationships will evoke specific feelings or states of awareness. In self-respectfully attending to these feelings, the person can maintain their grounding, an ongoing realistic sense of the self in one's world. In losing contact with this bodily process, the individual is left to the prey of fantasy and unrealistic ideals, illusions, goals, and perceptions.

BIOENERGETIC THERAPY: FINDING YOUR MOVEMENT

The goal of bioenergetic therapy is for the patient to find his or her own movement. This does not mean "You do your thing, and I do my thing"; it does not represent a therapeutic version of identifying oneself with one's spiteful rebellion; it does not mean any movement whether or not it is antisocial, individualistically in opposition to the communal good, or self-aggrandizing. It is not a reinforcement of egocentrism or narcissism. It is not some therapeutic ideology or utopian idolizing of the individual and the individual's sensations, feelings, or impulses, regardless of their nature or content.

In earlier discussions I said that life is movement. Protoplasm moves, and movement is an intrinsic quality of it. Similarly, emotion, at the core of the individual's life, is the perception of pulsation or organismic movement. The words *emotion* and *aggression* both signify movement.

An aggressive movement—the first gasp for breath—is the first act of every newborn. As the child grows toward adulthood, the aggressive movement evolves and branches out into wider circles of the society as it is invested in successive forms of learning, work activity, and social role. Similarly, the first early movements of reaching out for love and contact evolve developmentally through successive stages from infancy through adulthood.

This view points to the specific goal of bioenergetic therapy mentioned at the outset, finding one's movement. Virtually every individual who seeks therapeutic help does so because, in some fundamental way, their movement was stopped in some greater or lesser measure. In every case, it was stopped in a measure greater than the organism could tolerate. While we humans are extraordinarily malleable in terms of the sociocultural forms our movement can assume, there are limits beyond which the movement can be stopped, and the organism is put into intolerable stress. Character structure is the adaptation resulting when the movement is stopped, and it is also the structure that keeps the movement stopped. Trauma, fear, punishment, shame, guilt, deprivation, abuse, overly arduous sociocultural "training," exploitation of various kinds, family uprootedness, are only some of the ways in which children's movement can be stopped.

People in therapy or who have gone through therapy often give expression to the experience of the movement having been stopped in their lives and themselves. Writing of her hospitalization as an eighteen-year-old, a woman captures her sense of having been stopped:

[S]he was looking out, looking for someone who would see her.
This time I read the title of the painting: *Girl Interrupted at Her Music.*
Interrupted at her music: as my life had been, interrupted in the music of being seventeen, as her life had been, snatched and fixed on canvas: one moment made to stand still and to stand for all the other moments, whatever they would be or might have been. What life can recover from that?
I had something to tell her now. "I see you," I said.
. . . "Don't you see, she's trying to get out," I said, pointing at her.[32]

My formulation of the goal of therapy differs from that of Reich and Lowen. It is not incompatible with theirs, and it rests on the same foundations. The goals they propound—orgastic potency (Reich), pleasure, self-expression, and grounded maturation (Lowen)—are valid criteria for health. Another issue is involved here, however. Therapy is an interpersonal process. It is based on a relationship between therapist and patient. To respect the patient and avoid the exercise of power over the patient, the therapist must not choose any goal for any patient. Nor should the patient be expected to reach toward a therapeutic goal espoused by any school of therapy, even including such obviously valued goals as health, sanity, orgastic potency, and self-expression. It is up to the patient to choose and seek his or her own goals, to make up his or her own mind. It is not up to the therapist to presuppose the goal. The therapist is only a consultant in those choices, their meaning, and means of attainment. Nothing is more important for any person than to make up his or her own mind and make his or her own choices. Finding one's own movement allows one to make up one's own mind.[33]

Pulsatory movement was analyzed from various points of view in the previous sections. The therapeutic approach in bioenergetics consists in influencing each of those aspects or phases of pulsatory movement in direct and indirect ways. The techniques of the therapy directly influence the body's capacity for lively movement, its motility. Exercises and movements that directly engage the legs, helping to energize and break down tensions in them, directly foster grounding. Exercises and movements with the pelvis relate directly to sexual issues. Increasing the individual's capacity for deeper respiration enhances overall energetic level and capacity for feeling. Reducing chronic tension softens character armor and character attitudes. Bioenergetic therapy is designed not only to eliminate illness (neurotic symptoms), it is also meant to foster health. The criteria of health—orgastic potency, grounding, and self-expression—provide guides in therapy for fostering and evaluating the development of health. All these lines of approach foster the individual's capacity for finding his or her own movement in life.

Consider how the pulsatory grounding wave may offer a specific guide line to fostering the finding of one's own movement. The lower point of that wave, and what can indeed be called its root, lies at the base of the genital. This is also the literal, bodily root of any disturbances of sexuality. In bioenergetics, as in horticulture, to get the growth of a strong healthy organism, the root has to be free, healthy, and alive. In the human organism, freeing that root means freeing the sexual function as deeply as possible. Therapeutically, this is done both analytically and on the bodily level. Sexuality is analyzed developmentally and in terms of current functioning. At the same time, therapeutic work proceeds on freeing the bodily contractions that restrict the actual spontaneous sexual movements, feelings, and impulses. This aspect of the therapy fosters both the movement toward orgastic potency and toward the identification with the genital which is the basis of selfhood and, therefore, self-expression.

The essential condition for the progress of any therapy, however, is the engagement of the self in the process. The avenue for this engagement is self-respect, whether the person is "on the move" or "stuck." The problem of engaging the self and self-respect in the therapeutic process and what it means can be illuminated by considering a frequently expressed wish we are all familiar with, the wish "to find myself." Since biological pulsation is the basis of the self, it must be reestablished, enhanced, or freed, and the person must be in contact with it, in order for that self to be "found." This immediately establishes the bodily basis of the process.

One of the many things that makes therapy difficult is that, as often as not, the self that is "found," at least initially, isn't the one that we were looking for. A very fine young man, for example, came to therapy feeling he was a failure if he did not realize himself as the special genius his mother and father had made him feel he was or had to be. What he actually found in himself was a legacy of shame, abandonment, and a deep sense of confusion. This wasn't the self he was looking for, but these damaged and damaging feelings were the heritage of his family and the result of how his movement was stopped. Not only did these feelings have to be accepted, it was also necessary that he respect himself in the process. Very specifically, he needed to respect the terribly painful states associated with his sense of shame, humiliation, and failure. This was his bodily reality. Respect for those bodily realities *is* self-respect.

Here, in this process, is the essence of healing. Inherent in it is reestablishing contact with aspects of the self literally at the level of the tissues. This allows an actual change in the tissue, enhancing its pulsatory aliveness. Each such step supports enhancing the unitary pulsatory functioning of the organism: grounding and sexuality, selfhood and sexuality. Each step in respecting the bodily states associated with his shame, for example, fosters his ability to find his own movement in the world. For many people, such changes are prerequisite to finding the strength to sustain the stress of a sexual relationship and a social work function.

This is a difficult and demanding process. It involves a softening and reorganizing of the character structure. Usually this process is accompanied by breakthroughs of anxiety, energetic expressions, feelings, and autonomic reactions of various kinds. Sometimes these experiences are quite frightening, having the feeling of being on the edge of craziness, death, or breakdown. Sustaining such a process depends on the continued relationship between patient and therapist, the analysis of the transference and countertransference, a deep commitment to change on the part of the patient, and a deep capacity to be in the presence of primal emotion on the part of the therapist.

The process of establishing self-respect can begin in the first therapeutic encounter. Self-respect is not a goal to be reached; it is a body capability, an attitude, a process to be learned or relearned, and it can be acknowledged from the beginning. It is thus a profound aspect of the therapeutic process in which the individual is engaged from the beginning, and it is a process which can immediately be established in the full fabric of the individual's life.

In working with the body, the individual has the opportunity for the immediate acquisition of important tools of healing and change. The practice of working with the body fosters self-respect and promotes the movement toward health and toward finding one's own movement in the world. In addition to the therapy, we use bioenergetic exercise classes to enhance and support the therapeutic process and teach people to work with their body on their own. Since change is ultimately change in the body, and since change in the body occurs relatively slowly, it is necessary that people who want to change learn to take the responsibility for working with their own bodies. In the group classes, bioenergetic exercises are used which are geared to fostering the natural movement, aliveness, and pulsation of the body.[34] Through participating in bioenergetic exercise classes, the discipline of working with one's body can become part of a self-respectful daily practice. A self-respectful way of life allows for experiencing the simple joys and sorrows of life, the joys and sorrows that are common to humankind. This means less involvement with self-delusion and with the narcissistic illusions prevalent today in our society.

Part II

VIOLATIONS OF SEXUALITY

A violation of sexuality is an external influence in childhood development which is essentially disrespectful of the child in such a way as to interfere with and disturb the identification with the genital and eventually the capacity for sexual love and self-respect. Painful struggles to attain a degree of personal fulfillment are an inevitable outcome of the violations of sexuality. Part II catalogues a range and variety of the violations of sexuality and their outcomes. Sexual misery; genital incest desires; hate; sexual "craziness"; shock, genital injury, and dissociation; and shame, humilation, guilt, and self-hate are explored in the light of organismic functionalism.

The Sexual Misery of Our Time

> The first task would have been to become aware, fully aware,
> of the depth and complexity of human misery.
>
> —Wilhelm Reich

THE CLINICAL SEMINAR

For several years I led a monthly daylong clinic for bioenergetic therapists. Over those years, we had the opportunity to see quite a few people. Each individual we saw left a deep impression on me. We devoted three hours to a therapist and her patient, and we glimpsed the ongoing drama of a life in progress, the individual's character, and the therapist's often heroic efforts to be helpful.

Running through all these lives, with all their differences, I found a recurring, overriding common theme. Each life was marked by sexual misery. I came to call it the sexual misery of our time.

Misery is the word for what I saw, and it is truly a sexual misery. For virtually each of these men and women, the very quest to fulfill themselves brings misery—as much misery as fulfillment. These are men and women in their prime. Their quest to fulfill themselves with a partner is as much a part of them as breathing, and their misery is inescapable until they are able to sort out its sources in their sexuality.

These are not people suffering from inescapable sexual deprivation or moral prohibition. Their very pursuit of a sexual love relationship evokes pain, suffering, confusion, conflict—misery. Often, the very sexual acts in which they engage do not bring gratification or fulfillment; rather, they have been tormented by their very participation in the sexual act. Often, they are terribly confused by their tumultuous experiences and feelings with their partners. Being with their partners for any length of time creates deep tensions, anxieties, conflicts, painful ambivalence, dislike, distrust, rage, entrapment, and even hatred. The whole experience tends, too much of the time, to deteriorate into torment or torture.

As competent and mature as they may be, all these people are lost to themselves in a basic way. At a basic sexual level, they simply do not know clearly enough who and what they are, what they would desire for themselves, or what they aspire to be. Sometimes they feel that they do not know what their sexual orientation is: heterosexual, gay, or lesbian. Even more fundamentally, knowing perfectly well that they are male or female, they find that they have no idea, model, or conception of what it would be for them to be a man or woman in their own terms, terms that they could respect and identify with. Their basic quest in their therapies is to define these ends for themselves, to find their own sexual movement, and to be able to enter a sexual partnership with the possibility for pleasure, fulfillment, and love.

Parents and family members are, as often as not, models of how they wish not to be. At the same time, they continue to be so tied in with their own mothers, fathers, and siblings, that they are incapable of moving on in life to find their own loves and found their own families. Inevitably, there are all sorts of erotic, love, and love-hate attachments with these past family members, whether or not they now in fact live independently of them.

Sexual chaos[1] is the most apt way to characterize their developmental environment. The sexual chaos of the families in which they developed reflects nothing more or less than the sexual chaos of the culture. It is here, unfortunately, that we see with dread clarity how and to what degree the sexual revolution has gone astray. As Wilhelm Reich predicted, it has led to chaos.

The most fundamental feature of this picture is the lack of identification with the genital and the genital movement. The identification with the genital is conflicted, attenuated, disrupted, confused, broken, or crushed in some way. From this condition arises the other features of the picture I have drawn. The expression of an identification with the genital movement becomes convoluted, torturous, obscured, and replaced by substitutes. Self-respect, as an inherent bodily process, a natural part of life, is deeply eroded—by shame, guilt, humiliation, confusion, and trauma. It is replaced with ego facsimiles which can only be supported by constant social approbations of one kind or another. A sense of well-being simply based in the healthy body is lost, and in fact the body may be weakening, sickening, or subject to chronic fatigue. The individual no longer identifies with his or her body or feels connected to a bodily sense of self. The mood is one of complaint and negativity.

This is what I have seen in recent years. This description may sound unhealthy and disturbing, biased, or simply the kind of description that any clinic records might yield. I do not see the matter in any of these terms however. I see it as a description of a malaise pervasive throughout our culture.

Certainly, in the course of our work we therapists see a surfeit of suffering. It is not my practice, however, to see only the suffering of those who come to see me. I make it a point to see strengths, virtues, and health, as well; without seeing these aspects of the person, there cannot be forward movement. Thus, I also see the courage, sincerity, seriousness, commitment, and real strength it takes to fight for a better life. Further, personal suffering has to be seen in the context of the inevitable suffering that life brings to each of us.

More than all this, however, I do not see these individuals as ill, in any ordinary sense; nor do I see them as in any way the more pathetic or inept of our society. On the contrary, I see them as in every way representative of our society and culture, and in many cases they represent the healthier, stronger, and more self-claiming. These are people who tend to be educated, who have the time, energy, and money to devote to working for a better life, and they have the willingness to do so. They make sacrifices and set priorities to be able to pursue their therapeutic goals. It is not only their pain that motivates these people to pursue therapy. They have faith that they have something better to bring to life, that life is too precious to allow it to pass by without giving the effort to find peace and the ability to love. They have not given up on themselves or life, although, often enough, their strength is waning.

From this point of view, I see no reason to consider the individuals herewith described as other than representative of our time, our place, our culture.

PEOPLE FROM THE CLINICAL SEMINAR

Latch

Latch's case illustrates the sexual misery of our times. Latch was in his mid-forties, and he had recently asked a young woman, F, to marry him. He was in torment about the decision and his relationship with F. He had wanted to marry her soon after starting to go out with her. Now he said, "I'd be better off dead. I want my own life back."

He had the sense of his life being out of control, that there was an enormous amount of neurotic conflict in his life and that he lived on the edge of warding off disaster at every moment, as if everything were a major trauma. He was filled with self-hate. He had a compulsive need to be pleasing to women, at the same time he was deeply ambivalent, often hostile to them, and lived in fear of being controlled by them. Full of scruples and self-doubt, he questioned every feeling he had for F and was distrustful and suspicious of her. "How wholehearted am I about this? I feel like I'm playing a game. I feel authentic and then inauthentic. I'm determined to be myself under abnormal conditions. I'm never wholehearted. Am I brave or crazy? I'm always asking myself what is the right thing to do."

Yet, he felt good in her presence, felt love and excitement for her. He also suffered with premature ejaculation. He was afraid he'd be her "sex slave." He couldn't seem to tolerate the contact she wanted in lovemaking. He'd be swallowed alive, castrated. "Do I have to endure this terror to have what I want?" It was obvious to both himself and his fiancée that he cast her in the role of his mother, and neither of them wanted that. Of himself, he would say, "I only know how to play the fiancé." In such ways did he torture himself and anyone around him.

In spite of all this, Latch, with an advanced degree and a nice job, had been able to create a pleasant life for himself. He had aspirations to other creative work, but with his disorganization and lack of discipline, it was difficult to tell how realistic such aspirations might be. His torment and woes made him egocentric and self-occupied, and he seemed to have some unconscious presumption of specialness.

Once his beloved was his, Latch lost much of his joy in her, and he lost himself, sexually, as well. The prospect of sex as exciting, lustful, passionate, and fulfilling was lost or clouded in his torment; so was the possibility that with their commitment and love, their sexual pleasure in one another could be a real fulfillment. He could not keep his passion focused on her, and he was consumed by his own self-occupation instead. The torment, ambivalence, and confusion about all the terrible feelings he was having are abundantly evident.

Sexual misery is apparent enough in this description, and there are additional aspects to the picture. There was even lacking in his mind—or it had been lost or obscured—a clear picture of the possibility of a fulfilling love of his own: an image or story of what it might be to live in harmony, sexual pleasure, and companionship with a wife. This reveals not just an uprootedness from traditional values of family life. It reveals that the individual has lost connection with his own body as the source and model for sexual life and sexual relationship. He did not know what it was to be a man and enjoy it; and since he couldn't help being male, he was having to suffer it, at least for the time it was taking him to straighten himself out. This description of Latch illustrates the effects of a disruption in the identification with the genital.

I described character as an adaptation, and here we see such an adaptation at work. I make the same assumption any field naturalist makes when observing an animal in its native habitat: that it is more or less perfectly adapted to its environment, because its survival depends on it. What we observe in Latch is, in some way, an adaptation driven by exigencies for survival. However, inherent in human adaptation is a dilemma faced by no other animal in its normal environment. Childhood adaptation occurs in the early developmental environment, centered in a family or family substitute. Character is the adult structure that emerges out of this process. Character adaptation can, and often does, prove an impediment to adult sexual and reproductive functioning, rather than a preparation for it.

Sexual misery is the direct function of this ill fit between early adaptation and the exigencies, struggles, and opportunities of adult sexual life.

If we view the current behavior as a direct expression of an adaptation to an early environment, we can make inferences about the nature of the environment that would produce the observed behavior. I believe the two fit like lock and key.

The discrepancy between adaptation to the world of childhood and the world of adulthood and its effects is terribly apparent if we look at the problem in its simplest and most inescapable terms: as castration. What else do we call it when an animal has been prepared by its early environment to be unable to reproduce or successfully mate? This is a somewhat shocking way to express the matter, but it is hardly inappropriate. Before Reich wrote about orgastic impotence, Freud observed the reality of "the castration complex."

The discrepancy between childhood adaptation and adult sexuality plays itself out in sexual misery. The mating is constantly unsuccessful. For humans that does not necessarily mean not having offspring, although that is not an infrequent outcome. It does mean sexual misery: the quest for fulfillment as a man or woman results in as much misery as fulfillment and pleasure. Similarly, orgastic impotence does not imply physical castration, but the emotional and energetic problems are terribly real: disruption in the capacity for genital pleasure, satisfying orgasm, and sexual love.

The adaptational perspective is incomplete without an appreciation of the place of trauma. Adaptation occurs as a response to an environment's survival requirements. Normal development is a life movement, not simply a response to the exigencies of survival. The adaptation that results in character development is a response to trauma. In addition, the adaptation to an ongoing traumatizing environment creates an organismic stress in the child that in itself amounts to a trauma. While the child adapts "perfectly," in a sense, to its environment, the environment is still traumatizing, and the adaptation required also amounts to a trauma to the organism. The organismic changes required in such adaptations are ongoing traumatic stresses that perpetuate in the body the original trauma.

My perspective is that the adaptations we are seeing (which create the sexual misery) are reactions to trauma. I am calling the traumatizing factor "sexual chaos." Sexual chaos includes but is not restricted to sexual abuse.

Consider the origins of Latch's sexual misery and his lack of self-respect. His father died when he was thirteen, and he, in effect, became Mother's substitute husband.[2] "We had each other on a string," he says, "There were constant lovers' quarrels and fights." To end the fight, he would have to appease her, and he was "afraid she'd die if I walked away." He loved and hated her, was devoted to her, writing her poems and songs, and giving presents. He was aware of sexual feelings around her; he liked her breasts. He dreamt of intercourse with her. He'd say, "She wants to castrate me. She wants to dance her own dance with me." She was a "hard" woman and a "martyr." She had an underlying critical attitude toward him, was harsh, "controlling," and "on patrol."

The sexual chaos of the family must be reflected in Latch's own chaos: his torment, ambivalence, confusion, sexual misery, shame, guilt—the whole torturous drama. It would be an absurdity to believe that he could have created all that out of fantasy—as much as he is in fantasy.

The chaos is not hard to understand in light of Latch's relation with his mother. After his father's death, he found himself substituting for his father as husband for his own mother. Sexual feelings during that time must have been disturbing to Latch. As he entered adolescence, he still stood at the boundary of the incest taboo. It must have felt to him that his sexual feelings were threatening to cross that barrier. We find him in adulthood not with an unconscious incestuous wish, but with a disturbing awareness of having had sexual feeling in relation to his mother. This kind of experience creates in adulthood the disturbing feeling of not being able to tell the difference between Mother and fiancée. As it is, he feels that sex is "bestial . . . too powerful," something he can be humiliated for, and something that is shameful when he finds himself feeling an attraction to any woman other than his fiancée. His guilt is also reflected in his ambivalence, constant scruples, self-torment, and self-doubts.

The chaotic influence of this relationship with his mother goes even deeper. We might ask, If the man is aware of the sexual feeling for his mother, what is unconscious in this relationship? After all, once conscious, he need not be so disturbed in adulthood by such natural feeling. This question helps further clarify the nature of the sexual chaos in the family.

In essence, what is "unconscious" in Latch's account is his mother's seduction of him. As much as he describes his involvement with her, he doesn't describe her. He is too involved to see her, and, in addition, her seduction inevitably began too early for him to have the separation that permits such perception. She simply *was*—she was the given, the reality.

"Seduction" does not necessarily imply literal intercourse or genital stimulation. It does imply powerful interactions that have an enormous impact on the developing child because they are sexually stimulating. In Latch's case, seduction beginning before his father's death was exaggerated and reinforced after the death.

If a boy loves his mother and has a genuine excitement about her, what makes these feelings problematic? In and of themselves, they are the normal response to a loving parent. When such feelings become problematic, their problematic aspect cannot be considered apart from the parents' (usually both parents) reactions to them. In addition, falling in love with a parent is an altogether different matter from simply loving the parent.

Specifically, we can ask, in relation to the mother, what would make these feelings incestuous feelings? There is only one answer to this question. The sexual response of the boy for the mother becomes incestuous when the mother responds to them out of her own adult sexuality, or, when the mother evokes them for a response to her own sexuality, seducing the boy into falling in love with her. If the mother simply enjoys the child's feelings for what they are, his love for her, the feelings do not become "incestuous"; they do not take on dangerous meanings, developmentally disruptive meanings, conscious or unconscious.

Latch is describing a mother who usurped her son's sexual feelings, excitement, and his sexuality for herself. She did not leave it with him. She used it for her own needs, needs which were substitutes for her own direct sexual fulfillment. This is the seduction.

There were indications of developmental and adaptational disturbances before his father's death. At age ten he was frightened of the moon and his parents took him to a psychiatrist. Latch's father seems to have been as problematic for Latch as his mother. His father's behavior contributed as much as Mother's to the family's sexual chaos and to Latch's later misery.

Father, too, drew Latch in for his own needs, becoming his friend, telling stories, drawing pictures, and then turning on him, yelling, hitting, squashing him. How should we understand this inconsistent, cruel pattern and its contribution to the sexual chaos and Latch's sexual misery? There are two facets to it. First, there is Father's competition with Latch, and then, there is his identification with Latch, an identification which amounts to a homoerotic involvement.

The small son is routinely considered to be in competition with the father in the oedipal period. If such "competition" does indeed occur, what is made of it, both within the family and within the son, depends almost entirely on how the father responds. What real sexual threat is a five-year-old boy to a grown man—unless, of course, the grown man also feels like a five-year-old, that is, identifies with the child? I cannot understand Father's attacks on the child in any other way than as competitive retaliation. Within families, there are all kinds of rationalizations for such punitive measures; none of them are to be taken at face value.[3]

Father's retaliation has to be seen in the context of a triangle. If Mother's seduction of the son sets him up against the father, the competition becomes real and deadly. Then there is a deadly message that the boy and man read from the mother, "I love him (the son) more than you."

In this way, the father is thrown back into the feelings and insecurities of his own early years, and he competes with and identifies with his own son. (A comparable situation occurs for a mother when the father chooses his daughter over his wife.) Knowing something of the parents' backgrounds can help in understanding this multigenerational chaos. What we glimpsed of Latch's father's past also revealed sexual misery and efforts to resolve his own sexual insecurities.

The father identifies with his son. This means that feelings and memories of himself as a tender boy with budding sexual interests are awakened as he experiences his son's relationship with his wife, the son's mother. In this process the father takes a sexual interest in the son's sexual development, an interest in the service of his own erotic needs. The son, still a child and therefore open to his bodily feelings and passions, with his excited involvement with his penis and his own developing body, becomes an avenue for the father for resolving long unsettled sexual conflicts of his own. The love-hate relation with the son reflects Father's own ambivalences and struggles with sex, love, and passion, the excitements and misgivings about his own genital and genital feeling—all that he experienced in his own development. In this involvement with the son's tender genital development there is a homoerotic element, one that is likely to be a source of the father cruelly turning against the son, even as his, the father's, own genital development probably met with conflictive responses. This underlying erotic involvement is not that different from the mother's with the son.[4]

Out of such multigenerational erotic entanglements, chaos emerges for the child, who experiences it all in his own body, and can resolve none of it; and none of it gives him a clear direction *in his own right*. He has become usurped by the parents as a vehicle for resolving their own sexual chaos.

As if all this were not enough, there was yet another facet to the family sexual chaos which was the crushing blow to Latch. His feeling of himself in relation to father is of being squashed, berated, and spanked by the beloved; in relation to mother it is of being controlled, "on a string," used. For both relationships, this describes humiliation.

Latch's first experiences of sex and love were in the context of domination by and submission to more powerful figures. Power entered both parental relationships, and he was humiliated in both. In this context he learned about sex and love. For him, to love sexually is to experience humiliation. It is his humiliation which infuses all his woes and sexual misery: his fear of being swallowed up by the more powerful woman; his chronic sense of humiliation; his perpetual, subtle, hostile efforts at self-assertion; his loss of sense of self and feeling of enslavement; his self-torture and torture of the other.

His therapist describes his body as "bound, soft, neglected, with a distended belly and 'depressed' chest; strong legs, but flat feet; slouches in his chair." We also observed a split in the eyes, that is each eye with a different expression, breaks at the diaphragm and occiput, and tension around the pelvis that was very deep and gave the appearance of a chastity belt. The whole impression was of someone whose aggressive movement had been broken. He himself said that he felt as if he had a hole in his chest somewhere near his diaphragm. These characteristics are the bodily expressions of his submission and humiliation. His social presentation reflected a compensatory fantasy effort at specialness and grandiosity which had little force behind it.

The question raised earlier—What is unconscious here?—needs to be raised again. There was an element of craziness—insanity—in the abusive treatment Latch received from both his parents. How can a child look at and know a father's or mother's abuse and craziness for what it is? The child can only adapt to survive. In Latch's case, adaptation meant cutting off sexual movement, submitting, and trying desperately to make sense of chaos. Adapting to sexual chaos and humiliation produces an inner chaos. What is also unconscious in Latch is the murderous rage that inevitably resides behind humiliation.

Given the crazy environment in which he developed and adapted, it is hardly surprising that the stress of committing himself to a sexual relationship with the woman he loves made him "go nuts" and start feeling crazy himself. Actually, in feeling crazy, he is, for the first time, in contact with his own reality. He is finally experiencing the reality of his childhood—the insanity—that he was unable to face as a child.

Lorna

Lorna is a tall, graceful, athletic woman of considerable sexual beauty, a youthful-looking thirty-eight-year-old. Two years earlier she had been feeling panic about getting married and having children before it was too late. For a few years in her late teens she had a nice boyfriend, but for the many years since then there had been little in the way of relationships with men. She felt "life ended" for her when her parents divorced when she was eighteen.

Lorna now has a lover, a man who is extremely fond of her. Her sexual misery can be characterized in the expression, "She doesn't get it." She acts continuously as if she doesn't get it. She gets terribly upset about it all. "Is it me? I'm so upset about him. Tell me it's okay. What is happening in my relationship? Is it okay? Is it the end? Will it break up? Will he leave? Am I a passing thing? I have to protect myself. Something bad will happen. It'll turn out bad if I wish for anything." An underlying panicky feeling makes her question everything. She constantly questions everything in her life and looks with "big scared eyes and a hanging question."

Her lover says to her, "I don't see why someone hasn't nabbed you," expressing his delight, excitement, and his feeling of good fortune at having, himself, done just that. Above all, it is her lover's excitement about her that she doesn't get. Since she doesn't get it, she can't quite respond. As a result of this character constellation, she has remained single and childless, up to this point.

Lorna's sexual misery has quite a different quality from Latch's. His is characterized by humiliation, guilt, confusion, and ambivalence. Lorna's is characterized by a frozen quality, an inability to feel or respond, and by shock and dissociation. There was sexual chaos in her familial environment as well, but it had a different quality from Latch's.

It is impossible, I believe, to understand someone like Lorna except by looking at and seeing her, and I mean seeing her in bioenergetic terms. She is beautiful and sexually attractive. She also looks terribly frightened, and her face has a masked, unreal expression that gives her a haunted look. When she began bioenergetic work, she had a frozen, doll-like quality, and that has begun to change. It is only by seeing these qualities of her facial and bodily expression that we can understand her and what happened to her.

Lorna's history reveals that she was the sexually beautiful and exciting member of her family and evoked the interest of both parents. Her father, who is described as "infantile," infantilized her in turn, treating her and looking at her like a doll. Her mother obviously responded to her, too, and to Father's interest. Mother, who supposedly liked Lorna's two younger brothers, was critical and judgmental of her and made Lorna "feel like a prostitute." An educator, Mother carried a didactic and precise style into her everyday life. It was also an antisexual attitude, and Lorna felt she got the instructions "Do not love!" from her.

Lorna was caught between Father's excitement about her and Mother's hatred of her. The intensity of this trap had a horrifying effect on her, and thus we see her haunted look. The adaptational response to her horror was to dissociate herself from the object of their interest, that is the sexual beauty and aliveness of her own body. It's no wonder that in her present life she cannot entirely understand or respond to her lover's excitement about her. The necessity of her adaptation required her to surrender her identification with her genital feeling and dissociate herself from her sexual awareness. No wonder she "doesn't get it!"

In the sexual chaos of Lorna's family, Lorna's own sense of reality was subjected to a peculiar denial and distortion. While she was the sexual center of the family, each member of the family, in their own way acted as if they were not really responding to her sexually. Each family member in their own way diminished her, made her feel dirty, like a prostitute, or treated her like a doll, that is, an object without sexual feeling. Her beauty and aliveness that excited people was denied; they acted as if it didn't exist. As a result, these qualities were denied to Lorna. She guiltily dissociated herself from them, and she was left with the feeling that there was nothing much to her but her badness. At the same time the family conspired to act as if none of all this were going on.

The denial of her basic bodily reality sends the child into shock. Lorna grew up in a kind of unreality, something a child is incapable of seeing for what it is. While she is incapable of seeing the situation, she is also unable to escape it, and incapable of not responding to it bodily. As a result, she had to act as if she were neither sexual, nor beautiful, nor that anyone would be excited about her. This of course means dissociating herself from her own bodily experience and from her own genital excitation.

A previous therapist had actually reenacted her family trauma. In espousing the "healing of the inner child," he had denied her sexual maturity and attractiveness and had infantilized her, just as her father had. For a therapist to treat an adult woman or man as a child is to deny their sexuality and the reality of their adult sexuality. For a therapist to deny the patient's adult sexuality is to treat the patient as a child. In Lorna's case, such treatment could only deepen her shock.

The effects of trauma are clearly visible in Lorna. The masked, unreal quality of her face shows shock. Her dissociation from an awareness of her sexual attractiveness to her lover, her dissociation from her own genital feeling, and her dissociation from her feelings and a sense of her own body are all the effects of developmental trauma. Trauma also created her chronic state of sympathetic activation: anxiety, panicky feelings, chronic tension and worry, and a dread which is experienced as the constant anxiety that something terrible is going to happen. Her body is frozen in time. Even its youthfulness seems to be the result of her having been stopped in time.

To understand the nature of the original trauma, I have a simple rule of thumb: the cause (trauma) has to be both of the strength and of a quality to bring about the observed bodily and behavioral effects. To split an oak log for firewood takes a good blow with a heavy splitter; the job doesn't get done with a jackknife. How strong a force and of what kind is required to split the organic unity of a child's bodily experience of herself?

SELF-RESPECT IN THE CONTEXT OF SEXUAL MISERY

Growing up in sexual chaos undermines the development of self-respect. The misery of sexual misery is a direct function of the loss of self-respect. The degree and manner in which self-respect is disrupted or lost reveals the extent and nature of early trauma in an individual's life. Where self-respect is lost, it is replaced by such states as anxiety, guilt, shame, dissociation, and self-hate.

Lorna revealed a nearly complete lack of faith in her own self-regulatory processes. She didn't know her feelings and she couldn't trust her feelings. She anxiously and compulsively tried to get her therapist to manage her self-regulation in a way that she felt she couldn't. Trust in her own self-regulatory processes had been lost and obscured in her early characterological adaptation. Shock and dissociation took over the bodily processes of self-respect.

In Latch's case, too, the bodily processes of self-respect had been lost. In his case, humiliation had usurped the process of self-respect. Self-respect is replaced with depleting forms of self-hate. The stories of Lorna and Latch illustrate that self-respect cannot develop in adult life without the fundamental identification with the genital, genital feeling, and genital movement.

SOMATIC ILLNESS IN THE CONTEXT OF SEXUAL MISERY

Serious somatic illness complicates the picture in the cases of the two men that follow. Their sexual misery sheds light on the illnesses. It can be seen either as a primary contributing factor to the illnesses, or as a factor inhibiting getting well, or both.

Ray

Ray's therapist, Dr. T, is a cardiologist who studied bioenergetics out of a deep conviction that heart disease is often directly related to sexuality and problems with love. He felt that, in particular, the suppression of the deep pain of early heartbreak could be a causative factor in heart disease.[5] Ray actually had a history of congenital heart disease, and he had heart surgery as a five-year-old. When we saw him in his early forties, he had achieved success in a technical field, he was married, and he was the father of two boys.

Dr. T had an interesting hypothesis about Ray. As an adult, Ray had discovered that he had not been a wanted child, that he had been conceived out of wedlock, and that his parents had supposedly married out of necessity. Dr. T observed that Ray's whole life had been a struggle just to stay alive, and he believed that the deformation of Ray's heart had developed in utero as a function of the rejection that had begun at conception. Ray had reported a dream in which an umbilical cord had been wrapped around his throat.

Whether or not this hypothesis is correct, it is certainly true that Ray's life had been a survival struggle from day one. The struggle had exhausted him to the point of such distressed depletion that he literally cringes and writhes under the least further stress. Dr. T reported that when his nurse touched Ray's scar in the course of preparing him for a stress test, Ray went into shock. His voice sounded like that of an old man, and he complained of a lot of body tension and pain in his neck, pelvis, and lower back.

For Ray, himself, the saddest part of his life was his love life. This is what had brought him to therapy. He felt that his life had been devoted to the struggle for survival and the achievement of success. He felt exhausted by it, and it had not brought him the love he longed for. He longed to love and to be loved—for kind, tender contact, and for a greater depth of sexual feeling and fulfillment. He felt very attracted to his wife but did not feel that she was interested in him. She was a beautiful and exceptionally dynamic woman in his eyes, and he felt that "I am a loser, and why would she want to make love with a loser?" In this and in many other ways, he regularly beat himself down.

He fatigued easily and had little energy for lovemaking, and often when he did make love, the feeling and the orgasm were not very strong. He felt that he could have a greater capacity for sexual feeling, and he longed for that. His diminished feelings and despair were the result of the deep contraction that remained in his chest, around his heart, and in his pelvis. Massive chronic guilt is the final component of Ray's misery. It is produced and kept active by his deep contractions.

Ray's sexual misery is his unrequited longing for love and sexual fulfillment, a longing that his struggle to survive leaves him too depleted to realize. The underlying factor that destroys his self-respect is guilt, which he expresses and attempts to relieve by almost constant self-flagellation. His self-punishment can only undermine the body's movement to restore, refresh, and heal itself. His health and need to reconstitute his energetic reserves after more than forty years of struggle are constantly undermined. Needless to say, any organ weakness, such as that of his heart, would only be exacerbated by this destructive cycle.

As a boy, Ray had made a typical effort at trying very hard to be good, and his failure was also typical and inevitable. As an altar boy, he remembers a priest fondling him. He himself reported that he had little sexual feeling as a boy or adolescent and no masturbation. He was the "little boy who was not supposed to cry." His effort to be good, supposedly, was to "make up for being a burden to his mother." He idolized his mother, a "saint," who had been the "nurse" for him, as a child, and whose beauty and goodness had been imposed on by himself, the other children, and especially his father. His first memory is of soiling himself when Mother was pregnant with one of his siblings and feeling that—as far as any love from his Mother was concerned—all was over forever. He questioned whether he really had the right to live.

The horror, shock, and loneliness of his early life were so great that he not only questioned his right to exist, he developed delusional fantasies to explain the apparent mystery of why his life had been spared. He must have a special mission in life, a special gift to bring to the world. He felt there must be some mystical explanation. Through such fantasies a lonely, frightened boy assumed guilty responsibility for the misery of the loveless, rejecting, shocking world in which he found himself. With such pathetic speculations he tried to make sense of the nightmare and to invent a rational system in which he could make home life better "by being good." Being good in this way means to have no needs, no feelings of sadness or anger, certainly no genital feelings, and certainly no sexual activities like masturbation. Being unreal, such efforts are doomed to failure, and are actually only part of the constant cycle of guilt and self-punishment. The fondling by the priest would only have isolated him further and made the guilt deeper.

Several factors put Ray in between his parents and in the middle of a fatal rivalry with Father. He was the oldest child, he had special physical needs requiring more of Mother's tender attentions, and he was the one old enough to see his saintly Mother's treatment by Father. Father was violent and regal. Ray felt father could kill him at any time. Add to this an element of Mother's rejection, making her love conditional on Ray's good behavior, as if Ray could make up to her for his father, and we have a lonely, frightened, guilty boy, with a terrible yearning for love, closeness, and tenderness.

Then, as a five-year-old, when he knew he had to go into the hospital for a dangerous operation, Ray was prepared to die. He used every bit of energy he could "to try to live," but at that age, he could only have experienced the operation in the context of the very real battle for his life in which he was already engaged in his own home.

It is no wonder that his survival is a mystery to him, and that he still seeks some mystical explanation for it and for his life. His sexual trauma was thus compounded with a surgical one, and the surgical one may have been itself necessitated by the conflictive circumstances in which he was conceived and his parents married. He has had a heavy burden of fate to carry. The trauma is still frozen in his deep bodily contraction. Even a nurse's gentle touch can still send him into shock.

Alfred

Alfred's first visit to the clinical seminar revealed a young man in his mid-thirties in such dire straits that his mere appearance made us question if he would live another year. At his second visit with us ten months later, the downward slide seemed to have been stopped, and he was noticeably stronger, thanks in no small measure to the steady work and presence of his therapist.

Alfred had been diagnosed with chronic fatigue syndrome, still something of a medical mystery.[6] It had progressed to an alarming point. He was suffering from terrible anxiety, panic attacks, frequent terror, depression, and despair. He seemed to be simply falling apart and physically breaking down in such a way that if the breakdown didn't stop, he would die.

He was terrified he was dying, and he was living alone in a small studio apartment. Fortunately a number of friends had rallied around him and were taking turns preparing food for him. He couldn't eat without feeling ill, and, already slender, he had lost more weight. He was just able to get to one medical appointment a day, and take very short walks, but he had not been able to give up smoking a pack of cigarettes a day. His sleep was disturbed; he felt a wave of anxiety as he fell asleep and more anxious and out of touch with himself when he woke up. HIV tests were negative. By the time of his second visit with us, he was able to prepare his own food. Before his illness, he had held responsible caretaking jobs.

It was awful to see the quality of his anxiety, panic, and terror, and the way these permeated his everyday life. Relaxing was impossible: he expected at any moment to be tortured, abused, killed. He was literally afraid to breathe. He was desperate to run away somehow, to make this awful experience stop. "If I can't make it go away I'll lose my life. And I can't make it go away. I feel like I'm out of control, everything is crazy, a nightmare all the time." The person he had known himself to be was no longer there. He had lost all ability to soothe or care about himself, and he felt as if he needed to be held twenty-four hours a day.

Alfred's descent into this nightmarish state did not occur all at once, but in a steplike series of breakdowns. In his history, each of three major breakdowns was clearly associated with a crisis of sexual misery.

The panic attacks began four years ago subsequent to spending a vacation with his parents. He had spent some nights in the same bedroom with them. His father had made "eerie" noises in the night. From what I had learned of his early history, I gathered that this panic and anxiety represented the reliving of early trauma and sexual abuse.

In Alfred's family, the kind of sexual chaos seen in the families of Latch, Lorna, and Ray, reached its complete and most extreme expression. Alfred's memories of his earliest years reveal an environment chaotic, psychotic, and abusive in the extreme. He describes it as an Auschwitz,[7] a nightmare that never ended. The developmental disruption he was exposed to began with the disruption of his earliest bonding with his mother; disruption in every form continued throughout his early years.

He slept in a room with his parents until he was five. It is no surprise, then, that memories were awakened on the vacation with his parents in which he spent nights in their room.

He was an only child. He has the impression of having been tortured in his infancy. He has a memory of being stuck in a box in a closet, of being put in a car trunk, of crying alone in his crib. His father was a "madman" who couldn't tolerate anyone, or anyone else's needs, who would brutally lash out, a monster. Alfred was always terrified of him—terrified beyond words—and unsafe in his presence. I suspected Father had been psychotic in Alfred's early years.

He remembers being tied up and used sexually by an older male cousin from ages four to twelve. Strange memories of strange things being done to his body in a hospital are probably screen memories,[8] that is memory images which disguise through real or constructed imagery some other experience.

Another step in his breakdown can be traced to more recent events, the loss of a lover. This lover, a man, had left him in a way that made Alfred feel he had been rejected with indifference. The loss left him feeling helpless, hopeless, and full of an enormous longing. He literally did not have the energy to mourn this loss, and he was left terribly depleted. He had not had a lover since.

The depth and quality of his longing can be seen as a function of the disruption of the early bonding with his mother. Since these bonds were broken so early, they were left open, like an unhealed wound. The longing is an expression of that open break in the energetic integrity of the organism. In longing of that sort, the energy seeps out to the world, as the individual seeks another person as the source of repair and warmth, preventing the organism from building up its own energy resources. As the person waits and waits for the other, his strength is depleted and he gets weaker and weaker.

Alfred now finds himself astonished and "embarrassed" at the intensity of his need for his therapist, as he establishes with her something like the early disrupted maternal bond, a process that will allow restitution. In the past, each time Alfred reached out sexually to a partner, he was also reaching out for someone who would repair the early bonding. As a result, he was doubly vulnerable to any possible rejection and so vulnerable to loss that it threatened his survival.

Alfred apparently had operated for many years on the slimmest margins of available energy, and the process of depletion had begun years before. His mid-twenties saw the most intense bout of sexual misery. He had been upset and tormented by confusions around his heterosexuality. Finally, he simply couldn't stand the torment and decided he wanted to be with men. As if the confusion and torment weren't enough in themselves, he simply didn't have the energy to sustain the conflict in such a way as to feel that he had brought it to a satisfactory resolution. His decision amounted to a giving up, a resignation from the conflict; he just "put it away." The struggle had been depleting, not strengthening.

The most recent crisis followed an effort to reestablish a heterosexual relationship. Desire and affection had developed for a woman colleague. When she left their workplace, he fell ill, and was eventually diagnosed with chronic fatigue syndrome. It was at this point that he sought out his current therapist, a sympathetic and caring woman and one he could reach out toward and deeply need.

In previous cases we saw the healthy body processes of self-respect undermined and replaced by humiliation, guilt, shock, and self-hate. In Alfred's case, it appears that the biologically deeper breakdown of self-respect is expressed in illness. To the extent that chronic fatigue syndrome is an autoimmune response, here is self-hate on a cellular level. In Alfred's case, he had begun adult life with few resources emotionally and energetically. Further breakdown would necessarily effect him somatically.

THOSE DEPRIVED OF A SEXUAL LIFE

There are those who are deprived of a sexual life. This is what happened to Celia and Brown. It has also happened to many others. In saying they were *deprived* of their sexual lives, I mean just that. It has been their fate in life never to have established a relationship of sexual love for any period of time. Celia is in her mid-fifties and Brown in his late forties. Each has had brief sexual relationships. To say they are deprived of their sexuality implies that it was not their choice, as indeed it was not. Each often expressed their deep regrets, longing, and sorrow at being alone. Their sexual misery is their deprivation and loneliness.

As to the manner in which they were deprived, in the simplest terms, their upbringing amounted to domestication. In speaking of domesticated animals, we refer to the ones that serve us and the ones we keep as pets. Castration is a tool used in the domestication of animals, and it is not inappropriate to use the word when a child's upbringing has the quality of domestication. Gonads are not literally removed.[9] In the case of humans, the job can be done on the emotional and energetic level. The effect is just as real in the body.

The domestication of both Celia and Brown was so severe, austere, and thorough that the element of untrammeled freedom, wildness, and spontaneity that a person needs to find their way to fulfillment in the sexual arena was tamed out of them. I am horrified by the treatment of children that can result in this fate.

Celia and Brown both come from traditional, middle-class, white Anglo-Saxon backgrounds, of families which were staunchly traditional in their values and behaviors. Both were able to establish themselves in the professional world without too much difficulty. Both are good-looking, healthy, intelligent people.

In each person, there is a specific damage to self-respect. Celia had the feeling that she is the one who simply cannot have a love of her own. It is just not for her, as if that were some absolute law. In Brown's case, he has a deep sense of shameful ugliness. He is in fact much above average in looks and physique. In both, these feelings can be traced back to their developmental years and were so deeply ingrained they were terribly difficult to shake. The fate of being deprived of a sexual life is not unique to Celia and Brown. It is all too common.

I believe a universal credo is needed: Children have a natural right to their sexual lives. They have a right to a developmental environment which protects and makes possible the development of an adult sexual life. To domesticate a child to deprive it of its potential for an adult sexual life is one of the most basic deprivations to which a human can be subjected. It is the right of children to be allowed to develop in a manner which allows them to become sexual adults whose normal quest for sex, love, and a loving sexual partner is not itself a source of misery.

GENITAL INCEST DESIRES

> One feature of the popular view of the sexual instinct is that it is absent in childhood and only awakens in the period of life described as puberty. This, however, is not merely a simple error but one that has had grave consequences, for it is mainly to this idea that we owe our present ignorance of the fundamental conditions of sexual life.
>
> —Sigmund Freud

TWO MEN, TWO LIVES, TWO VIEWS OF OEDIPUS

In the stories in the preceding chapter we see people with difficulties in love, difficulties whose roots can be traced to their experiences with their first loves, and their first loves, we understand, are their parents, one, or the other, usually both. Difficulties in love were first described in this light by Sigmund Freud, and it is easy enough now, in the light of Freud's discoveries, to see these stories as unending Oedipal dramas. In doing so we gain insight and understanding, even though such dramas are not exactly what Freud meant by an Oedipus complex.

The original formulations of the Oedipus complex contain serious distortions about sexuality. This is not to deny core truths in Freud's formulations. Wilhelm Reich revised the conception of the Oedipus complex in important ways. My purpose in reviewing their formulations of the Oedipus complex is to shed light on issues pertaining to the themes of sex and self-respect.

Freud elaborated the theoretical structure in which the Oedipus complex is embedded, over the course of thirty years. Those embellishments and elaborations show us what Freud did with the initial insights he attained in his self analysis and what they meant to him. Reich, who was born forty-one years after Freud, made something vastly different from similar insights into himself.

If Freud wrote from the point of view of civilization, Wilhelm Reich wrote from the point of view of nature. If Freud wrote from the point of view of control, equilibrium, renunciation, and the mind, Reich wrote from the point of view of impulse, expression, fulfillment, and the body. In the end Freud wrote from the point of view of death, Thanatos, as it appears in his theory of the two great instincts, Thanatos and Eros. It was on this point that Reich broke with Freud theoretically and wrote from the point of view of life and life energy.[1] More different approaches, more different truths, and more different lives can hardly be imagined.

Both men had a deep human and clinical appreciation and understanding of sex and of the relations between the sexes, but their appreciations differed vastly. Reich was a sexually passionate man. His views of women were not dominated by the kind of nineteenth-century patriarchal ideas Freud insisted on institutionalizing in his theories. Sexual life for Reich was always a real, immediate concern in a way that Freud perhaps masked in his own life. Freud's long, abstemious engagement followed a bourgeois pattern[2] that Reich could never have followed. Reich also had a deep appreciation for the sexual life of children and adolescents; it was real to him in a way that it never seems to be for Freud, the very man who wrote the first treatise on "infantile sexuality."

Underlying these differences were vast differences in their personal histories. Freud's elaboration of the meaning and theoretical structure of the Oedipus complex reveals the meaning and feeling tone of Freud's own story. We see what it meant and what it was like to become a man in the society of late nineteenth- and early-twentieth-century Vienna, what it meant and what it was like for a profoundly intelligent and intellectual Jewish man of single-minded ambition. We see what it meant and what it was like for such a man in an irresistibly bourgeois, authoritarian, anti-sexual, and patriarchal society. It was from the position of one who had weathered and was still struggling with these experiences that Freud approached his early profound and hard-won insights into his own unconscious Oedipal wishes—to desire his mother and wish his father dead. It was out of these experiences, and his continuing ambition and determination to be a famous man of attainment in that very society, that he continued to elaborate a theoretical structure to contain and make sense of these early, disquieting insights.

Wilhelm Reich, too, achieved hard-won insights into his own Oedipal tragedy.[3] However, the kind of world Freud knew had been turned topsy-turvy and crumbled before Reich was twenty. He was a soldier in World War I by eighteen, and he had already felt the tragic death of both parents, a tragedy for which he felt a central responsibility. An orderly bourgeois existence, bounded by Victorian certainties concerning the relations between men and women was something he never knew.

Their lives as young men were utterly different. Freud was hard work-ing, ascetic, and single-minded in his ambition and in his effort to establish himself in his career and achieve fame. He knew one woman in his life whom he met at age twenty-six and married four years later when he felt he could maintain a household. Reich was very much a modern man in this one regard: he knew many women and he knew the full measure of sexual misery and sexual excitement.[4] Equally ambitious, extraordinarily brilliant, as original a genius as Freud, always amazingly productive, his life was chaotic in his youth, and tumultuous throughout.

Reich's family situation had been very different from Freud's. Reich's father could be rageful, jealous, and frightening to a small child; he appar-ently was frightening even to the peasants who worked for him.[5] Reich's childhood, and his adolescence too, had prepared him not so much to adapt or rebel, but to be outside of, alienated from, the societal structure—patriarchal and authoritarian—in which Freud had labored so mightily.

Freud and Reich each gained hard-earned, deep insights into their own childhood sexuality. From similar ore emerged different metals. While Reich never criticized Freud directly, he did produce a surgically sharp cri-tique of the underlying world view and cultural experience out of which Freud's views arose.

CRITIQUE OF FREUD'S VIEW

Freud's description of the Oedipus complex took the male as the paradigm case, and it never worked as applied to women. This ground is now well known. The rumpus, of course, centered on "penis envy" and the basic idea of woman as a failed (i.e., castrated) man. In all of the discussion about Freud's psychology of women, however, one essential point has been omitted. If a theory of sexuality is incorrect for women, it cannot possibly be correct for men.

The denigration and mythologizing of women (e.g. as "the dark conti-nent,") in Freud's writing arises out of and expresses anxieties about women common to the culture of which he was a part.[6] However, we know also that these very attitudes toward women represent a distortion of the sexuality and the sexual attitudes of the males who hold them. They express not only the males' anxiety about women, they also reveal the men's hatred and fear of their own sexuality, and a theory about men that embodies these attitudes is a distorted theory.[7]

Freud's view of sexuality, then, hides and expresses a distorted concep-tion not only of female sexuality but of male sexuality as well. The core of that distortion can be seen in a critical examination of the conception of the castration complex and its relation to the emergence of the superego. The castration complex was soon added to the Oedipus complex. It not only fit clinical data, it was essential in understanding the "passing of the Oedipus complex."[8] The castration complex plays a crucial role in development, a necessary condition for the formation of the superego, the structure through which the child becomes a civilized person with a moral sense. The important mediating process here is "identification," the mechanism through which the child's ego was "built up" by relations with socializing adults. By 1923 Freud had described "the more complete Oedipus complex, which is twofold," which takes account of the inherent bisexuality of children.[9]

Of the castration complex, Freud says, "Now the view we hold is that the phallic stage of the genital organization succumbs to this threat of castration." He felt that actual threats "more or less plainly and more or less brutally . . . uttered" and then "the sight of the female genitalia" bring home to the male child the real possibility of castration, the actual removal of the prized penis. These threats and experiences occur in the context of masturbation, and they move the child to relinquish claims on his mother and they are "replaced by identification. The authority of the father or the parents is introjected into the ego and there forms the kernel of the superego, which takes its severity from the father."[10]

What this really means should be made perfectly clear. It means that the male child's development is normally to be dependent upon being terrified, usually by the father, but possibly by the mother or other parenting figure, terrified to the degree that he expects to have his penis removed. This is the real meaning of the castration complex. There should be no mistaking this. Furthermore, this is to be considered normal development. The exact conditions of the dreaded castration may be quite ambiguous in the boy's mind, but the fear and guilt will always center around any (masturbatorily fantasized) claims on the boy's mother.

Only adult denial and rationalization could disguise such a horror in a theory of the mind. What is for the child a terrifying and horrifying reality is converted, by theorizing adults, into a realm of childish fantasy and "mental work," as if it were no more than the ordinary frustration of childhood. For the child, this horror is reality, plain and simple, or it would not effect development. Further, as reality to the child, there must be external actualities to which he is responding—actualities which, however the adult world disguises them, are terrifying to the child. However the threat of castration is established in reality, it is a terrible threat, and it means that a child is terribly frightened, frightened enough to believe his penis will be removed. We are given to understand this as normal development, requisite to becoming a moral, civilized person. This viewpoint is no less awful than the idea that penis envy is the central event in the girl child's development.[11]

It is to be understood that sons are to be threatened in a deathly way by fathers, and that fathers and sons are to be deadly rivals. Unfortunately, this is not uncommon, because fathers project their own sexual fears, wishes, guilts, and delusions into the child. However, this does not make it a healthy development. Freud enshrined this development in the formation of the superego, the structure which is to allow the child to become a civilized man.[12]

It would seem to me to be more accurate and more believable that an individual becomes moral and civilized in spite of having been terrified and made to feel guilt about sex and his own body. This basically was the position of Wilhelm Reich. Allowing a child to maintain pleasure in his own genitals is a better guarantor of morality than fear.

The enduring effects of castration anxiety and superego formation eventually emerge as guilt and bodily tensions in the pelvis. They make reestablishing the pleasure and full feeling of genital sexuality extremely difficult in adult life. These, however, are not the only developmental results of castration fear. The restricting and blocking of healthy sexual feeling and movement leads to secondary, substitute sexual drives—power, prestige, ambition, competitiveness, and sadism. These all have an egocentric and asocial element and can be overtly antisocial. The preservation, on the other hand, of the capacity for sexual pleasure, for example through respecting the masturbatory freedom of the child, leads to a healthy sociality.

The threat of the actual loss of the penis became an essential element in Freud's theory of male sexuality. How could Freud and his followers have accepted the idea of the castration complex so blandly? To me, it makes sense only if, in some fashion, it was—the fashion. In the patriarchal society of Freud's time, I have to assume that threatening boys *was* the fashion, and that was the way that the young men became—and stayed—involved with and submissive to the male authority and the whole apparatus of authoritarian conventional society. Freud himself, through the medium of his ambition, was nothing more nor less than enslaved in those conventions. His years of asceticism and sacrifice must have made sense to him in light of the possibility that thereby he would achieve the freedom offered by fame. What fame he achieved as the years went on seemed to give him little pleasure, and it served mainly to enmesh him more deeply in the struggle of maintaining and establishing his findings, his theory, his organization.[13]

In the final analysis, Freud's story of the Oedipus complex is more Old Testament than Greek, more of Abraham and Isaac[14] than of Oedipus in Thebes. Alice Miller has approached the study of the story of Abraham and Isaac through artists' depictions of it. She says:

It is astonishing at first glance that not one of the artists . . . was tempted to give this dramatic scene an individual, personal stamp. . . . Why did all of these artists accept the story as valid? The only answer I can think of is that the situation involves a fundamental fact of our existence, with which many of us become familiar during the first years of life and which is so painful that knowledge of it can survive only in the depths of the unconscious. Our awareness of the child's victimization is so deeply rooted in us that we scarcely seem to have reacted at all to the monstrousness of the story of Abraham and Isaac.[15]

It is a very sad thing to say, but I am making exactly the same statement about Freud's theory of the castration complex and its relation to the Oedipus complex. "Our awareness of the child's victimization is so deeply rooted in us that we scarcely seem to have reacted at all to the monstrous-ness of castration theory." I would add that, in our distorted conceptions of male and female sexuality, it is considered "masculine" to act as if no such grievous threat had ever occurred, even as a small child. Denial of this sort is maintained through loyalty to the father and later to those who hold their authority and power by virtue of that same loyalty and denial. In this way a great tradition is carried on and ensured, each generation of men in a sense waiting their turn to subject their sons to that to which they have been subjected. There are alternatives to this tradition, as Miller, too, goes on to point out, ones that are neither destructive nor senselessly rebellious but rather are affirming of life.

REICH'S REVISION OF THE OEDIPUS COMPLEX

Wilhelm Reich made a radical departure from Freud in his interpretation of the sexual core of neurosis. Before he broke with the psychoanalysts, Reich wrote a paper which already revealed just how differently he saw things. In this paper, titled, "The Characterological Resolution of the Infantile Sexual Conflict,"[16] when he says anything at all about the Oedi-pus complex he is straining to accommodate Freud, and he says nothing at all about the superego. Instead, he describes the origins of character: "The character armor is formed as a chronic result of the clash between instinctual demands and outer world which frustrates those demands. Its strength and continued *raison d'être* are derived from the current con-flicts between instinct and outer world."[17] This description of the origins of character, it should be noted, is quite close in meaning to Freud's seduc-tion-trauma theory of the origins of hysteria. It has to do with actual events in the life of a child. There is little limit to what might be conceived of as a "clash between instinctual demands and outer world." Included would be physical and sexual abuse, sexual or emotional exploitation and overexcitation, harsh punishments, shaming, prohibitions, discipline, conflicts, neglect, antisexual attitudes, a hostile family environment, and so on. This clash is of such a quantity and quality as to cause a "chronic," that is, lasting, effect. Once that chronic effect is established, it continues the conflicts in a "current" status in the organism; they are ongoing. They are not lost, "submerged," "dissolved," "passed," or, for that matter, repressed.

Reich goes on to describe the organismic position of the character armor as lying "at the boundary between biophysiological instinctive life and the outer world."[18] Reich might have taken the opportunity, here, to follow the direction already taken by Freud, as in *The Ego and the Id,* into the devel-opment of the structural model of the mind. He in fact is taking an entirely different direction. He is moving toward "biophysiological instinctive life" and sees the ego poised—not in balance between id and superego—but between the biological life of the organism and the outer world. Freud, in a sense, retreated, withdrew into the realm of the mind. In his typical stormy fashion, Reich forged ahead, confronting "the world" head on.

The crux of Reich's argument and a point from which he further diverged with Freud is in the following remarkable statement. "At the core of the armor's definitive formation, we regularly find, in the course of analysis, the conflict between genital incest desires and the actual frustration of their gratification."[19]

The Oedipus complex is given an entirely different focus here as "the conflict between genital incest desires and the actual frustration of their gratification." It more closely describes the reality of what actually happens in a child's life. The focus is bodily: genital desires, gratification, and frustration. The term *actual frustration* refers to real life events, events which prevent the expression and gratification of genital desires. The threats for masturbation and the frightening fathers that Freud wrote about are examples of what create "actual frustration." In using the term *actual frustration* in relation to genital incest desires, it should be understood that there is no implication that genital incest desires should be gratified with the incestuous object.

Reich's shift in the meaning of the Oedipus development gave a clearer focus to the therapeutic endeavor, and it gave clearer guidance on the path to freeing excitatory movement for its fulfillment in the real world. Not long after this paper, Reich's therapeutic focus of freeing the excitation moved from the psychological realm to the bodily—freeing the body to increase its capacity for excitation.

In later years, Reich did a comprehensive study of fascism, authoritarianism, and the patriarchal family structure.[20] It was the latter, he believed, which is the source of the sexual distortions that Freud described as the Oedipus complex. In turn, authoritarian and fascistic social structures are fed by armored sexuality formed in the patriarchal family organization. Character, as the residue of the sexual traumas of childhood, is seen as an armoring, a hardening, a limitation on life; it is not seen as the psychic vehicle for maintaining civilization.

A true ethic, healthy work, and the capacity for love are achieved, if at all, in spite of character. If submission to the father out of fear—castration anxiety—is involved in character, that fear is to be freed, felt, expressed, and the inhibited anger and rage is also to be expressed in the safe confines of the therapeutic setting. If the boy or girl submitted in the face of an angry, terrifying, rageful, jealous, or psychotic father, that was an adaptive strategy in the face of a real threat.

The authoritarian agency of the father and his institutions are not monuments to which one forever owes allegiance, in such situations. They are irrational and are regarded as the source of the frustration of instinctual movement, and their inner vestiges are to be removed from body and psyche. If there is to be authority, it is to be rational authority, based on love, work, and knowledge, not on submission out of fear of castration and death.

TRAUMA THEORY

Freud's seduction-trauma theory is often mentioned, but seldom presented. One of his original statements deserve citation.

[T]he specific cause of hysteria . . . is a premature sexual experience with actual stimulation of the genitalia, the result of sexual abuse practiced by another person, and the period of life in which this fateful event occurs is early childhood up to the age of eight to ten, before the child has attained sexual maturity.

   A passive sexual experience before puberty: this is the specific aetiology of hysteria.[21]

In turning from these views, Freud also turned from the external to the internal world, and from a potential critique of society to a stoic accommodation to it. Reich, by focusing his attention on the conflict between the incestuous genital desire and its actual frustration, prepared himself for the eventual recognition of muscular armoring as a characterological expression, and by seeing the body, he returned to the outer world and a critique of society.

   We saw examples of the effects of the sexual seduction of children in the previous chapter. While these stories did not necessarily involve what Freud called "coitus-like processes," there is no question, in my mind, that they do involve "actual excitation of the genital organs," and the appropriate word for the manner in which that excitation occurs is "seduction." With their dependence and responsiveness, children are easily seduced. Such excitation occurring in the phase of childhood sexual identity formation is sexual, and it is experienced at the time the child is identifying with his or her genital. The effects are lasting.

   The sexual misery of any given individual requires an understanding of just what kind of violation they were exposed to. Violations include, in addition to overt sexual abuse, physical abuse, seduction without overt sexual abuse, emotional exploitation of all kinds, exploiting the potential of children for shame, guilt, and humiliation, hatred of the child which can be expressed in various ways, many forms of neglect and deprivation, raising children in family atmospheres that are violent, horrifying, or terrifying (apart from or in addition to that of the outer world), disrespect in every conceivable form, harsh punishment and discipline sometimes in the guise of moral or religious dogma, and traditional genital mutilations. Violations include exploiting the child's liveliness, sexual energy, sexual responsiveness, innocence, beauty, tenderness, and erotic sensitivity. Violations include seducing the child into being the tender confidant, "pal," or companion. All of these produce violations of sexuality and all have lasting negative effects on children who take them into adult life and, more likely than not, perpetrate similar violations on the next generation.

SEXUAL CRAZINESS
VERSUS SEXUAL PASSION

> Where id was, there shall ego be.
> —Sigmund Freud

AN EXAMPLE OF SEXUAL CRAZINESS

A picture of ordinary human sexuality both disturbing and exciting emerges out of Wilhelm Reich's work. There is the disturbing picture of armor limiting and distorting our capacity for sexual love. Chronic organismic tensions originating in the early sexual conflict between genital incest desires and their actual frustration constrict and counter the biological drive to build a healthy charge and allow periodic discharge. The tension created in this battle can feel like torment, engendering deep frustration, conflicts, and even despair. At the same time Reich's vision of the self as an organismic expression of the natural energies of the body offers the possibility of fulfillment and pleasure in the degree to which we can soften our armor and surrender to our feelings. If Freud's conception of the Oedipus complex and infantile sexuality were met with shock and resistance, Reich's view of our sexuality has been even more difficult to come to terms with. Yet, increasingly, what he described is being integrated more and more—albeit in piecemeal fashion—into popular and professional culture. From his work we can gain insight into what we see and experience. Consider the distinction between sexual craziness and sexual passion.

The kind of sexual craziness I have in mind is quite common. I am not referring to extreme cases. Many examples could be offered. Here is one.

Tim

A young man in his early thirties, Tim saw me twice for consultation. He felt less than free sexually with his woman companion; he felt he was always playing the father for women. He found that he was often very afraid of men and often wanted to fight them.

Tim was his mother's darling. "She was all over me. She took away my manhood." As he talked about her, he was startled to find himself getting an erection. Father, who was alcoholic, was away from home for long periods of time. Tim remembers that when Mother explained sex to him and a sister, she had them both open their pajamas for the comparison.

I was impressed by his "pretty boy" look and the expression of boyish innocence that masked his face. I did not feel inclined to take for granted either his innocence or his benignity, and I suggested that the innocent expression disguised its opposite, that is, a sexual awareness that had been developmentally precocious. His head was not well associated with the body, and the feet were collapsed and undercharged. He had done sufficient weight training to build a body to fit the "pretty boy" image.

There had been some petty criminality and a strong tone of self-destructiveness in his history. For several months during his therapy he had inflicted wounds on himself, cutting his arms and occasionally his chest in the effort to relieve an awful feeling; and he had thought of killing himself. I talked with him about guilt about a "secret crime." He replied, "I replaced my father with my mother."

In our second session, his rage and his craziness exploded. He had thought about his "secret crime" and told me that he had been very rebellious as a teenager, refusing to do anything his parents expected of him. I asked him to face me, raise his fist, look right at me and say, "I won't do what you want!"

Right away he could feel in his fists that he wanted to hit. His face did not show that. He kept smiling. I encouraged him to let it show in his face. For a split second, he opened his eyes and a startled look of craziness and fear showed in them. Later he told me he could feel the craziness in his eyes.

I encouraged him to allow the expression of his feeling, and the murderous feelings broke through. He became red in the face with rage and practically flew off the ground. For a moment I thought he might lose control and go after me. He was making sounds and the word *kill* started coming out. I directed him to hitting a pillow on the bed. He went at it furiously, muttering, "Kill, kill, kill . . . ." Then in a kind of subdued whisper he started saying, "Kill my father . . . fuck my mother, kill my father . . . fuck my mother." He hit the pillow for a good while, bent forward to ground himself, cried briefly, and gradually quieted down.

I suggested one further piece of work. I asked him to bang his pelvis on a pillow and say, "Is this what you want?" He did this for a long time, fully aware that it had to do with his mother. He kept saying, "Rape." A few times he stopped, felt and examined his penis, and said, "It's mine." After a while he talked about the extreme shame he felt for his genitals for having been excited about his mother.

Tim is not psychotic; in his daily life, he functions within reality reasonably well. Yet there is a kind of craziness in him, too. When it broke through for a moment, I saw it in his eyes, and he felt it.

The craziness consists, in part, in the potential for the explosion of a murderous rage and the ease with which it can be triggered. However, there is more to it. When Tim comes close to his sexual passions, he loses contact with present reality to a degree, and his actions emerge from memory, from the time in which his passion was directed toward his mother and father. The craziness is this loss of present reality and the blurring of the boundary between inner and outer.

With such strong emotional, bodily memories, it is difficult for him to tell the difference between time past and time present, between the lover of today and the mother of the past, between a man of today and the father of the past. As long as there is a necessity to control those passions, the individual is unable to give in to love and sexual excitement in a realistic, full, and pleasurable way.

If Tim presents an unusual picture, it is only because he is able to express his incestuous and patricidal feelings so openly. He is not intellectually versed in psychology and is, to that degree, unselfconscious in his expressions. I might have chosen as an example someone who presented essentially similar material after two or more years of therapy, but it would have been the same material.[1] The point I wish to emphasize is that, regardless of the structure or timing of the expression, the type of relational distortions of reality found in Tim's life are so extremely common as to be "normal."

Is the word *crazy* pertinent here? I believe it is. The dictionary definition of "crazy" carries the meanings of cracked, (sometimes used as slang for crazy), insane, and wildly enthusiastic, as in, "I'm crazy about you." The last use indicates the demotic understanding that between passion and craziness there is a thin line. All three of these meanings apply in the present usage. The "crack" involved here is the separation between the individual's passions and his or her connection with present reality. Important figures in Tim's life, become targets of the passions belonging to his past, making his current life, in significant ways, a psychodramatic stage for his private inner dramas. The word *crazy* here does not denote a psychiatric diagnosis, and I do not intend it to be one.[2]

SEXUAL CRAZINESS AND GENITAL INCEST DESIRES

Desire presses for expression. When desire is attached to the incestuous object, there is a press toward that which is crazy, since incest generates a form of craziness. Neither moralistic judgment nor psychiatric diagnosis is intended here.

Reich's formulation, refers to the "conflict between genital incest desires and the *actual frustration* of their gratification." The word *actual* indicates a real body state, a state kept dynamically alive by an ongoing, chronic conflict. Is there some implication in Reich's formulation that the conflict should or could be ameliorated by gratification of the genital incest desires? No. Of course not. Not if that means engaging in genital sex with the incestuous object. That would be incest and insanity. This is clear enough.

When a parent responds from the position of adult sexuality to a child's excitement, the child's sexuality is inappropriately brought into the adult realm, and genital incest desires are created. Bodily excitation arises in the child as a result of the adult's response. The parent's input heightens the tensions and frustration that must be held in the child's developing character. The characterological conflict between genital incest desires and their actual frustration thus contains and holds a quantity of energy generated not only in the normal course of child development. Additional energy is derived from the incestuous sexual inputs of the parental figures as well. The resulting characterological structures can be truly explosive and crazy-making.

As the excitation becomes stronger, it becomes a kind of foreign intrusion into the bioenergetic system of the child, an alien excitation. It is an excitation which, by its nature, cannot be discharged. The child cannot be the adult's lover because of the incest taboo, and also there are obvious bodily, energetic, emotional, and psychological discrepancies between child and adult. The child is not sexually mature, its body is simply smaller, and its whole energetic system for the charge and discharge of sexual excitation is immature. Similarly, when the child is taken into the arena of adult sexuality, there is an enormous power differential between child and adult. The child is dependent on an adult world. Even when the adult is psychologically or emotionally infantile, he or she is physically mature and in an adult social role. All of this creates a profoundly disturbing, frightening, and confusing effect on how the child will experience his or her own body, feelings, and excitation in a sexually charged environment with a parent.

The outcome is an arousal which cannot be discharged, and this creates a hyperactivation of the sympathetic nervous system and muscular tensions, both of which become chronic. This is the actual frustration; and it becomes an organismic fixation, a functional system that cannot be shifted and yet still keeps demanding relief. There will be a specific quality and degree of excitation, which the organism is always striving to both discharge and hold, and the individual will repetitively seek relationships and conditions which seem to offer propitious opportunities for such discharge, but they are impossible to obtain.

Because of the taboo and frightening circumstances under which the excitation arose, the organism must not only hold the excitation but even ensure that discharge shall never occur. In this state there is a chronic undischarged, frustrated excitation which feels alien and bad in the body.

These are the conditions which create and sustain sexual craziness. The individual is desperately driven to discharge tensions which cannot be discharged, or to desperately sustain an unbearable state of frustration. Finally, it must be understood that ultimately the focus of all this tension, confusion, fear, and frustration will be the genital itself. These are the bodily realities.

The frustration is maintained by muscular tensions, always including tensions in the pelvis, specific tensions in the genitals themselves, and tensions in the neuromuscular structures supporting the whole genital apparatus. These latter tensions play a central role in maintaining the character structure. Sometimes people are aware of these tensions. A woman who identified herself as a lesbian was aware of the deep tensions in her vagina which made heterosexual intercourse painful for her.

A man had been aware all his life that tensions around the base of his penis created the sensation that his penis was separate from his body. Those sensations began in his boyhood. He remembers swimming with other boys and feeling his penis "evaporate." In contrast with being aware of the genital tensions, one woman, caught in the erotic excitation of both parents, did not have any memories of sexual awareness in her own body until she was in her twenties.

A child's excitation, augmented by a parent's sexual excitation, will press for discharge and will engender incestuous fantasy even when there is no overt incest. Overt incest, of course, further traumatizes and complicates the child's development. Overt incest engenders, not less, but more, actual frustration, of an even more horrible sort.

Desire presses for expression. Genital incest desires exists at "the core of the character's definitive formation," and they press for expression. Here is the source of sexual craziness. In both overt and covert incest, then, there can be seen the potential for a *feeling* of craziness or insanity, a *fear* of craziness, and an *actual* craziness. Sometimes, to become sexually freer in adulthood, each of these possibilities must be experienced, as different aspects of the core conflict are contacted in the course of an ongoing relationship.

This discussion sheds some light on the significance of childhood masturbation. The sexual life of childhood is lived out in play, fantasy, and masturbation. Masturbation gives pleasure, relieves tension, and fosters the child's identification with, pleasure in, and trust in his or her own body. Masturbation can relieve, within limits, the excess of excitation that may build up within a child in the context of different relationships. The inhibition of masturbation intensifies conflicts about genital incest desires, fostering the incestuous fixations and generating chronic frustration and tensions. I believe this is what Freud may have had in mind when he wrote that, "masturbation represents the executive agency of the whole of infantile sexuality and is, therefore, able to take over the sense of guilt attaching to it."[3]

These ideas suggest a revision of Freud's famous aphorism, "Where id was, there shall ego be."[4] The revision is, Where sexual craziness was, there shall sexual passion be. For, where the individual can feel and express his or her sexual passion, he or she will not be crazy in the least.

Freud's image of the id as "a chaos, a cauldron of seething excitement"[5] is well known. I propose that Freud saw (heard) things in this light because he was in fact seeing (and hearing about!) sexual craziness. In this light the id became a concept for categorizing and seeming to contain much that was chaotic, seething, and charged with held excitement, and at the same time incompatible with social functioning. Freud could maintain a distance and separation from the material he was hearing, the sexual craziness, by understanding it as the expressions of a more or less separate, more or less buried structure of the mind. He could present this structure as separate from and antithetical to the "civilized" structures of the mind, and this distance and separation served him, his patients, and the young science of psychoanalysis.

DELUSION AND REALITY IN LOVE

An idealized sexual fantasy—in essence a delusion—plays a central role in the state of sexual craziness. Such delusions are commonly associated with love. They have two aspects. One aspect informs the individual (unrealistically) of his or her "true" sexual potential (under the right circumstances and with the right partner), and the other creates an image of an (unreal) ideal partner.

The idealized sexual fantasies are the linchpins that hold the individual into his or her sexual craziness. The individual unconsciously holds the idealized fantasy as if it were the secret to fulfillment, thus maintaining the delusion that the fantasy could be realized in life. However, the idealized fantasy is always accompanied by its degraded polar version. Phallic supremacy is accompanied by fears and secret feelings of impotent failure; irresistible beauty is accompanied by feelings of whorish ugliness. As long as the idealized delusion is retained, the individual is in continuous conflict due to the regular and inevitable emergence of the degraded image and its accompanying feelings of shame, failure, worthlessness, degradation, ugliness, and so on.

Fantasy sustains a heightened energizing of the cranium, removing the individual from a realistic appreciation of the genital function. This further disturbs the possibility of actual sexual gratification and fulfillment in love. The ensuing heightened frustration and tension fuels the fires of the disturbance.[6]

I believe the idealized sexual fantasies take typical forms in men and in women. In the case of the man the delusion has very directly to do with the fantasized power of the genital: phallic power, hardness, strength, aggressiveness, superiority. In the case of the woman the fantasy has to do with the fantasized power (attractiveness) of the whole surface appearance of the body. This difference is not simply a matter of culture. It is based on the evolution of the female and male body. Margulis and Sagan note that "[e]volutionary biologists generally agree with Darwin, that in most species of animals the female does most of the choosing of mates. Humans differ from most other mammals in that females generally have the most striking appearance."[7] The human female's striking appearance is formed by evolutionary pressures.

Breasts and a new pubic modesty [hidden estrus]—the very subtleties that had made it impossible for male hominids to completely control the sex lives of female ancestors—now became sought after as distinguishing marks of the feminine, the very charms of women.[8]

We assume that foremothers once had periodically colorful labial and buttock swellings but somehow lost them. That with the universal adoption of clothing—including the "clothing" of permanently protubertant [sic] breasts—the loss of estrus was transported from body to mind, from the physiology of females cyclically coming into heat to the consciousness of women choosing when they wanted to be most attractive.[9]

Evolution thus brought attractiveness of overall appearance into the mind of women in close association to her central biological function in life and to her identity. The male body evolved under the influence of different pressures in this regard. "The average length of the erect penis of a man is some five times that of an adult gorilla. Human testicles, which hang down, are also considerably larger than those of gorillas and orangutans, two of our closest relatives."[10] The larger genitals gave the individual's sperm greater likelihood of successful fertilization. Male preoccupations with phallic power thus seem to have an evolutionary basis as well.

Individual development and emotion-laden experience go hand in hand with evolutionary developments. Individual development is organized around the identification with the genital. From early childhood on, the genital provides feelings of pleasure, although in some that feeling is intensely inhibited. How could we not desire that our whole life should be informed, in some sense, by such delight and pleasure? In particular, why would we not cherish the dream that a particularly delightful partner would heighten that pleasure to its fullest (imagined) potential?

Under the circumstances of modern life, delusional idealization becomes virtually inevitable. Impinging on the developing adolescent are the pain and conflict of real life, an almost certainly damaged sense of self, and a glut of erotic imagery from multiple sources. To individual and evolutionary development, these factors add a powerful distorting force. The distortion pushes the individual away from self-respect and body reality to a more delusional, driven version of love and sex.

A fantasy becomes the ideal through which any actual life experience—including those with every partner—is evaluated. It is difficult to escape the effects of the distortions and loss of reality caused by the sway of these fantasies, because they are so real to the individual. The delusion is, after all, built on real bodily experiences, that is, genital sensations and feelings. The problem is those experiences have been rearranged in a distorted way as part of the adaptive effort to deal with traumatic incestuous relationships.

SEXUAL PASSION

Tim's story reveals that, in sexual craziness, one's lover evokes feelings once felt for or in relation to one of the incestuous figures of childhood. Also evoked, then, will be the individual's reactions and attitudes that represent the effort to manage such feelings (character reactions). When the potentially explosive, crazy emotions, passions, and attitudes associated with the incestuous figure erupt, they can wreck havoc. For that matter, efforts to avoid them can wreck havoc as well, through avoidance, inability to make a commitment, or inability to love at all. In this way, various passions of the sexual dramas and tragedies of childhood are played out in adult life, often with a good deal of pain, disrupted relationships, and devastation of any capacity for enjoying a loved partner.

Sexual passion is the alternative to sexual craziness, and sexual craziness can be transformed into sexual passion. Genital desires can be freed from the incestuous figures. These goals require identifying and working with "the actual frustration" in its bodily form.

The key to this process is fostering the individual's identification with his or her own genital feeling and movement in life's here and now reality. This can be accomplished when it is recognized that, however contorted the form, an individual's effort at managing his or her sexual life contains within it the basic, organismic drive to reestablish the genital identification and free the sexual movement toward its fulfillment.

Confronting the bodily tensions associated with the genital apparatus inevitably means confronting frightening and painful feelings, and, at some point, a feeling of sexual craziness. The tensions associated with the genital apparatus will also underlie shame, humiliation, and guilt, and they will reflect how parents reacted to the child's genitalia and genital feelings. When genital tensions can be reduced, sexual craziness will yield to sexual passion.

Masturbation, from childhood throughout life, is an important mechanism for pleasure and gratification and as a means of relieving genital tensions. Sometimes, however, tensions in the genital apparatus can be so severe as to interfere with masturbation. Shame about sex, guilt about incestuous genital desires, and humiliation sometimes appear more immediately and directly in masturbatory experience than elsewhere. A young woman was unable to bear the feelings she had when she touched her own genital. She could masturbate only by rubbing herself on the bed. In his youth a man had been similarly unable to touch his penis and had to cause friction in other ways. Fears of sexual craziness are associated with these disturbances.

Since sexual craziness lies at the core of every character formation, it is inevitable that it will be encountered in the course of therapy. There's no escaping it. The therapeutic task always returns to the focus of freeing genital desire and feeling from the incestuous objects and, on the bioenergetic level, of fostering and grounding the downward movement of the excitatory wave. On the way down, that excitatory wave has to go through the pelvis and the genital apparatus. There is no other way *down*.

When a deeper level of excitation invades the pelvis and genital apparatus, symptoms may become exacerbated, and the person may enter an emotional state aptly called "sexual craziness." Feelings of being crazy, a fear of going crazy, and uncharacteristically wild behavior are not uncommon. The conflict between genital desires and actual, chronic frustration may be experienced intensely, and the frustration may feel intolerable. As the individual moves through and integrates these experiences, sexual craziness is replaced by the capacity for sexual passion.

SHOCK, GENITAL INJURY, AND DISSOCIATION

> The road between vital experiencing and dying inwardly
> is paved with disappointments in love.
>
> —Wilhelm Reich

In the previous two chapters I explored the deeper roots of sexual misery. Adaptation to the conflict between genital incest desires and their actual frustration results in organismic changes. Sexual craziness, expressed behaviorally and as a part of the personality, is one common outcome or effect of this adaptation. In such adaptations, there has been a violation of the child's sexuality.

In this chapter I describe very briefly three other organismic effects of the violation of sexuality in childhood. Shock, dissociation, and genital injury also have roots in the conflict between genital incest desires and their actual frustration. They occur in the context of the relationships in which the child is forming its sexual identity and identifying with the genital. The organismic realities of shock, genital injury, and dissociation reveal the true meaning of the "castration complex." They are all profound interferences in self-respect and make fulfillment in love profoundly difficult.

SHOCK

I was witness to the reality of the bioenergetics of shock soon after I began practicing bioenergetic therapy. Tom, a young man who came for therapy, had a look that reminded me of a stunned ox, as if he had been hit between his eyes. His father was violently abusive. This father beat his son with his fists or strapped him regularly and, on more than one occasion, had thrown potentially lethal objects at him.

To work with Tom's shock, I tapped on his forehead quite firmly with my fingertips just above the midpoint of the eyebrows as he lay on the bed. Following this, a movement emerged from the numbed state. He flinched uncontrollably, and I asked him to make an effort to open his eyes. As his eyes were mobilized, he began to relive bodily the memory of his father's abuse, accompanied by a torrent of fear, anguish, helplessness, and pain. This was repeated many times in the course of his therapy.

There is, then, such a thing as shock that becomes established in the body as a chronic state. Shock creates a numbing in the organism and a blanking out of pain and terror.[1] It is not difficult to momentarily send people into shock. A sudden very loud, sharp noise in a roomful of people can send many of them into shock.

What happens if a child, in the course of its development, is repeatedly thrown into shock? Tom's look of a stunned animal is the answer to that question. The effects of shock on his mental and emotional functioning were pervasive. Every positive movement in his life was forced against an invisible resistance and was terribly difficult. Since first seeing Tom, I have observed shock in many others.

Shock stops organismic movement. The long-term adaptation to shock is a chronic overall numbing that effects the functioning of the organism literally at both ends, that is, sexually and mentally. Mentally, the effects can be seen in various kinds of difficulties with cognition. Tom, an intelligent man, often struggled to make coherent sentences. Other people in shock can appear extremely unaware about the significance and effects of their actions because they do not have a feeling grasp of what they are doing.

The effects of shock on sexuality and sexual life are equally pervasive. An individual may go to extreme measures to break out of sexual shock in order to feel alive again, to have sexual feeling and excitement. At one point in his life, Tom had made quite a frantic effort to do so.

An "acting out" of a fantasy is not uncommon for those who are trying to break out of shock. Sometimes forays into forms of sexuality at variance with the person's usual lifestyle have that significance. A woman who offered services to men who had foot fetishes was a workshop participant on one occasion. I suspect that both she and her clients were trying to free their sexual feeling from shock.[2]

Those deprived of a sexual life (see Chapter 4) are often victims of shock. Such was the case with Nora, a young woman who suffered life in a state of cold shock. Nora was a woman of exceptional sexual beauty, who, seeking a feelingful, warm life, was always "on" sexually. Nonetheless, over the course of her youth, she had not been able to break out of her shock to a degree sufficient enough for a relationship to develop with any of her admirers.

All of these, and many others, are lives lived in shock. Unfortunately it is not necessary to go to a war zone or a hospital for war veterans to see victims of shock. For many, life in their early years was war enough, and they, in effect, remain captives behind enemy lines, in the shock induced in their own families of origin. One of Nancy's repeated images of her life in her family, and hence her life later, was of being "staked out," tied to a stake, bait for the wolf who would come to tear her apart.

Shock of the kind I am describing can be generated as late as adolescence, as in Ellen's case. A physically and sexually developed young woman at fourteen, she had attained her full height and was lively, physically active and competent, beautiful, and sensual. She had joined a dance group, and boys and young men were very interested in her. She was excited and enjoying life enormously. At this time, her father, a man of stern, authoritarian discipline, went crazy about her behavior: if he wasn't going to have her, it seemed, no one would. He actually locked her in the house for six months, allowing her out only to go to school, and the next academic year he sent Ellen to a convent school. She had dearly loved her father and was thrown into shock and confusion by his betrayal of her life. She no longer knew which way to turn in her life; the sense of joy and excitement about herself and life were smashed.

Ellen's early adult life was typical of those who are sent into shock as children. Their life goes on, but rather than living life and feeling it, they *do* life. In Ellen's case, she did many of the same things women of her generation did: college, Peace Corps, marriage, children, a successful career. As her children were growing, she realized she felt inexplicably trapped. She sought help, escaped her marriage, and after several years of hard work to restore her feelings, also found love. Hers was a long road to personhood, and a cursory summary hardly reveals the pain, courage, and hard work that goes into restoring life to a body that spent most of its early years in shock.

The quality of "doing life," as I call it, is characteristic of the life of one who is in shock. The numbness in their body allows them to function as members of society, but it is a functioning that is not an expression of a feeling self. It is more like a program. The bioenergetic adaptation to shock effects the organism at both ends, head and tail. The individual's cognitive and sexual functioning is effected. This means that there must be armoring in both head and tail (pelvis).

The brain, the ocular segment, and the neck are all effected. Tom, for example, had a remarkably thick neck, and I have seen other very muscularly developed necks in other shocked individuals. In addition to these conditions, I believe that the brain itself is effected by chronic shock. I speculate that it is effected through the conditioning of the autonomic nervous system, and then also by virtue of the fact that in experiences of shock, the central nervous system is overwhelmed with stimulation which it cannot immediately process and integrate in its usual ways. These two effects, I would assume, influence neurohumor pathways, transmission, and production which have profound implications for mood and emotion.

GENITAL INJURY

Adaptation to shock also involves armoring in the diaphragm, abdomen, and pelvis. This armoring encapsulates and maintains a genital injury by disrupting the energetic unification of the genital with the rest of the body. Identification with the genital is interfered with, effecting both sexual identity and sexual experience. The result is a genital injury just as truly as if the damage were perceptible to visual inspection.

As a nine-year-old living in a rural area, Tom engaged in a disturbing practice. He would hide himself by the road at dusk, and when the road was clear he would lie down in it with his genital exposed. When a car came along, he would hide again. He was never hurt or observed at this dangerous practice.

A variety of psychological meanings can be seen in a childhood practice of this sort. If we look at it in bodily, bioenergetic terms, its meaning is clear. A body will express what is in it: in this case, a sense of genital injury. Tom's genital injury, a sense of disturbance in his genital being, is expressed in this practice. As a bodily expression, it is an effort to find a movement that would allow him to energetically integrate his genital with his body and with the rest of his experience of himself. In this sense, it is a positive, integrative, and self-affirming effort. At the same time it expresses the injury, his guilt, and expectation of punishment.

The sense of genital injury is often sensed or expressed as a form of castration. "Withered" and "pathetic" were two words a woman often used. She had felt deep vaginal tensions as well. A man of middle years experienced his penis as separate or cut off from his body. There are those who are unable to touch themselves in masturbation. The replacement of the reality of sex with an idealized sexual fantasy also expresses genital injury. The basis of all these reactions lies in some degree of disturbance of the energetic integration of the genital. Sexual excitation, charge, and discharge are interfered with in some measure. Feeling, sexual pleasure, and the fulfillment of sexual love are interfered with. All of this amounts to nothing more nor less than real genital injury. That physical damage is not visible does not change the fact. Underlying genital injury is traumatic shock with attendant feelings of fear, terror, and the threat of death still frozen in the body.

DISSOCIATION

Dissociation is currently seen as an effect of trauma.[3] The basic mechanism of that trauma can be understood as a functional expression of the bioenergetic changes involved in genital injury. In chronic shock, the energetic connection of the genital with the rest of the body, that is with the self, is disturbed. The genital actually is dissociated, partially, energetically, from the rest of the body. This is the organismic basis for the psychological and behavioral aspects of dissociation. The functioning of the genital apparatus, in terms of excitation, feeling, charge and discharge, is interfered with. Genital feeling itself is interfered with; usually it is diminished and, often, at the same time, displaced or replaced by feelings of shame, disgust, dirtiness, and badness, and images of dark and awful things.

The deepest implication of all this is the loss of the energetic foundation for a cohesive integration of the self. With the break in the energetic connection between genital and body and consequent disruption of the identification with the genital, there is a break in the core organization of the self. This is the biological, bodily reality of dissociation. The self is split, because the self is the body, and there is a split in the body at a basic level. Without the integration of sexuality based on an identification with the genital, unity and integration of the self is not possible.

There is a subjective experience of dissociation. People often say, "I am not in my body." This phenomenology is accurate in the sense that it is the ego that is dissociated from the body. In essence, this subjective experience is the upshot of the person identifying the self with ego consciousness. As a result of trauma, the identification with the genital and with bodily experience and feelings becomes dangerous or unbearable. It is as if the person were to say, "My being here is threatened, and I'll deal with that by making this body—where these terrible things are happening—not me. This is not me." In this way, the person "takes up residence" in a world that is more or less make-believe, living, for example, in a social persona or an alter ego. The body, in the meantime, goes on—in a sense, normally—about its biological business. The body will, after all, continue its regular biological processes. Subjectively, it is the body that is to a greater or lesser degree alien, because the self, as a survival adaptation, has restricted itself to a narrow range of ego consciousness. In this sense, it is the ego that is dissociated from the body and sexuality.

I do not confine the term *dissociation* to traditional psychopathological phenomena such as multiple personality disorder, because the phenomenon of dissociation is more widespread than the diagnostic categories. Many lives today have a dissociated quality. As I described earlier, many people "do" their lives. Their movement does not come from within. It represents a social adaptation from which the person, in his or her depths, is absent. Such was the case with Nancy for many years.

"PHIL, MY LIFE IS TOO HARD": NANCY'S STORY

So Nancy declared some months after the beginning of a therapy of some years. She was simply telling me the plain truth.

Nancy's story and the process of her therapy illustrate shock, dissociation, and genital injury. From her childhood on, Nancy had to disavow her sexuality, her genital feeling, her attractiveness to men, her own excitement about men, and her own sexual life. Her self-respect was brutally compromised. This adaptation seems to have begun before she barely had time to establish the identification with her own genital.

Indications of dissociation are apparent in Nancy's accounts of her adolescence. She had grown into a young woman of exceptional beauty. Seeing her was enough to make men fall all over themselves. To all of this, she herself was an outsider. She found no pleasure in her beauty nor in men's response to it. She felt they wanted only to use her, not merely sexually but also as an adornment for their own egos, and she felt they had no ability or interest in seeing or knowing her as a person. So, too, the religious counselor whose help she sought at nineteen had been unable to resist her, kissing her at their first meeting. They married, and after that she "turned off" whatever it was that had caused the constant flurry of male excitement around her. Her sexual life with her husband was never happy for her.

Nancy was forty-two when I met her, just after her marriage of twenty-two years had ended. Her first two or three years of therapy were a constant struggle with exhaustion, self-castigation, fear, a wish to give up and die, and a craving for a safe place to "crouch" long enough to heal. Themes of shock, genital injury, and dissociation emerged quickly in the first year. The likelihood of sexual abuse emerged later, and more focused memories, probably of sexual abuse, emerged after four or five years.

She expressed her sense of genital injury in the phrase "my big raw wound." She had been betrayed in one way or another by every man in her life, from her father on, every man who had been important to her and upon whom she had needed to rely. With the exception of one brief, happy sexual relationship, she lived a sad, celibate life, for some years after her divorce. Her guilt and the effort to atone had, in fact, emerged in Nancy as a young girl.

The worst of Nancy's problems was that she had a sheer genius for self-flagellation. She jokingly referred to it as her "life's work," and named her therapy "The Case of the Brilliant Beater." She could slide into a virtual orgy of self-punishment at the drop of a hat. She had the "brilliant" ability to take *any* occurrence involving another person, however minor, as an occasion out of which to create a vast empire of self-blame, self-reproach, a demonstration of her worthlessness, unloveableness and so on.

"It's all my fault," she would say. "Every move is wrong." She had the feeling something "evil" was in her. All of this implies a self-hate system absorbing vast amounts of energy.

A fear of being killed—for any noise or anything "bad"—emerged in the first weeks of therapy. After two years, the image and sensation of being threatened by father's "big fists" emerged. As the third year of her therapy began, she expressed her situation succinctly: "The essence of me seemed to elicit punishment, and as a result I tried to deny who I was." These images emerged in the course of bioenergetic work.

From the beginning of her work, I had asked Nancy to lie on the bed and kick.[4] Nancy had been frozen in her body for many years when she began bioenergetic work. Her body was tight, underweight, and her whole appearance conveyed frozen terror. She looked as if she could break. Over time her body changed a great deal. It softened and filled out, and she became remarkably stronger; she enjoyed working with her body and had a talent for it.

After even a little kicking, her body would go into a kind of convulsion, and she would look like she was frozen in terror, unable to make a sound. I would usually encourage her to scream, which gradually she could do more and more fully. This released feelings of terror, horror, and images of punishment. Her eyes would go off, and shock, terror, and horror would show in her face in pitiable and frightening ways. It is appropriate to call these experiences body memories from her childhood. She would even speak in the voice of a child, as if the experiences were here and now, although she was fully aware of where she was. Bodily movement allowed these experiences to find expression. She would say, "I had no idea it was that bad."

Memories of punishment and threat of death emerged after any intimation of sexual feeling or movement. On one occasion the topic of her "acting as if she didn't know what to do with a man" came up. Her body went into a violent autonomic reaction even as she sat in her chair. She began choking, convulsing around her abdomen, and almost fainted. She rose out of the chair, began stomping, screaming, and crying, "Help me!" She expressed violent images of punishment and of her badness. She would be killed, slapped around viciously by demons; she was a danger to the world. After she calmed down, she said, "I can't pretend any more how bad it was. I was the softest and fullest [of the children] and I was attacked for it."

It did seem, in fact, that she had been the sexual choice of both parents, and they both turned on her for it. "They did something terrible to me and wouldn't let me make a sound." Screaming time and again helped her to release herself from that enforced silence. Outcries would emerge of her fear of her mother, and then she would go into speaking in her mother's voice.

I'm nothing. I'm supposed to do what I'm told [cowering and cringing]. I might do something bad and get killed. If you're nothing, you're not supposed to take liberties like getting above your station. Down in the dirt is your station! You worm, don't stand up. Don't take liberties with me, young lady. You forget your place. How dare you take liberties, you nothing!

After six years of therapy, clearer memories and images emerged on one occasion in a striking way. As Nancy lay on the bed one day, I suggested that she reach up with her hands, and, after a moment I asked her to see what it would feel like to grasp my hand. As it happened, perhaps due to the tentativeness of her movement, Nancy grasped, not my whole hand, but the first two fingers. Almost immediately she went into a state of shock and horror. She said later, "I knew it was a penis." In sessions after that the memory of the "two fingers" became more penislike (without repeating the exercise), and "spit in my mouth." She experienced these sensations many times in later sessions.

With someone in shock, the smallest movement, sound, or word can throw the person into actively reliving his or her shock. Nancy's childhood was, at times, a living nightmare, sending her into shock and dissociation. Once she described shock as "much worse than being afraid." In the voice of the child again, she said, "If you do it one more time I'll die. I can't take it. But I didn't die." She went on to compare her feeling with someone being tortured by a master of torture who just keeps his victim on the edge of death, without letting her even have the escape of death." Significantly, she added, "This is where it came from—my feeling that I'm bad, wrong. I feel I did something wrong and should be punished."

She described her situation very succinctly at one point in one of the later years of her therapy. "It was like you were sliding out of your mother and no one is catching you. No hands were there to help me. I wanted something, and I got 'two fingers.' I needed something and if I didn't get it, I'd die. And if I asked for it I'd be killed."

For months she came to sessions saying she felt dissociated and crazy. "It's not me talking," she would say. Nancy had considerable talent in her professional work, and she felt she did good work, but she would say, "It's not me who is doing it."

The genital injury is gradually healing. As healing on the bodily level occurs, this allows for the emergence of memory and the achievement of understanding. The body changes are the basis for the emergence of memory and gaining understanding. A scream might start the healing, because the scream frees long held chronic tensions and frozen autonomic reactions. The healing proceeds as the energetic movement deepens in the body.

In an early week of therapy Nancy described herself as retreating into a tiny point in her body, somewhere behind her sternum. This mental image is a perception of a real withdrawal and contraction of energy, feeling, and movement from the periphery of her body, especially pelvis and genitals, into the core. The deepening and expansion of the energetic movement in her body was experienced as that point gradually becoming larger and larger until, on occasions, she could feel herself "come out all the way to the edge of my body."

The terrible difficulty for someone like Nancy who was shocked, threatened, and sexually abused is that each step of the way in warming and enlivening the body is accompanied by terror and panic. The subjective feeling of danger is not entirely eliminated until the person is capable of strong sexual feelings. It is not easy to reach this goal. The character adaptation evolved to avoid threatening dangers that must be emotionally faced and experienced, dangers such as the threat of death, sexual abuse, horror, terror, and emotional disintegration. We have the strength to do this as adults, in order to free ourselves, and we can know that the worst has long since happened and is in the past.

CONSEQUENCES FOR SELF-RESPECT AND FULFILLMENT

Chronic shock and dissociation paralyze the individual's healthy bodily basis for self-respect and therefore for personal fulfillment. This is painfully evident in Nancy's life. She fulfilled what we might think of as her genetic mission—that is to bear a child—even though as a person, she found herself dissociated and unable to find personal fulfillment in her bodily self, from adolescence on. In shock, the body will live its life, but as a person the capacity for personal fulfillment is disturbed. It is my impression that, in some measure, this is the fate of many people today. This is part of the sad story of our time. Bioenergetic work with the body may restore aliveness, feeling and the capacity for self-respect and personal fulfillment.

THE HATED CHILD

The sexual behaviour of a human being often *lays down the pattern* for all
his other modes of reacting to life. . . . [I]f, for all sorts of reasons, he
refrains from satisfying his strong sexual instincts, his behaviour will be
conciliatory and resigned rather than vigorous in other spheres of life as well.

—Sigmund Freud

THE FACE OF HATE

As a therapist, I have worked with many people who, in their childhood,
were hated by their parents. I am not referring to a passing moment of
hatred. I am referring to a consistent hatred, a consistently hateful attitude,
or consistently recurring hateful episodes. The effects of being hated are all-
pervasive and devastating to the developing child. There is an element of
hatred in all violations of children's sexuality. There are several aspects to
the face of hate that bear directly on issues of sex and self-respect.

It is painful and difficult to look in the face of hate. Yet hate is part of
everyone's experience. To be hated evokes an immediate and natural inclination to avoid, block out, not experience, or retaliate. These inclinations
make hate difficult to understand as an experience. There is a kind of
inherent inability to see hate for what it is. In therapy, there is a very deep
resistance to uncovering, seeing, and experiencing the reality and effects of
hatred.

The idea that parents might hate their own child is shocking. In fact, I
believe it can only be characterized as unnatural, because it literally goes
against nature to hate one's own offspring; it goes against the survival and
flourishing of one's kind. It also goes against the natural, soft, warm
response evoked by the immature infant and child. Few people can or
would acknowledge that they hate their own child. Nevertheless I know it

is a common occurrence. I can see it any day I'm on the streets or in the shops. Consider this example from everyday life which reveals some facets of the face of hate.

For a couple of years I would occasionally see a particular mother and daughter on the street near my office. The child was a lovely girl of five or six. My attention would be drawn to this pair because I would be horrified by what I saw. I saw the mother violently hating this little girl. It took the form of a direct, abusive assault, mostly verbal, but the mother would grab the child's arm and bend over her so as to direct the full force of her hate into the child's face. Shamed to be seen to be hated by her own mother and assaulted for her presumed badness, the little girl was obviously in shock and was barely able to maintain herself. Passersby would go their way as if this were an ordinary occurrence; I fear it is.

This aspect of the face of hate reveals a similarity to sexual craziness. The mother was acting as if she were disciplining a recalcitrant child whose "bad" behavior was driving her to her wits end. Indeed, her behavior gave every evidence of her inner state. To understand the effects of hate, and all violations of sexuality in childhood, the differences in roles and developmental conditions of parent and child must be considered. The parent, having passed through the developmentally critical years, is now the developmental influence on the child. The parent has physical and emotional power at her disposal in dealing with the dependent child, immature child. The child's immature ego has not developed skills for handling hateful assaults. The rage of a full grown adult is a real danger to the child of five or six, whereas the child's anger is not a real threat.

While the mother has maintained herself sufficiently so that her behavior has a facade of normalcy, there is nothing sane about overwhelming a small child with physical threat and a torrent of verbal abuse. My purpose here is not to castigate a nameless mother but rather to see clearly: to look into the face of hate, to see it for what it is, and to see the insanity in it.

The emotional tone of the mother's abuse was not in accord with a little girl's reality or the realities of her behaviors. The child, a person in her own right, has her own inclinations, her own bodily experiences, and she was being sent into shock because of her mother's response to who and what she is. The mother's behavior is too discordant with the biological expectations[1] of the child. When that is the case there is often an element of craziness in the behavior.

Tricia

Tricia's story reveals other facets of the face of parental hate. Tricia was the second child, and she was hated supposedly because a girl had already been born, and the parents wanted a boy. The craziness in this is evident immediately.

The mother's cruelty to this girl passes comprehension. Tricia was a particularly beautiful, blond, fair-skinned girl. Her first experience of sexual intercourse occurred in a horrendous context, engineered by her mother. On one occasion, when Tricia was sixteen or seventeen, her mother punished her for some very minor infringements in a grotesque manner. She took her to the roughest section of the city, where, as a fair-skinned blond in a predominantly black neighborhood, she would be noticed, and left her. It was late at night, many miles from her home; she had no money and no idea how to get home. She called a man who had been making advances, and she "paid" him for a very indifferent "rescue" by allowing him to have sex with her. When she arrived home the next afternoon, the mother made no inquiries as to how she had gotten home or what had happened. This and other similar incidents indicate that this mother had the witchlike wish to sexually destroy her beautiful daughter of whom she had a crazy envy.

As an adult Tricia was perfectionistic and driven. She worked not eight hours a day but instead ten to sixteen, turning out difficult technical reports days in advance. Her unrelentingly superior work aroused resentment even from her supervisors, and she once again found herself the object of hate, which, given how hard she was trying, was incomprehensible to her.

Once hate is seen to be a factor in the lives of children, its devastation is quickly understood. What is more inimical to life than hate? Being hated in any consistent way over time is utterly devastating to the developing sense of self, the capacity for self-respect, and for finding fulfillment in love.[2] Even for an adult (especially if hated as a child), the experience of being hated is awful.

To look into the face of hate and gain some understanding, we need to ask some fundamental questions. What is hate and how does it arise? Why do parents hate their children (when they do) and what is it they hate? What are the connections amongst hate, incestuous relationships, and sexual craziness? What are the long-term organismic and developmental effects on sex and self-respect?

WHAT IS HATE?

There is an intuitive inclination to see hate as the opposite of love, as if it were love converted into its opposite. Lowen, for example, says, "It is not difficult to understand the polarity if one realizes that hate is frozen love, that is, a love that has turned cold."[3]

Hate must arise then, when love is turned against or thwarted in particular ways. Lowen suggests[4] that betrayal, as betrayal of the love a child offers a parent, is the particular condition which turns love to hate. Lowen's analysis[5] is based on Reich, who wrote, "frustrated love is transformed into hate."[6]

One of the profound contributions of Reich's work is that it accounts for the actual biological mechanisms of that transformation. The expression of love and reaching out to the world is transformed into hate by the organismic changes of armoring and character development. As impulses move from the core toward the world, they are transformed in the effort to break through the armor. The armor is made up of all kinds of character stratagems, inhibitions, and muscular tensions which function as defenses against anxiety. What was once soft, natural, pulsatory, warm, and flowing must become hard, effortful, ego driven, and inevitably contains an hostile element. The hostile element has its source in the unexpressed anger and rage involved in the development of the character armor. Hate and cruelty are thus directly related to distortions of love and sex, and their origins often lie in the core conflict between genital incest desires and their actual frustration.

Elie Wiesel contrasts compassion and hatred.[7] This contrast is a reminder that hate is not simply a feeling. It involves a total way of looking at the other. To feel hate for another is to see them as bad, evil, or malevolent; the other is seen in the worst possible light. To feel compassion for the other is to see the other's humanness and potential for goodness. Similarly, when someone is viewed with love, they are seen in the best possible light, and their goodness is experienced.

There is a similar contrast between hate and respect. While hate is not exactly the opposite of respect, it does *annihilate* that which respect would promote in the child's development and being. The natural, organismic development of self-respect is annihilated by hate. Repeated exposure to hate will induce in the child the development not of self-respect but rather a form of its opposite—the self-hate system which will be a central aspect of character. The self-hate system, as I shall describe it below, is the prototype and the foundation for shame and guilt.

Henry

That hate is love transformed into its opposite is demonstrated by its effects. If being loved gives us a feeling of beauty, warmth, and rightness in the world, hate gives us the feeling of coldness, ugliness, and of being wrong in the world. Henry was apparently hated from early infancy.

I am beyond the species. That is my experience. I am so diseased that I am beyond the species. I am the one to be attacked by my own species. Thrown to the wolves. Thrown out. That is my experience.

I feel frozen in my body, and emotionally withdrawn, so withdrawn that I don't feel it as such any more. My energy is very far inside and forgotten. I am frightened all the time, except when I am not alone.

I have the feeling that I just don't know what I could say or do that would be appropriate or would answer what was said or asked of me. I get panicked, and I don't feel all right. I don't know how to interact with people.

I feel I've given up on myself; I'm hopeless; life is pointless. Being wrong is a threat to survival all the time. I feel fragmented, a physical feeling of fragmentation until I see the whole problem and understand. This makes life hard.

If I could have expressed feelings as a child, I would only have had anger and fear. I was living in a cold world. There was nothing to express. Everything was cold and frightening. It was all the same. Miserable.

So Henry poignantly expressed his isolation, coldness, and sense of always being wrong—all effects of hate, effects opposite to those engendered by love.

WHY DO PARENTS HATE THEIR CHILDREN, AND WHAT DO THEY HATE?

Some years ago, while working on this material, I realized I was avoiding the question of why parents hate their children. I came up with the realization that such hate is "unnatural," and though I found that helpful, I still felt timid about asking this question.

When I realized I had been unable to explore this question, I had to ask myself what was keeping me from addressing it. What I came up with surprised me, and it also gave me the beginnings of an answer. What I came up with was the following series of further questions. Is it because there are so many reasons for such hate that to ask the question would only pose the job of cataloguing a monumental list of human ills? Or is it that one is not supposed to know? And could it be that the question is not supposed to be asked, because it is assumed (in some bizarre way) that parents in our society have the right to hate their children in the same way they have the "right" to kick their dog—after all, it's "theirs"?

I suspect the answer to all three questions is "yes."

If all this sounds like a pessimistic view, don't forget that we are talking about hate. The reasons for and the sources of hate can be illuminated more deeply only if the initial resistances to asking the relevant fundamental questions can be overcome.

With an understanding of the relationship between love and hate, I believe it is not difficult to give a simple and direct answer to the questions: Why do parents hate their children (when they do), and what is it they hate?

When the developing child is hated, what is hated is the child's sexuality and capacity for love as a male or female. Children, from their early years through adolescence, have a natural movement, softness, beauty, and innocence of sexual expression. They have it, that is, if it has not been destroyed. It is the pulsation itself, the aliveness itself, that is hated.

A parent whose own sexual beauty and softness was violated and destroyed, who had to harden and turn against it in him or herself, will inevitably turn against it in his or her child. The parent hates in the child what he or she hates in him- or herself. A father or mother who cannot tolerate the softness and bodily movement of their own sexual feelings will hate that quality in the child and set out to destroy it. It is actually the child's very movement toward the other in the expression of love and its closely associated excitement that is hated. Love is met with hate, and this form of turning against love turns it into hate.

Hate is derived from love; or perhaps it is more accurate to say that what might have been the basis for love becomes the basis for hate. Hate, like love, is an expression of the basic excitation of the organism, the basic organismic pulsation. Excitation in a developing child does not occur in a vacuum. From birth onward it is organized in relation to the important figures of a facilitating environment through movement and reciprocal movement. Two basic qualities to that movement are reaching out and aggression. From the beginning the child reaches out to the environment (parents) for love, to establish contact, receive nurture, engage holding, and to stimulate exciting engagement. Aggression does not signify something destructive. It has the meaning of *moving toward*: moving toward the object, the other person, the world—in the service of meeting whatever need is involved. As maturation proceeds, patterns of reaching out and aggressive movement in the world develop, mature, and become more complex and differentiated.

Parental response can enhance the pleasures of these movements or produce pain and frustration. Frustration, even sometimes pain, in themselves are not necessarily traumatic, but they easily can be induced in such a way as to be traumatic. Repeated experience of pleasure in a relationship allows for the development of love and the capacity for love. Repeated experiences of painful, traumatic frustration lead to hate. When the developing child's reaching out is turned against in a painful, traumatic way, it learns to hate, and the aggression will come to have a destructive element. What might have been an impulse to touch, hold, love, becomes an impulse to hurt, torture, or kill.

HATE IN THE INCESTUOUS RELATIONSHIP

With its themes of infanticide, parricide, incest, hubris, and self-destruction, it should not be hard to find a place for the theme of hate in the Oedipus complex. The more strongly the child's relationships with parents take on an incestuous quality, the more likely it is that hate enters the picture, and where an incestuous relationship is present so too is some quality of sexual craziness.

While there can be overt sexual incest, there are also relationships which could be called "covert incest." When the parent responds with his or her adult sexuality to the child's love, the relationship becomes incestuous. This is very common, perhaps more common than otherwise. There need not be overt genital contact. In all likelihood, there will be some kind of physical contact that carries an erotic charge.

A very pretty young woman described how her father would have her lie with him on the couch while he watched television. His embrace was so intimate that he would even wrap his leg around her. I find it hard to imagine that she did not feel his penis pressing against her. I would call this an incestuous experience for the daughter.

The incestuous relationships of everyday life are readily observed. One hot summer day, near where we live in New England, my wife and I were watching the horse-pulling contests at a county fair. We were thrilled by the beauty and strength of the horses. As we sat in the bleachers, we also watched, with a somewhat horrified fascination, a father and daughter who sat nearby. The girl, between fifteen and sixteen, sat right between her father's knees on the board just below him. Their bodies grazed each other in an unconscious, erotic dance. She was restless and jumped up from time to time to run after a shirtless boy about her age who was selling ice cream, only to return to the intimacy with her father. By the father's side was a younger boy we assumed to be son and brother. He looked disconsolate and confused.

Both parent and child in this sort of incestuous, erotic dance tend to act as if the sexual feelings and erotic tone are nonexistent. Here the father acts as if he had no erotic feeling for the girl, despite her sexual liveliness and adolescent blossoming. The daughter definitely must act in the same way. The contradiction between the facade and the father's bodily movements, and her own bodily experience, which she is still in touch with to some degree, will make the girl feel crazy inside. Further, this daughter is caught in a trap. If the father were to respond in a genitally overt way, she would be jeopardized and made crazy. As it is, he responds with hidden excitement through covert behaviors, and, to control his guilty excitement, must overtly deny her attractiveness, her sexuality, and her being. It is this trap that is most crazy-making.

However, it is not only the daughter that will feel crazy. In the case of the father, there is a discrepancy between facade (denial) and the reality of his bodily movement (sexual), and this discrepancy is an expression of the virtual craziness of his behavior. While the father is not likely to experience this craziness, its reality will inevitably effect him, and the effect is to evoke hate for the girl. The incestuous eroticism causes problems enough for the child, and on top of that she will be hated. In addition, jealousy will also inevitably lead her mother to hate her as well. She thus gets hate from both parents. She is hated by the very parent who is excited by and excites her—her father—and she is hated by the other parent, her mother, for the very aliveness and excitement to which the father is responding. The situation is exactly the same, *mutatis mutandis*, when mother and son are in an erotic dance. When, as happens, there is an erotic relationship with the parent of the same sex, the child can be caught in a similar trap.

The hated child's situation always has to be looked at in the context of the sexual relationships with the parents. Children in these situations are both hated and driven crazy, and the destructive impact on the developing self can be massive. Covert incest of this sort should therefore be considered a form of sexual abuse.

Examples of covert incest where the child was also hated are very common. Among any number of others, I can mention David. He bathed with his mother until the age of thirteen and regularly observed her naked around the house. When he innocently mentioned these baths to his schoolmates, their derisive laughter informed him that something was amiss. As a child, David experienced abandonment, neglect, and outright cruelty and exploitation by his mother, all of which were extremely hateful. In other instances, the child's incestuous relationship is with the same sex parent, and sometimes that parent is unpredictable and violent. I use the word *unnatural* to describe the behavior of such parents.

THE SELF-HATE SYSTEM

The self-hate system is the most significant characterological development of the hated child, and inevitably it is present in the personality of the adult who was hated as a child. I call it a system, because it is an active, organizing function of the ego. It is not simply a matter of the person hating themselves; that is there, and that is bad enough. As an aspect of the ego, the self-hate system actively organizes perceptions and understanding of any event in the service of actively experiencing self-hate and bad feelings. Under the auspices of the self-hate system, no stone is left unturned, no event is unscrutinized, no interaction, even of the easiest sort, is free from providing sources, reasons, and causes of self-hate. The self-hate system can make of anyone a virtual genius at reorganizing experience in the service of this kind of pain.

It seems understandable enough that the hated child becomes the self-hating adult, but it is not as simple as might appear. If we only said, "The child hates himself because his parents hated him," this would be correct, but it would overlook the development of the self-hate system as a mechanism of the ego. Oddly enough, in the long run, the hated children come to hate themselves because, for all their efforts, they are never able to win the parents' respect and love. If we put this development into a "logical" set of thoughts, it would be: "My parents hate me, so there must be something wrong with me (bad feeling in the body); since I am bad, I will try to be better (delusional ideal); I will try to be what (I fantasize) they want me to be; I am trying as hard as I can (ego drive); they still hate me; therefore I am hateful after all."

Such "logic," of course, makes no realistic sense. It reveals how the self-hate system of the ego is an effort at making sense of experience that otherwise is beyond reason. While the self-hate system is an aspect of the ego, organizing perception and experience, the feeling of badness is already present as an underlying bodily feeling. The self-hate system represents a developmental, adaptive effort to accommodate parental hatred without perceiving the hatred for what it is. The self-hate system is built up in the ego on the underlying bodily feeling of badness and fear. The mind estab-

lishes structures which explain feelings whose sources have been lost, while
the feelings remain very real and present. Similarly, the self-hate system of
the ego actually protects the individual from awareness of the unnatural
and unbelievable hatred of the parents, their craziness, and the emotional
and bodily effects of the punitive and abusive behaviors arising out of the
hatred.

When the child's natural reaching out for love and its natural aggression
are met with hate or a chronically hateful environment, it is an unbearably
painful experience. Reaching out, as Lowen says, is an "impulse that is at
the heart of life."[8] It is an expression of the very aliveness of the organism.
A shrinking back and contraction becomes the chronic state of the organism. Natural movement is stopped throughout the organism, and on a deep
level they remain stopped into adulthood. Conditions of hatefulness can sur-
round the child at birth, and they can occur in adolescence. How and when
the stopping is effected will have a determinative effect on the individual.

Such bodily changes necessitate alternative modes of reaching out, moving aggressively in the world, and feeling and expressing excitement and
love. These alternatives are compensatory adaptations which become the
individual's characteristic way of being in the world. While they are less
efficient, offer less pleasure, may be self-defeating, or even require the
renunciation of normal modes of expression, they are adaptive necessities
and become the person's "second nature."[9]

The capacity to experience the body in a pleasurable way or to build a
life based on a pleasurable bodily orientation is significantly diminished in
this state. When the ability to experience good feelings is radically limited,
movements within the body that would ordinarily be experienced as pleasurable are no longer experienced in those terms. The child's sexual excitement itself, and even more broadly, the basic expansive, reaching-out
movements of the organism, come to have, in the child's own feelings, a
bad, dirty, or dangerous quality. Expansion itself comes to be experienced
in some negative way as a form of unpleasure, and it is soon terminated.
The basic feeling remaining is one of badness.

This leaves the person in a state like Henry's, who "knows" he is hated
on almost any occasion of human contact. Life goes on in the expectation
of being hated and trying to ward off hate. Such is the manifestation of the
self-hate system. To the degree the individual is able to work and be socially
productive, it is often on the basis of a rigidly ego-driven life sometimes
supported by a rigid belief system. Such an individual sets out to "do" life
and to make it work. Underlying are deeply held "convictions" that one is
hateful, deserves to be hated, and is sure to be hated at the very next
moment, and these convictions are accompanied by the omnipresent terrible fear of again being hated and an intangible feeling of having done something terribly wrong, without knowing exactly what. Someone in this state
is driven for the rest of his or her life to try to do whatever is necessary to
avoid ever again having the terrible feeling of being hated.

Good feeling in the body depends on the energetic pulsation that moves through the body from head to tail, sometimes experienced as sexual feeling, sometimes as pleasure generally, and sometimes just as feeling good. The development of sexual identity depends on the energetic movement entering, filling, and pulsating through the whole genital structure, pelvis, and pelvic floor. The feelings that result from this energetic development are the basis for an identity as a man or woman. It is just this movement that is stopped in the hated child. Problems in sexual identity and expression arise when the full movement is stopped in any measure.

Yet those hated as children arrive at adulthood with an underlying feeling of badness. This feeling of badness, when it is experienced, is experienced as residing in the body itself, as if permeating the tissues. If the feeling of badness is not consciously associated in the mind with sexual feeling and behavior, practically everything the individual says and does nonetheless indicates the reality of this association in the mind. The underlying feelings of badness provide the basis for maintaining the self-hate system in the ego. Guilt, shame, and humiliation will become entrenched aspects of this system and this way of being.

The self-hate system offers a negative reflection of self-respect. The development of self-respect is based on the capacity for good feeling on a body level, and the capacity of the ego to perceive and organize experience in such a way as to maintain and regulate that good feeling. It is an active ongoing process based in the natural movements in the body, enhancing and sustaining them in an ongoing process.

The self-hate system undermines self-respect. It organizes experience and perception in such a way as to show the badness of the self. The results are attitudes and behaviors that diminish and even destroy good, healthy bodily states and feelings, and enhance bad feeling states. The particular mode of these operations are subtle and have endless variations. The object of the self-hate system's hate is always the body, and in particular the body's movements toward expansion, excitement, pleasure, and the reaching out for love. Fulfillment in sexual love will be jeopardized, sometimes to a tragic degree.

OTHER DEVELOPMENTAL EFFECTS OF HATE

Four other specific developmental effects of hate should briefly be mentioned. They are all functions of disturbed self-respect.

Hate and Rage. It should come as no surprise that the hated child becomes the hating adult. Unfortunately, the hatred is often expressed in such a way that the individual does not consider it hatred. It is lived out in all kinds of potentially destructive, self-destructive, perverse, or distorted ways. The impulses behind these movements may be intensely murderous. If the feelings of badness, dirtiness, evilness, and so on are experienced as being *caused* by those presently in the person's life, the hate will be experienced as being justified. For those with very deep feelings of badness, it is often terribly difficult to realize that no one in their present life could possibly be the cause of such feelings.

Denial. Denial signifies a separation of feeling from perceptual memory. It implies that what was seen and experienced was so horrible that the child could not bear the reality, and the perception of reality is lost. What is denied is the horrible, simple fact that the parent truly hated the child. Denial becomes a trait in one's character in the sense that one becomes characteristically unable to see, to assess and understand certain aspects of one's own or other people's behavior, especially if it is hostile.

There is a physical basis of this process, part of which is a set of very deep tensions in the head, upper neck, and around the eyes. To break through this denial, the eyes must be opened to the hate. I ask people to open their eyes, lift their hands protectively and say, "You really hated me!" Seeing, in memory, the hate in the parent's eyes, is to remember what it felt like to be hated. It is a terrible feeling, close to being annihilated. Denial is often expressed as disbelief: "I can't believe it!" This is a characteristic and understandable reaction.

Shock and Dissociation. The person hated as a child for his or her sexual aliveness may be in a state of chronic shock (see Chapter 7).

Sexual Confusion and Chaotic Self-Regulation. A child exposed to the hate of parents is exposed to diverse and contradictory excitations. He or she develops tensions and tendencies to excitation of diverse and contradictory kinds which make self-regulation and fulfillment through an ordinary, stable relationship, difficult or even almost impossible. Driven by the organismic need for discharge and the effort to attain some kind of steady self-regulation, such an individual may be driven through life in all kinds of more or less wild ways. Self-regulation must be slowly established through learning self-respect step by step.

The topic of hate, to our great sorrow, is a vast one.[10] I hope that by discussing hate for what it is and by looking into the face of hate, some understanding is brought to an important element in the development of many people. I hope that armed with knowledge and the courage to see, we will one day have the strength to counter this inhuman aspect of humanity.

SHAME AND GUILT

Conscience is no doubt something within us, but it has not been
there from the beginning. In this sense it is the opposite of sexuality,
which is certainly present from the very beginning of life,
and is not a thing that only comes in later.

—Sigmund Freud

SHAME AND GUILT IN RELATION TO GENITAL INJURY

As chronic conditions, shame, humiliation, and guilt are disturbing and
destructive. They insidiously pervade life, invade any and every experience,
undermine every effort, and infiltrate the self, creating a depressive state.
Inwardly, they are in an irrational pursuit of the self, no matter if the person
is a good citizen or bad, and they do not make a person better. Many
seek help to free themselves of them. They persist like parasites in the
blood. Undermined and angered by them already, individuals may be able
neither to allow for the cleansing experience of remorse or justifiable
shame nor to accept rationally the bitter pill of a humiliation brought on
by personal acts or the hands of others. Shame, humiliation, and guilt cloak
themselves in elaborate claims of rational justification and remain installed
as sharp, piercing, and bitter affects which carry their own claims to an
indisputable, painful reality. They lead us to endless arguments of self-justification—with
ourselves and others. They rob us of joy, pleasure, relaxation,
health, and fulfillment. Rationality, true moral goodness, mercy, and
forgiveness are not adequate to expunge them from our systems. They can
remain the unconscious habits of a lifetime. They infiltrate and overtake
the processes of self-respect.

I view shame, humiliation, and guilt as violations of sexuality. These
processes enter the person and the person's life directly in relation to the

degree of disruption of self-respect and the capacity for sexual love. How do these debilitating conditions become so firmly entrenched in our systems? Why are they so difficult to change?

The analysis of shame and guilt in this chapter relates them to the basic pulsatory processes of the body, to genital injury, and to character formation. In this analysis, shame, humiliation, and guilt will also be seen to be variations on the self-hate system (see Chapter 8). In the light of this analysis it will be understandable why these conditions are difficult to change.

The study of shame and guilt illuminates the study of self-respect. Shame and guilt, in all their variations, are the result of the disruption and distortion of self-respect. In every way, shame and guilt are mirrors of self-respect, except that shame and guilt engender pain and contraction whereas self-respect engenders pleasure and expansion. Just as shame and guilt form complex systems within the personality and character, so does self-respect. Just as shame and guilt are bodily processes, so is self-respect. Each has to do with the regulation of pulsation and how the self is organized in relation to that pulsation.

Charles

A discussion of one of Charles's dreams graphically reveals the relationship between shame and genital injury.

I am working at a hamburger joint like a McDonald's, and I am in the front of the store, and I have to protect a broken down woman from a tough man. I go to the man and am able to hold back his arms. The man leaves and I go into the shower room. I find, in a very matter of fact way, I've had to cut off the head of my penis, where all the feeling is. I hold it in my hand to save it. There is blood all over the place. I am trying to stand so that no one can see this.

I was disturbed by the primitive, bloody image of self-castration, and I felt some urgency in learning what he was telling us about himself through its agency.

In fact, this dream symbolically captured his sexual development and his adaptation. As a teenager, he had worked in such a place, and found himself surrounded by "cute girls." This was more torment than pleasure because, with a severely castrating, humiliating father, he was not only very shaky in his feelings about himself as a young man, he was also tormented with guilt and shame about masturbation. It was not hard to find his severely depressed mother in the broken down woman he was trying to protect. It seems he had to protect her by his own castration.

As we touched on these themes, all of which had been explored in earlier sessions, it was also clear that none of this explained the emergence and presentation of this disturbing dream now, at this time. Something, I guessed, must have recently happened which he could not put his finger on, but it was something that had to be ferreted out to calm his worry— and mine. I began thinking out loud about how prone he was to terrible experiences of shame and humiliation, often arising when dealing with authority at work.

To our mutual relief, the secret emerged. As it turned out, he had been humiliated by his boss in front of another man during the day prior to the night of the dream. Although he felt he stood up to his boss, the experience had made him feel "this small" (indicated in a gesture showing about a half inch between thumb and forefinger, a gesture reminiscent of the dream image in which he held in his hand the "head of my penis"). Interestingly enough, he had told me how he was "trying to go head to head with my boss, not head to chest," that is to feel on the same level as his boss as a man, rather than feeling like the humiliated small boy. In his dream, he had lost his other head altogether, and was doing his best just to save it. Hardly anything is more shameful to a man than being exposed to other men as castrated. The strength of his shame and humiliation had sent him into shock.

I cannot imagine a more graphic depiction of the inherent relationship between shame and genital injury than this dream.[1] In guilt, too, there is an inherent relationship with genital injury. Such a relationship is explicit in Freud's establishing the castration complex as the vehicle for the "passing" of the Oedipus complex, instituting the formation of the superego, the capacity for guilt. Genital injury is the basis for "castration anxiety," the anticipatory fear of being hurt on a deep sexual level. This fear is based on deep tensions in the pelvis, contractions that create the energetic disruption of the genital apparatus, genital injury.

Genital injury is a disturbance of the basic pulsatory movements of the organism, and therefore shame and guilt are the results of and reflect that disturbance. Shame and guilt must be understood in terms of the organism's chronic adaptations to the pulsatory disturbance of genital injury. Chronic adaptations of this sort are called character formations. This formulation carries a further significance. Shame and guilt are the organism's mechanism for handling and managing within allowed limits its fundamental excitatory capabilities.

PERSPECTIVES ON SHAME AND GUILT

Effects on a Life

Charles and Nancy (see Chapter 7) are kindred souls. We see in their lives variations on the profound, pervasive encroachments of shame and guilt. They are both self-made persons. Both, highly intelligent, achieved a high level of creative, professional competence in different fields without benefit of formal education. Shame and guilt interfered with their capacity to pursue conventional educational pathways.

The relationship between genital injury and shame and guilt is evident in Nancy's story, as it is in Charles's. As a child she had very little experience of pleasure and good feeling in her body. Her guilt found expression in an eternal expectation of punishment: "It's all my fault; I did something wrong and should be punished." The depth of her shame was constantly recorded in her feeling that she was a worm, especially in relation to those she needed for acceptance and love.

In his shame and guilt, Charles also had symptoms of chronic shock. Any environmental conditioning which permanently interferes with underlying pulsatory mechanisms and movements must exact a deep price from the organism, a price often expressed in the symptoms of chronic shock.

Ordinary Meaning versus Clinical Entity

In psychoanalysis, the study of guilt was introduced early and paralleled the study of sexuality. Shame was a later entry, and a more problematic one, requiring elaborations of theory which Freud accomplished with the introduction of concepts of narcissism and the ego ideal.[2] In recent years, with pioneering work by Andrew P. Morrison[3] as a stimulus, shame has achieved center stage on the clinical scene.

There has been a perceived need for theoretical understanding of guilt and shame, even though the ordinary meaning of the words is perfectly clear and precise. Why should this be so? What is the problem? These are the first questions that need to be answered.

The answer is simple enough. The clinical entity and the reference of the ordinary words are not the same. In the clinical, psychotherapeutic setting and in the theories which purport to guide that setting, the focus of study is a clinical entity, that is, a set of behaviors and feelings and an aspect of the whole personality of the individual, an aspect which forms a system within the personality.

The ordinary meaning of guilt, for example, refers to either "the act or state of having done wrong; or a painful feeling of self-reproach resulting from a belief that one has done something wrong or immoral."[4] If we refer to Nancy's story, we see nothing so much as an inflamed, living example of an individual living her whole life with a painful feeling of self-reproach resulting from a belief that she has done something wrong. Her state, to that extent, certainly fits the criteria for guilt. No theory is needed to justify, clarify, or explain that much. The question is how this state became *chronic*, how she came to find herself in it to begin with, and how it came to encompass essentially her whole being and color her whole life. A theory is called for to explain all this.

The same questions can be raised in regard to shame, "the painful emotion arising from the consciousness of something dishonoring, ridiculous, or indecorous in one's own conduct or circumstances."[5] A person without the capacity for such reactions would be seriously compromised in social life. However, if we look at Charles's reaction to his boss, we see a different matter altogether. We see a shame proneness and a humiliation proneness of such depth as to be a social handicap of quite a terrible order; it constitutes a dominating aspect of his personality. Those who have under-taken to either rid themselves or help others rid themselves of paralyzing shame or guilt know full well what an extravagant undertaking it can be: to the heart of darkness and back again. The first clarification necessary, therefore, is to be aware of the differentiation between ordinary meaning and clinical entity.

Guilt and shame, as aspects of ordinary life, are developments repre-senting an innate capacity for sensitivity to others and to one's place in the social group. In the clinical setting the examination of guilt and shame reveals people whose innate capacity for sensitivity to others has been exaggerated into a crippling distortion of their whole being. The capacity to respond as a member of a social group is distorted into a personality structure maintaining the individual in chronic states of shame, humilia-tion, and guilt. The theoretical problem has to do with understanding these personality structures.

The exploitation of the innate capacities for shame and guilt leading to characterological states begins in childhood. Shame and guilt are consis-tently linked with violations of sexuality. The issue becomes one of domes-tication rather than facilitating development. A guilty, shamed person is a more readily domesticated one, not only in childhood but in adulthood as well. Seeing, understanding, and respecting the child's sexuality is the way to avoid violations of sexuality in childhood, and the creation of chronic states of guilt and shame.

Stopping the Movement

Clinical shame and guilt must first of all be fundamentally compre-hended as bodily processes. Traumas and violations of sexuality provide the building blocks to make chronic guilt, shame, and humiliation. Punish-ments, threats, shaming, humiliating, exploiting, putting-down, abusing all stop energetic movement and create very real bodily pain and tension in children. It is easy enough for that pain and tension to become chronic, and soon these bad feelings are interpreted as badness. Then adaptive mecha-nisms are brought into play to accommodate to both the bad feelings and their interpretation. Guilt and shame are actually an aspect of these adap-tive mechanisms.

The synthesizing functions of the ego—the same as those that create the character itself—use that real pain and tension to develop a system for modulating energetic expression, and they weave a system of beliefs as a part of that creative synthesis. The depressing, burdensome, burning, sear-ing, agonizing, unbearable, and tormenting experiences that accompany guilt, shame, and humiliation are not brought about by the belief systems. Those unbearable experiences are already present in the body, from child-hood, and the beliefs are the outgrowths of children adapting to, and mak-ing the best of, unbearable, real interpersonal events. The integrating and synthesizing functions of the ego use the results of traumas and violations of sexuality—bad feelings in the body—to establish the self-hate systems. From this derives the power of guilt, shame, and humiliation.

The same conditions which create genital injury create shame and guilt. Shame and guilt reflect and express fundamental violations of sexuality. Shame and guilt are often directly determined by the reactions of the facilitating environment to the child's genital, genital expression, and expression of sexual nature generally. Shame and guilt develop as adaptive responses to chronic stopping or interference of sexual movement and the identifications with the genital and genital movement.

Normally, the organism reaches out to the world, seeking pleasure, excitement, fulfillment of sexual aims, and happiness. Within the ordinary possibilities of the given culture, the individual will seek gratification, contentment, and personal fulfillment. Shame and guilt are inhibitions of these movements in constant, gross or subtle, but pervasive ways. More accurately stated, shame and guilt are the mechanisms whereby the inhibition of the organism is achieved, maintained, and regulated. In this sense they are bodily processes; they are not derived from cognitive structures or beliefs. The beliefs associated with shame and guilt are not the cause of the unbearable feeling. They are the result. These beliefs, which seem so real, are the ego's effort to manage, interpret, and make sense of, a painful bodily state. The belief structures are secondary offshoots of an inhibitory, painful, contracted state, already established on a bodily level.

In childhood, excitatory movement is contained within the vital connections with parents, siblings, other family members, and other adults in socializing and caretaking relationships. Examples of excitatory movements are explorations of the environment, play, seeking contact and love with adults, practicing bodily skills, and masturbation. All such movements at one time or another elicit various forms of containment by adults, and such containment requires modification of the child's excitatory process and sometimes the inhibition of it. It is obvious enough that there are various ways of doing this, and not all such ways result in a chronic inhibition or stopping of the child's movement. When containment frustrates and temporarily stops a movement, a healthy vital connection allows for the discharge of the frustration and tension without punitive consequences for the child.

It is common enough, however, that the movement is stopped in such a way as to be a violation of sexuality and create chronic shock, shame and guilt. It is not difficult to understand why all this occurs with such frequency. Within the context of the child's vital connection with a parent the child has an emotional and sexual significance for the parent that evokes the parent's shame and guilt, and the parent's response, out of his or her own inhibitory mechanism, is to stop any of the child's behavior perceived as bad and shameful. These parent-child shame-guilt dyads are as common as day and night. They reveal that the arena in which the stopping of the child's movement occurs is often a subtle one in which the parent cannot really perceive the realities of the child, the child's situation, or his or her own (parental) behavior.

A Father and Son

Mr. Masters and his son, Steve, age eleven, are an example of this kind of explosive dyad. As a child himself, Mr. Masters had been drawn into a highly sexualized relationship with his infantile and needy mother; he had also been physically beaten and threatened by his father as well as stepfather. He was nonetheless, a highly energetic, brilliant businessman, with a wife he loved and an older daughter. He lived, to some extent, in a sexualized fantasy world, a reflection of his mother's constant provocations, and was constantly aware of every sexual possibility. He adored his lovely, competent daughter, and he had a terrible time with his small, less successful, provocative son, who, with a child's sure aim and sensitivity, picked up his father's preference for his sister. This drove the boy wild, and Mr. Masters, for his part, was driven crazy by any of the boy's difficulties. In perceiving Steve as needy, vulnerable, and inept, he saw in Steve all that he himself had to suffer and surmount as an abused child and all that he had learned to hate in himself. In his ambivalence, he loved the boy, was constantly enraged at him, and felt shame and revulsion for him. In short, Mr. Masters saw his own hated, humiliated self in his son, the self he had to overcome as best he could so as not to drown emotionally and be lost for good. His therapy, for a significant period of time, focused on this all-important relationship with his son, which of course directly reflected his relationship with himself.

Differentiating Shame, Guilt, and Humiliation

It is tempting, it seems, to make theoretical hay over the psychological differences among shame, guilt, and humiliation. I believe the differences are far less important than the commonalities: the stopping of excitatory movement, the creation of pain and tension, the establishment of that pain and tension as a chronic body condition, and the establishment of the self-hate system. Shame, guilt, and humiliation all reflect real pain and tension established on a chronic basis during the developmental years. They are all functions of actual punishments, restraints, threats, fears, shaming, and humiliation in the context of vital connections which did not allow for the adequate discharge of the pain and tension and the restitution of good feeling.

There are a variety of ways in which we can feel badly about ourselves. We can feel badly about ourselves for what we do, say, feel, think, or even intend. We can feel badly for what we are, our very being. We can feel badly within ourselves or in relation to another or in relation to a group or ideal. Furthermore, these bad feelings can become very complex or can become embedded in a complex matrix of other behaviors, feelings, actions, tendencies.

Inevitably, we have ways of protecting ourselves from the bad feelings, and the ways we have of protecting ourselves tend to become very complex patterns of behavior that are difficult to sort out. It has been said that shame leads to hiding ("I hid my face in shame") and guilt to confession, making the one more difficult to discern than the other. However, both can be hidden, because it is often difficult for people to actually contact their deepest guilt, even when its effects are discerned by an outside observer. We all go to the greatest lengths to relieve ourselves of guilt, shame, and humiliation.

The phenomenological differences among these ways of feeling badly about one's self are important. While guilty constriction grips one person, a pervasive sense of humiliation may sweep through another. These subjective differences contribute to the different usages among the family of words reflecting guilt, shame, and humiliation. Then there are important developmental differences in the ways in which the chronic sense of shame or guilt originates that accounts for the different experiences. Movement can be stopped in a child at any age. The differences among guilt, shame, and humiliation have to do with the particular way in which the movement is stopped, who does the stopping, and the conditions under which the stopping occurs, including the child's cognitive development, the development of language, and the development of sexuality.

Viewed developmentally, the way in which the parent stops the child's movement makes a difference. Punishment and threats of punishment have a different feel than shaming. When the use of power enters the relationship, the feeling is also different, and the effect is humiliation. Shaming and punishment are acts, acts performed on the child and in the context of a relation with a child. A look can shame as well as words and deeds. All these effect expansion and aggression and can create states of tension and pain. Chronic shame and guilt in adulthood reflect both the tension and pain. The tension is reflected in body tensions, ego drivenness, and other behavioral compensations for guilt and shame such as compulsive work or drinking. The pain is reflected in the chronic feelings of badness and the pangs of experienced guilt, shame, and humiliation.[6]

The meanings of the words *humiliation* and *shame* reflect bodily experiences.

humiliate. (1) to make low or humble in position, condition or feeling; and (2) to lower or depress the dignity or self respect of . . . to mortify.

The "to make" and the "to lower" imply, in the case of the parent-child relationship, the use of power in the relationship. The meaning of the word *mortify* is particularly suggestive.

mortify. (1) (obsolete) to deprive of life; to kill, put to death. . . . Also to make as if dead; to render insensible. (2) to kill (in transferred and figurative senses); to destroy the vitality, vigour or activity of.[7]

There is no more total stopping of movement than killing it.

The closely related, apparently milder word *embarrass*, "derived from French, has to do with to block or obstruct in various derived meanings, such as to encumber, hamper, impede,"[8] also refers to stopping movement.

"The origins of the word 'shame' are believed to lie in early Teutonic words that mean 'to cover.'"[9] The bodily reference here is to the basic bodily response to shaming: the tendency to drop the head, hide the face, hide altogether, or to turn events into secrets. The words—*shame, humiliation*, and *guilt*—all capture and reflect basic emotional, bodily, expressive realities.

In shaming, a child will see him- or herself as reflected in the expressive manner of the other with whom there is a vital connection. In childhood these reflections will all have to do with the body and movement and body functions, with particular sensitivity in relation to the genitals and the child's sexuality. Parental response to genitals, genital feeling, and all expressive aspects of the child's sexuality, including their physical appearance, will be recognized by a child for what they are, not intellectually but rather in terms of its own, that is, the child's, bodily response. Shaming involves the child seeing and experiencing a devalued image of him- or herself reflected in the mirror of a parent's expressive behavior.

There is another element to shaming, as well, that makes it a powerful tool of influence. In essence, shaming disrupts, and potentially breaks, the child's vital connection with the parent. This is usually experienced as the loss of love or its threat. The threat of the loss of love in a vital connection is life threatening for a child. The vital connection is literally a child's life support system. Shame threatens to remove that life support. Any child threatened on that level is vulnerable to disruption on the deepest biological level. Life itself is threatened. Mortification, in this sense, is literal and real. Shaming thus directly influences the child's pulsation. Such effects are readily observed. A praised and approved of child, expands visibly, drawing him- or herself up, expanding outward, and moving freely with good feeling. The expansion is visible. A disapproved child, shrinks, hides, pulls in; the contraction is visible. Pleasure accompanies the expansion, pain the contraction. These are bodily effects on the deepest level of the organism.

The behavioral peculiarities of the shamed individual[10] can be more clearly understood in the light of this analysis of shaming. A child will soon learn the parameters within which he or she can safely navigate without being subject to such painful experiences of ostracism from the safe haven of the vital connection. He or she will soon learn to identify within him or herself what can be safely expressed and what must be hidden. Long practice and experience will generate a complex system of behaviors which include secrets, defenses, ego ideals, and interpersonal stratagems.

The shaming behavior of the parent may range from outright horror and ostracism to more subtly communicated discomfort and distaste. Children involved in incestuous relationships with one parent are inevitably subjected to humiliation not only by that parent, but the other parent as well.

Humiliation is added to the picture when the parent, in addition to sham-ing, actively subjects the child to a lowering of its station by asserting power over him or her, putting the child "beneath" the parent.

Shamed persons are exquisitely sensitive and uncomfortable socially because of the way shame arises as a reflection from the other. They thus tend to hide themselves by avoiding social situations and the avoidance of exposure through self-expression.

Where they exist as chronic states, shame and guilt tend to be inevitably intertwined in the personality. Shaming threatens the disruption of the vital connection, putting the child outside the vital connection, a kind of social ostracism and a severe punishment in its own right. In the case of punish-ments that lead to the creation of guilt, shaming is inevitably involved. The child ends up feeling bad about him- or herself and with the guilty feeling of deserving the punishment as well. Punishing, of course, can also put the child outside the protective boundaries of the vital connection. Thus the same bodily influence is present as in shame, a form of ostracism and the attendant sense of shameful devaluation of the self. A feeling of shameful unworthiness can thus accompany a guilty belief that one deserves punish-ment, and a guilty feeling of deserving punishment can accompany a shameful feeling of a devalued self. The intermingling of the two is part of the torment.

THE COGNITIVE PECULIARITIES OF SHAME AND GUILT

Earlier I pointed out that the belief systems associated with shame and guilt are not the cause of the unbearable affects associated with shame or guilt; they are the result, the outcome, of the movement having been stopped. Herein lies the first cognitive peculiarity of shame and guilt. Subjectively, one tends to believe one feels guilt or shame because of a belief taken as a truth. In reality, the beliefs are a kind of second thought, after the fact. The belief systems are in fact, an effort to explain the pain of the movement hav-ing been stopped. They reflect the way the ego uses the mind to make sense of a given condition. Once established in this way, the belief systems main-tain guilt and shame and have a pervasive influence on the personality.

The subjective, painful experience of shame or guilt will be inwardly understood as the result of the belief system, but this subjective perception is misleading. The one who in some deep way feels bad about him- or her-self will, in the effort to manage the pain, seek and find an explanation for the bad feeling, an explanation that serves only to obscure the real pain and its real source. A woman said, "The only way I could understand [my painful experience] was to think there was something wrong with me." Out of these convoluted constructions arise the cognitive peculiarities of shame and guilt. '

Those chronically burdened with crippling guilt and shame often do not recognize them for what they are. Often enough it takes the analytic and empathic skills of a therapist to help the individual not only identify his or her own shame and guilt but in addition learn to recognize their complex ways of dealing with, avoiding, and compensating for shame and guilt. Why should this be the case?

Guilt, for example, can appear to be "unconscious," and unconscious guilt can be dangerous. Mrs. Y, a visitor to the clinical seminar (see Chapter 4), came seriously close to injuring herself, as her therapy deepened. This frightened her, and she fled an earlier therapy. A similar experience was reported by a man who underwent a useful psychoanalysis as a young man, and described going through a period of life-threatening behaviors. Self-inflicted injury appears in Tim's story (see Chapter 6). Nancy (see Chapter 7), although raised to be a good Catholic girl, was quite unaware of her guilt.

Perhaps familiarity with depth psychology has made such discordancies of conscious awareness seem more or less "natural." There is, nonetheless, a peculiarity to this kind of behavior which I believe can be identified somewhat more specifically and clearly.

Both shame and guilt, as affective experiences, occur embedded in a cognitive, mental, network of beliefs and assumptions, about the self and about the world. They are not, in adults, affects that appear apart from this cognitive system. Let us call this cognitive system a "belief system," since that is what it is. The individual's private belief system, which supports shame and guilt experiences, will blend with more generally shared beliefs—moral, religious, cultural—common in the society. Private beliefs are disguised in this way. Nancy's religious training provided her with materials in which her private belief about her badness had been disguised in childhood by her "religious" beliefs about her sinfulness.[11] The belief system, for most people, becomes so embedded in the personality and mind that it is transparent. It is no longer seen any more than a fish sees water.

The belief system constitutes, in part, what in psychoanalytic theory is considered the ego ideal and the ideal self. Shame is understood as the affect that arises from the failure of the real ego or self to realize the ideal. Morrison summarizes this viewpoint: "I believe that the ego ideal—and particularly the ideal self—provides a framework for understanding shame from an *internal* perspective. . . . It is *failure* to live up to this ideal self — experienced as a sense of inferiority, defeat, flaw, or weakness—that results in the feeling of shame."[12]

A consideration of this statement will reveal another facet of the cognitive peculiarities of shame (and guilt). The ego ideal or ideal self are considered mental "structures." They are made up of loose networks of fantasies, illusions about the self and others, beliefs, and assumptions which guide and organize perceptions of the self and others. They are understood to be anchored in and formed in the realities of childhood, not in the realities of current life. The ego ideal and ideal self are thus delusional and semidelusional and are unrealistic guides to perception and action. In this light they are directly implicated in the struggle with reality perception of the shamed and guilty individual.

The most immediate example of the struggle with reality in shame and guilt is the virtually universal struggle with the question, "Why do I feel so awful? Am I really as bad, awful, and inferior as I feel myself to be?" What is real? Nancy assumed, "It's all my fault," but again and again she would struggle with why she felt so terrible, and so does every other shamed, guilty person. There is a poignant awareness of the discrepancy between the terrible feeling (with its accompanying beliefs) and the perception of reality (e.g., "I'm not *that* different from anyone else."). These disconcerting experiences, which take many forms, are at the core of the perceptual world of the guilty and shamed, the results of delusional beliefs long sustained and no longer subject to realistic evaluation. When perception is guided by fantasies, beliefs, and expectations formed in childhood, they cannot lead to realistic perceptions in adult life.

There is another cognitive peculiarity revealed by the idea that the painful affects of shame arise when one fails to meet the measure of the ideal self. The question still remains as to how we should understand the pain caused by this "failure." After all, the contents of the ideal self construct are in essence fantasies, images. How does comparing the self with a fantasy cause suffering? One might say it initiates self-reproach, and this is painful. Here is the heart of the issue, and the cognitive peculiarity. Self-reproach does not cause the pain. It is an indirect expression of the pain and it is an effort to manage the pain. Self-reproach manages the pain of shame and guilt in many ways. It is an intellectual effort to control and explain; it gives the illusion of control and that one can change the matter; it is a restitution for a lost relationship; it protects the individual from breaking down in sorrow and grief; and, finally, it gives a purportedly rational explanation of an emotional (non-rational) process. Thus the pain is managed, and the mind, while not set at ease, is provided a familiar, understandable disturbance, and, so it seems, the individual has some much needed guidance on how to make himself feel worth more than two cents: try harder, do more, be better.

A child whose movement is stopped experiences pain. The pain may range from discomfort to terror and the threat of death. Real pain experienced in the context of vital connections—caused by punishment, shaming, and other trauma which stop the child's movement—initiates the long developmental construction of beliefs to make sense of what is irrational and senseless and to manage the pain. The belief systems which form the contents of the ego ideal and the ideal self transform and disguise the nature of the pain. In reality, the pain of chronic guilt and shame is the original pain experienced in childhood. It is a body memory. It was real pain, and there was no escaping it. In the course of development, if the pain cannot be discharged and the tension released, the mind will wrap it in a complex web of beliefs. The pain remains, however, as a body memory.

These beliefs are so familiar to the person from such an early age, and they have determined reality for so long that they seem like reality and are unquestioned. They are difficult to ferret out. (We can recall Nancy saying, "I can't pretend it wasn't that bad.") These belief systems about the badness and inadequacy of the self become embedded in the personality of the individual. They seem to be the very engine of his or her social life forever—leading him and her to live in pain and suffering based on one overriding belief that life is meant to be this way. The idea that life is to be enjoyed becomes not only totally foreign but an anathema.

The basis of what I have been describing can be seen in subjective experience, and anyone who is experiencing painful self-reproach can observe it for themselves through an introspective experiment. In a state of self-recrimination it is usually easy enough to identify the mental self-accusations, all the terrible things one is saying to oneself—how worthless, how much a failure, just how bad, awful, inept, and so on. Having identified the inner mental voices, it is possible to pause, breath, feel the body and distance one's self, if only for a moment, from the self-accusatory voices. If one can do this for a moment and focus one's attention on one's breathing, one will in all likelihood experience an even deeper sense of pain, pain like an ache, for example, that might be located in the throat, chest, or around the heart. This is the bodily pain, present as a body memory, probably since childhood. If one stays focused on these sensations, it is then possible for crying to break through, and one will find relief. Crying that breaks through in this way may become very deep and go on for a long time with the feeling, "I could cry forever."

In this introspective experiment, one can experience the separation of pain and belief system (shame related self-accusations). Separating the belief system out will in fact allow the pain to deepen and become more real. It is then also possible to experience the pain as something that exists in one's self apart from all of one's ideal expectations. This process also allows one to evaluate and sort out one's ideal expectations for one's self and perhaps to realize that most are unrealistic and most are a futile effort to alleviate the pain that will continue as long as those ideals are held.

SHAME, GUILT, AND CHARACTER

Shame and guilt are self-hate systems. They are established in the person in the same way as the self-hate system (see Chapter 8), and I consider them to be nothing more nor less than variations on the self-hate system.

If Jack tells Bill, "You are worthless!" it would not be hard to understand this as an expression of hate. Jack intends to mortify Bill, lower Bill's esteem for himself and remove his good feelings. If Jack tells himself, "You are worthless!" and says it to himself in such a way as to lower esteem and deprive himself of good feeling, that is self-hate. His "intention" toward himself is self-mortification, to make himself closer to being dead, which is just what is done by the removal of good feeling, and this is what hate would intend.

As self-hate systems, guilt and shame become established aspects of the ego, broadly determining the way in which the world is perceived, experienced, and understood. They are the final developments of character, essentially sealing into the body the underlying bodily adaptation to early trauma.

Shame and guilt are embedded in character and are the principal mechanisms of character functioning. Shame and guilt are violations of sexuality, and as such, they are disturbances of the basic pulsatory movements of the organism. They also reflect the organism's chronic adaptations to those disturbances, the character formations. Shame and guilt are the organism's regulatory mechanism for managing, within allowed limits and forms, fundamental excitatory capabilities. Shame and guilt are the mechanisms whereby the individual's movement—excitement, self-expression, sexuality and aggression—are maintained within the characterologically determined limits.

Spasms of either guilt or shame often follow moments in which a person has allowed him- or herself a degree of self-expression—sexual or otherwise—greater than usual. In therapy, the shameful or guilty sense of having been too expressive is often revealed in comments such as, "I was too much" or "I was too out there." Shame and guilt are thus mechanisms for monitoring, and they signal the activation of controls on all forms of excitatory movement including ordinary good feeling. This kind of inhibitory monitoring contrasts with the monitoring of self-respect. The mechanism of self-respect supports expansion, movement, pleasure, and good feeling, just those states which shame and guilt are geared to limit, inhibit, and prohibit. Shame and guilt are thus seen to be expressions of the disturbance of the processes of self-respect eventuating from the violations of sexuality.

Peggy

Peggy is a married woman in her late thirties. Inquiry into her unhappiness often yields the announcement, "I am no good for anything." Exploring this announcement leads to finding out what it is like for her to live with her expectations of herself. It feels like a sword over her head, like torment, like torture; it is a terrible way to live. At this point, she says, "I feel so worthless," and she begins to cry. This is an important shift, because it is a shift from self-hate to a direct, feelingful expression of the pain of experiencing her shame. Her crying becomes sobbing, and out of her sobbing, a scream emerges.

Peggy moves to the couch where she can sob and scream. As she sobbed and screamed she felt the pain of the fear and threat she had lived under all her life. After she quieted down she had the insight that actually feeling her "worthlessness" was like leaving herself vulnerable to being hurt terribly, an experience of genital injury.

Screaming, sobbing, and experiencing her pain and terror frees her body from the tension that has been there since childhood and that has been maintained in her adult life as characterological adaptation. These changes in the current bioenergetic status of the body allow the autonomic nervous system to calm down and the restoration of normal energetic pulsation. This latter is indicated in calmer, fuller breathing, and a calmer, easier bodily feeling, all of which is a movement toward the restoration of well-being. The source of the large amount of tension energetically discharged is the actual bodily basis of the self-hate system, the actual source of her current guilt and shame.

Following this work, Peggy feels able to approach her anger and to express it. First she hits the bed with her fists, mobilizing her capacity for aggression and her breathing. I suggest she use the bioenergetic stool to further mobilize the full movement of the energy along the length of the body, from the eyes to the genital. As Peggy moved, an enormous amount of rage came out, and a strong energetic movement through her pelvis was visible.

With temporary dissolution of the shameful failure to meet an ideal, with mobilization of aggression through the pelvis, the therapy session moves into the deepest layers of the character: the genital injury. Peggy's real ongoing struggle is with sexual fulfillment with her husband. As fantasies and feelings are explored, Peggy realizes she has terrible feelings in her body and expects bad experiences as she approaches the possibility of sexual surrender.

At this point Peggy finds it helpful to express a strong "No!" by vigorously, kicking the bed, screaming, "It's mine!" She then sadly realized her No had been a necessary way of preserving her self-respect. The acknowledgment and expression of the "No!" is essential in establishing self-respect. The next, and even more challenging step, is to find self-respect in the "Yes!"

SHAME AND GUILT AS REFLECTED IN THE MIRROR OF SELF-RESPECT

Health

Andrew Morrison has some interesting remarks on well-being and the absence of shame. He talks about "the affective impact of the absence of shame, especially to someone familiar with its ponderous effects. To healthy pride, then, must be added a representation of the feeling of well-being that accompanies the absence or reversal of shame—something approaching euphoria."[13]

The "representation of the feeling of well-being" is what I would call ordinary good body feeling, hedonia, perhaps, rather than "euphoria." If I say that "well-being accompanies the absence of shame," I might also say with greater emphasis that the absence of shame "accompanies" well-being. However, health does not "accompany" the absence of illness, and indeed, it is more than the absence of illness. Ordinary good feeling reflects not only the absence of shame and guilt; it also reflects a body that is free of the chronic characterological conditions underlying them. Most important, it reflects the functioning of self-respect. Surely a "reversal of shame" does approach euphoria, for those of us so burdened, but ordinary good feeling is something different from that as well. The latter is the actual, healthy functioning of self-respect.

Ordinary good body feeling reflects the healthy functioning of self-respect in the individual. This is a state of health. In a state of health, the ordinary pulsatory functions of the body are relatively unimpeded by characterological constrictions, a freedom deeply reflected in the capacity for full sexual surrender. On a daily basis, and equally deeply, it is reflected in an ordinary sense of well-being—"good body feeling." There is nothing more precious than this state, as Morrison implies, and as anyone knows who has lost and regained it.

As a therapy, bioenergetics seeks to help the individual restore good body feeling through the restoration of the body's pulsatory and excitatory capacity. The direct approach to bodily, bioenergetic functioning offers an additional positive avenue for therapeutic endeavor, and it offers the only avenue to the basic core of the problem which exists on the body level.

Healing, Restitution, and Delusion

The basic childhood trauma leading to the development of the self-hate system is the stopping of excitatory movement. No childhood can or need be entirely free of events which will stop the child's movement at times. In ordinary healthy life, the adequate discharge of fear, tension, and anger within the context of a vital connection permit adequate healing, and the event will not be traumatic. Repeated patterns of traumatization (like fighting and "making up") are unhealthy, even when the pattern involves some form of discharge (as by crying) on each occasion. The repetitive pattern itself becomes chronically established on an organismic level. When tension, fear, and anger cannot be discharged, the events become traumatic and their effects chronic. The organism then resorts to using its energies and bodily resources to adapt to the chronicity, establishing tension and autonomic hyperactivation on a permanent basis, factors that are the basis of character formation.

Movement is prevented as long as chronic characterological constriction is present in the body. The self-hate system does not create that constriction, it manages the pain, monitors excitatory movement, and interprets the bad body feelings. It gives a meaning and content to the chronic pain that began with the original trauma.

The self-hate systems (whether self-hate, shame, or guilt) all contain, distort, disguise, and ultimately block the organismic drive to reestablish health—movement, good body feeling, well-being, and the basic pulsatory processes of the body. The form of the blocking is contained in the self-hate systems in a manner directly reflecting the way in which the excitatory movement was stopped in the context of the child's vital connections. Thus the shamed individual has an exquisite sensitivity to the quality of contact with others. The efforts driven by shame are all geared to reestablish the kind of love and contact once promised by the vital connection and, at the same time, restore a sense of bodily intactness and well-being. The preoccupations accompanying such efforts have to do with being and/or doing better and more, approaching an ideal of self or other.

In guilt, the self-hate system reflects punishment in relation to the more aggressive aspects of excitatory movement, and there is a congruent preoccupation with punishment and potential harm on a bodily level. The drive is to reestablish, in the face of an inhibition, the aggressivity and to retrieve intact the stopped excitation. The preoccupations are with doing/acting versus not doing/not acting.

Given the opportunity, an organism with any degree of health will seek to heal a trauma, and restore healthy good feeling. Healing of trauma means the reestablishment of good body feeling. An organism stopped in childhood, will resume the process of healing in adult life, given the opportunity, and people will take up at a later age from where they were once stopped. There will still be the necessity to discharge fear, tension, and anger in order for the good body feeling, the sense of well-being, to be reestablished and for movement to be freed. There is a bioenergetic drive toward this discharge. As long as the organism lives, it will have a capacity to reestablish its pulsatory self-regulation and self-respect.

The self-hate systems stand in a complex relation with the organism's drive to restore movement, self-respect, and healthy functioning. The self-hate systems *express* that drive, but in extraordinarily convoluted forms which are nothing more nor less than delusional departures from reality; the delusional constructs become restitutions in and of themselves; and the delusional constructs in the end serve to support the inhibition of the real restoration of feeling and health.

Ultimately, the self-hate systems are restitutions for the vital connection and for the support, contact, love, respect, and developmental opportunity that should have been available in the vital connection. As delusional systems they encompass every possible form of unreal expectation for the self: perfection, purity, goodness, always doing more and better than what one has done, renunciation of pleasure, and so on. They also encompass, and back their claims with, every possible kind of grotesque self-accusation and degraded self-image.

Because of the relationship with genital injury, the contents of the idealized, delusional restitutions always contain a genital ideal, sometimes explicitly, sometimes in hidden or symbolic forms (see Chapter 6). Mr. Masters had a strong tendency, which he knew in one part of himself to be delusional, to see himself as the prince of lovers of the western world, the one whom every princess desired. A woman, who in every way had everything she needed in her life, was still tormented because in her opinion she had never been "beautiful." This delusional idea persisted in spite of the fact that she loved her husband and he loved her and found her "sexy."

Guilt is overcome and good feeling established through reestablishing aggression—the capacity for direct movement toward a goal. Healing the genital injury is accomplished through addressing the fear associated with it—the castration complex. These considerations apply in the case of shame, too. In both cases, the relinquishing of unrealistic expectations for the self (delusional restitutions) is addressed as the need for mourning, grieving the original losses of parental love, support, appreciation, and respect. The grief, in this context, tends to be experienced as an acceptance of the injured, degraded, devalued self, a sobering self-perception which paves the way for the perception of the self as ordinary—not needing to be ideal (special)—and healed.

Narcissistic Injury

I consider the stopping of the movement and the resultant genital injury to be the basic narcissistic injury. Guilt reflects a narcissistic injury based in genital injury just as surely and as deeply as do shame or humiliation. The self-hate systems are inevitable outcomes of these injuries, as are other aspects of narcissism. Developmental timing, manner of causation, and who did the stopping all determine subsequent outcome. As an aspect of character, narcissism is distinguished by the flourishing of images of restitution centering around all kinds of idealized versions of the ego, the self, or another. Some such restitutional efforts will accompany any version of the self-hate systems.

Does the Organism Turn Energy against the Self?

This question is raised by the formulation of the self-hate system construct as well as by historically earlier formulations of guilt. The answer to the question is "no." There are two basic organismic movements, expansion and contraction. In expansion, the organism moves out, toward the world, and energy flows from the core toward the periphery. In contraction, the movement is away from the world, in toward the core. Character structure is a chronic contraction, and the self-reproach, self-beating, and so on, which are the cognitive components of the self-hate system express and support that contraction. The pain and contraction is already present in the body.

Characterological contractions tend to deepen with time, unless the individual takes steps to free him- or herself from them. A living organism is not static, and over time it either deepens the expansive or the contractile potential. Some of the debilitating aspects of aging are a function of contractions originating in early life and becoming more rigid in later years.

Attitudes expressed by the self-hate system foster the deepening of the contraction. Over time, the individual may become more aligned with the inner voices of self-blame. It is not uncommon to hear people express—

often with dismay—a growing awareness that, in spite of themselves, as they grow older they become more like one or both parents in ways disagreeable to themselves. Negative ego attitudes are then directed against the self, just as they were by parental figures early in life, supporting the original contraction, deepening a bad feeling in the body, and supporting behaviors that contribute to the further rigidification of the original character contraction.

Self-Respect in the Mirror of Shame and Guilt

Nothing more clearly illuminates the functioning of self-respect than shame and guilt. As self-hate systems, shame and guilt permeate the organism on cognitive, emotional, and biological levels. Self-respect is not simply the absence of shame and guilt. It is the expression of the functional system of self-regulation that also permeates the organism on all those same levels. In shame and guilt, there are cognitive mechanisms of control and regulation expressive of a negative movement or attitude and supporting pain and contraction. In self-respect, there are cognitive mechanisms of control and regulation supporting positive movements and attitudes supporting pleasure and expansion. Painful affects in shame and guilt are, of course, mirrored by pleasurable, peaceful ones in self-respect. The bioenergetic contraction in shame and guilt is mirrored by expansion and free pulsation in self-respect.

It makes sense to assume that the way to ensure the development of self-respect in a child is to respect him or her. The study of the self-hate systems and their origin in violations of sexuality, however, demonstrates conclusively the significance of respect as a dimension of the most profound importance in the developmental environment of children. All of the violations are forms of disrespect. Respect is the alternative to the violation of sexuality. Respect ensures a facilitating environment in which the child's organism can develop a healthy self-regulation of excitatory movement within its social world. Respect for the child's sexuality is the core of such a respectful attitude.

Part III

TOWARD A SELF-RESPECTING SEXUALITY

Part III explores the possibilities of developing a self-respecting sexuality in childhood and adulthood. The facilitating environment for children's development is analyzed from the point of view of sex and self-respect. In adulthood the greatest opportunity for such development lies in the evolution of a self-respecting sexuality within a couple. An exploration of the issues involved in living one's sexuality suggests difficulties and opportunities for a self-respecting sexuality in today's world. The latter includes consideration of a sexual ethic.

THE VITAL CONNECTION

REALITIES OF CHILDHOOD

Freud's work revealed childhood sexuality to educated Europeans and offered a view of the development of sexuality illuminating the lives of both children and adults. Reich deepened Freud's insights and enormously advanced the understanding of sexuality in childhood and adult life. His revision of the Oedipus complex, his discovery of armor, his description of the organismic functions of sexuality, and his arguments for the legitimacy of adolescent sexual life and against patriarchal family organization were major contributions to the understanding of our lives. At the same time, one aspect of the life of children was poorly comprehended by both Reich and Freud, and that had to do with the relational context of child development.

I have been using the term *vital connection*. Development, including sexual development, occurs in the context of the child's vital connections with his or her parents. The outcome of development depends on the presence and quality of the vital connection. The development of a self-respecting sexuality depends on the presence of vital connections supporting such a development, and that implies parents respectful of children's sexuality.

Vital connection[1] is derived from the term *vital signs*, that is, heartbeat, breath, reactivity, blood pressure. A vital connection is one that is essential to life. Without it, the basic pulsation of life loses a vital support and may either cease or be diminished. The connections, for a child, are always other people, usually the parents. Adults, too, need vital connections. The connection for adults are also other people, a spouse, partner, lover, friend, and they may also be a group, a pet, a place, a kind of work, or an organization.

A network of vital connections literally supporting the pulse of life is the biological container of the child's development as a living organism. In the womb the vital connection is through the placenta and umbilical cord and its various vessels. Once out of the womb, the baby needs the vital connection with the mother with his or her mouth, skin, and eyes. In each phase of development, the quality of the vital connection is defined by the contact, holding, support, nurture, and loving response offered by parents and caretakers. Adolescence and the early adult years prepare us for establishing vital connections with other adults on other terms. Adulthood is not a time in which a person does not need vital connections with other human beings. The pain of loss when a vital connection is broken or lost is bodily, and it clearly reveals the biological reality of the vital connection. A loss effects the whole body, and sometimes life is threatened.

In the phase of childhood sexual identity development, children need the vital connections as much as ever. The child needs vital connections which accommodate the new and stronger excitation. Only by accommodating the stronger energy and the new feelings will the vital connections with each parent foster and support the child's sexual differentiation and the development of his or her sexual identity.

Hitherto, the vital connection has been primarily dyadic; the paradigmatic vital connection is mother-child. The paradigmatic situation in the phase of sexual identity formation is a three-person unit. The three-person network among the two parents and the child becomes the vital connection for the child in the period of sexual identity formation. Where there are siblings and extended family, they too, in these years, eventually become part of the network.

Christopher

Christopher is a lively, feelingful little boy whose mother is a colleague. She told me the following story which provides a reminder of the realities of childhood and an example of the healthful containment of the tensions and feelings arising in the three person network during the period of sexual identity formation. One morning, as Christopher was coming into the kitchen, his mother asked him, "What would you like for breakfast?"

Christopher: Bumble bees!
Mother: Ouch!
Christopher: Why you say "ouch"?
Mother: That would hurt.
Christopher: Well, then we'll have the cat!
Mother: Well, then I suppose we'll have to kill him and fry him.
Christopher: (thinks; doesn't appeal to him): Eww, no. I know. I'll get a gun and I'll kill Daddy. He talks too much!

Mother realized, in retrospect, that she became a bit anxious at this point and began to explain to Christopher how little boys can have angry feelings when father interferes with their time with mother. She observed, however, that Christopher, still thinking it all over, wasn't paying much attention to her.

His loving mother soon had reason to guess that Christopher was annoyed with the way his father had buzzed in after work the evening before, dominating the family scene with his own stories, and breaking up Christopher's monopoly on his nice mother. It is not difficult to see Christopher's feelings and tensions as classically Oedipal: his angry, even murderous competition with his father—for whom he also feels affection—arising out of his love and attachment to his mother. D. W. Winnicott, for example, understands these tensions as a precursor to guilt and as presupposing a castration complex. It is a kind of tension he claims "belongs to healthy life."[2] It is illuminating to look at this story in this regard; however, let's leave aside these ideas for a moment and look at it from another angle.

What belongs to healthy life is this interchange itself, one in which Christopher has the respect and freedom to express his views and feelings, including some very angry feelings along with some interesting dietary fantasies. The freedom to express these feelings presupposes the *absence* of a castration complex which would have considerably inhibited the expression of Christopher's annoyance.[3]

The basic condition of healthy life is that Christopher's relations with neither mother nor father were threatened by his lively opinions and feelings. The vital connections with both parents sustained his tensions and his freedom to communicate his feelings. Having a relationship within which to express his feelings, he was also spared the necessity of communicating them through actions that might end up bringing real retaliation. Similarly, he was spared expressing them through nightmares, bed-wetting, school phobia, or other symptoms by which intimidated children express their anger. So goes healthy life for a child.

Between three and six years there are sexual and other biological developments in boys and girls. The energetic maturation of the organism proceeds from the head down. Energetically the genital becomes integrated into the full pulsatory charge of the organism. This concept parallels Freud's conception of psychosexual development, except that it refers to organismic development.

The energetic integration of the genital is dependent, in particular, on a strong competence in the use of the legs. As the child has his feet on the ground, and can use his legs for free, pleasurable locomotion, like running and even dancing, then the grounding charge can move through the whole body. As this happens, the genital can become energized and integrated in a new way. At this stage of development, the child's affectionate feelings also take on new meanings.

I am not implying that boys and girls do not have feelings in their genitals before this point. That is not the case at all. What is implied is a maturation and an integration of the genital into the whole pulsation of the body. At this point the child's identity as a boy or girl coalesces through the identification with the genital. The meanings and implications of the genitals for adult life are glimpsed more clearly. There is a new awareness of sexual being, and the child's capacity for loving, now organized around the identification with the genital, is prototypical of the form it will take in adulthood. Love now has a more defined masculine or feminine quality, and the child may have passing fantasies, dreams, or feelings of exclusive possession, jealousy and competition. Excitement, often focused on the parent of the opposite sex, has a new quality. It is stronger and more focused genitally.

A FURTHER ANOMALY IN THE OEDIPUS COMPLEX

Consideration of the role of the vital connection in childhood brings to light a further anomaly in the Oedipal phase. The focus, in the classical formulation, was on the boy's conflicts and tensions in relation to his father. What of his relation to his mother? In the classical interpretation, it is taken for granted that the boy will have a passionate attitude toward the mother of such a sort that the father is established as a rival. This implies a peculiarly intense relation with the mother. The peculiarities of the assumptions here have been so frequently repeated that the oddity of the emotional situation implied has come to seem normal. To have such an intense excitement and passionate attachment to the mother is itself an extreme tension and not conducive to healthy development. It creates "actual frustration," as Reich described.

When this occurs (as in the case of Latch), what we are seeing are the effects of a kind of seduction on the part of the mother. That means the mother's response to the boy's development is giving it a sexual meaning and a degree of sexual excitation that brings it into the adult arena. The tension is caused by the heightened charge that the mother's excitation creates in the child. Referring to his excitement about his mother, a young man said, "I was all dressed up and had nowhere to go." This is an overexcitation, and it leaves the lasting and frightening impression that all sexual excitement and sexual relations will have that quality.

In Christopher's relationship with his mother, we see the potential for such a relationship. However, his mother is neither so seductive with him nor indifferent to his father as to set him up in such an intolerable tension with her or with his father. Lucky Christopher is free to express his feelings and go about the business of growing up. When he does get "dressed up" later on, he'll know where to go.

In the classical descriptions of the Oedipus complex, the tension in the relation with the mother has been both overlooked and taken for granted, as if it were in some way natural to masculinity. This is simply not true. What this tension does establish, however, is the conception that manhood is an intense competition of the most basic, primitive sort. It is win or be castrated. The female, the mother, is there to offer herself in this competition, to, in a sense, train her son by drawing him in to a seductive liaison in which the males are opposed in their efforts to win her. This meaning, like an unspoken secret, is implicit in Freud's description of the Oedipus complex.

In this culturally enthroned family complex also lies the heart of the narcissistic dilemmas of our time. Each man, as each little boy, is left to strive to be the star, the number one. But here is where it becomes very clear that the situation also applies to the little girl as well. She too is put in the position of striving to compete for number one place. In her case it is often to be accomplished by winning the number-one man, the all-powerful father, and thus she is trained from the time she is a little girl to be a mother who can entice men to the competition, to raise the knights who will battle for her favors and honor her by offering their sexuality before her altar in the guise of noble deeds.[4]

The phase of the development of sexual identity does indeed have everything to do with sexuality. It is the time when the child is becoming a self—as boy, or as girl. Selfhood defined by sexuality is emerging. What is at stake is what *kind* of boy and what *kind* of girl will emerge. Developmentally premature resolution of these issues are forced on children today. Before they are off to school, boys and girls have already had to establish the nuclear ideals of masculinity and femininity as the starring winners of the first and greatest competition. They have had little time to simply be boy or girl, the same as others, the same, but younger, than the mother and father.

Freud and psychoanalysis helped the culture to take children's sexuality seriously, at least to a level. When it comes down to it, however, children are still not taken seriously in their real lives. There is only one way to do so: Respect their feelings and sexuality as fully as any adult's. In Freud's time, I suspect that children had very little occasion on which to express their affective life in the context of the kind of communicative relationships available to Christopher. It is no wonder that so much was repressed—so little was communicated. As the dependents of those who raised them but who did not share their life, children were of a different estate, a different land, like Lilliputia, and were expected to stay there "seen and not heard" until they were ready to enter the adult state. In Freud's generation and later, it was not uncommon for fathers to have been emotionally distant from their children and, often enough, from their wives, too. It's no wonder there was need for a talking cure, so many people, from childhood on, had forgotten how or never learned to communicate in the domain of emotion and relationship.

CHILDHOOD SEXUALITY AND SELF-RESPECT

What is needed is a model for childhood sexual development based in and directed toward "healthy life," to use Winnicott's felicitous phrase. Such a model must be firmly grounded in respect for children's sexuality. Children's sexuality, from the beginning of life, must be understood in light of the reality that one day, not only will they be adults whose fulfillment will rest largely on their capacity for sexual love, but their self-respect as well will be established only through respect for their sexuality from the beginning of life.

Such a model for childhood sexual development will define the traumas described so clearly by Freud and Reich, not as givens of childhood but rather as deviations from the healthy, real traumas and violations of sexuality. The terror of castration, described by Freud,[5] far from being the necessary force to create "civilized man," will be seen for what it is—a trauma and violation. Similarly, the tensely held overexcitation described by Reich as the conflict between genital incest desires and their actual frustration will also be seen as a deviation from the healthy, and a violation of sexuality.

Respectful recognition of children's sexuality demands what has hitherto been impossible on a very large scale: the sane acceptance and understanding of masturbation from infancy on and the place of a sexual life in adolescence. The cultural antisexual anxiety and hatred still so prevalent need not deter that large minority of relatively healthy adults and parents who desire a healthy life for themselves and their children and who know perfectly well that sex and a sexual life are a core aspect of it. While guiding a child wisely and patiently over time takes more time than punitive suppression, the time spent is rewarding for all concerned, leads to happier possibilities for the future, and fewer prolonged neurotic conditions in adult life.

The model Freud described leads to identifications with a frightening parent, identifications which, supposedly, go to "building up the ego," and a concomitant willingness to live according to the norms of society. These identifications arouse out of the early vital connections under the same conditions which form the basis for the self-hate systems, neurotic inhibitions, inability to assume responsibility for life, and depression.

Healthy development can occur only in the context of vital connections in which the child's sexuality and his or her own movement and excitements are respected, supported, guided, and given the opportunity for development. The basis for respecting a child's sexuality is a clear recognition and understanding that the child's relation to its own genital lies at the core of establishing its identity as boy or girl, man or woman. A healthy development must be grounded in the child's identification with his or her own genital and genital movement. For this to happen, the child must develop free of entangling incestuous involvements and also free of having been routinely terrified in his or her normal course of development. Parental or other adult intrusion, either through punitive morality or overcharged excitation, creates a violation of sexuality and an organismic disruption which effects the child's development throughout life.

A positive identification with the genital leads to a positive sense of gender and a healthy life. There is every reason to believe that a life pattern begun with this grounding will be one in which the individual is capable of love and social contribution. To my mind, it is the only conceivable way to engender strength in personal virtues and attributes valued by both the individual person and by the community.

A FACILITATING ENVIRONMENT FOR SELF-RESPECT

The malleability of a sensitive child is nearly boundless, permitting all these
parental demands to be absorbed by the psyche. The child can adapt
perfectly to them, and yet something remains, which we might call
body knowledge, that allows the truth to manifest itself in physical illnesses
or sensations, and sometimes also in dreams. If a psychosis or neurosis
develops, this is yet another way of letting the soul speak.

—Alice Miller

ANALYZING THE FACILITATING ENVIRONMENT

Self-respect and healthy sexuality in adulthood are the outcomes of a developmental process beginning at birth. For the adult to be self-respecting, the child must have been respected, and for the adult's sexuality to be healthy, the child's sexuality must have developed without violation. Self-respecting sexuality is the red thread[1] of development. It emerges from the biological core, and it is the central and main theme of development from birth to the sexual maturity of the reproductive years.

Sexuality is a fundamental organizing principle of development. At any stage of development and at all levels of the organism, the developmental process is being organized by and around the function of sex. An implication of this view is that the respectful fostering of that development is an equally inherited and inherent organizing mechanism in parenting, unless it has been otherwise disrupted in the adult in the course of his or her own development.

I view the person as a sexual organism from birth. I consider that the first six years of life have a definitive impact on sexual development. These years literally shape and form the organism on a bodily, bioenergetic level, and it is through the shape and form thus laid down that the individual lives his or her life.

I envision a maturing organism in a facilitating environment. In essence, the facilitating environment consists of the child's vital connections, and the network of vital connections surrounding those primary vital connections. In the good-enough environment, the positive outcome of the child's organismic development is fostered. In the case studies I have presented, we see outcomes that are not optimal or positive in various ways. These outcomes reflect environments that were not good-enough because they were disrespectful and violated the sexuality of the child. The impact of the early years was traumatic.[2]

I offer an analysis of the facilitating environment based on consideration of an optimal outcome. The optimal outcome is an adult man or woman living a life with some consistency from a position of self-respect and who has the strengths and capacities necessary to find, establish, and sustain a sexual love relationship with another person. The facilitating environment is analyzed in terms of fostering or interfering with the expression of sex and self-respect. Self-respect is an organismic function inherent in health. It reflects a harmonious organism, a person whose relations with him- or herself foster bodily feeling and the full underlying life of the body's pulsations. The positively facilitating environment sustains throughout development the capacity for having and living by feelings, pleasure, and sexual love.

The aspects of the facilitating environment to be examined lie in the child's interpersonal domain. The question to be kept in mind in examining this interpersonal world is, simply, What constitutes respect for the child and his or her sexuality?

To analyze the facilitating environment, I use a simple schema. I discuss childhood in terms of three periods,[3] and I consider five dimensions of the facilitating environment in each period. In addition to the periods and dimensions, I also discuss, very briefly, some aspects of the kinds of "body knowledge" (and body memory) acquired during each period.

Three Periods of Childhood
    1. Baby period: birth to eighteen months
    2. Intermediate period: eighteen to forty-two months
    3. Sexual identity period: forty-two to sixty-six months[4]

Five Dimensions of the Facilitating Environment
    1. Contact
    2. Holding
    3. Support
    4. Nurture
    5. Sexual response

The "periods" are arbitrary sections of time (not "phases"), delimited for the sole purpose of creating the opportunity for examining cross sections of the years of early development. The five "dimensions" of the facilitating environment are artificial; they are an analytic tool. Any given inter-action between a mother and baby might be analyzed in terms of each of these dimensions. At the same time, that dimension is only an aspect of the interaction, not something that exists on its own, independently of any of the other four. The "dimensions" suggest ways of looking, seeing, thinking, and describing.

The concepts of body knowledge and body memory grow out of a bioenergetic understanding of the long-term effects of the individual's early facilitating environment. Each person, by the time they are five or six, has acquired knowledge that will have the most profound significance for their life. This knowledge is not in an intellectual, verbal form. It is body-knowl-edge. It is the individual's truth. In the earliest years, on a bodily level, we learn what life is and what it is to be with other people. The body does not just contain that learning, it becomes that learning. Most of this knowledge will never be expressed in words. Often, only in the specialized situation of therapy will the individual find words for body knowledge and an aware-ness of body memory will emerge. Sometimes marriage or other close rela-tionships function similarly, allowing body knowledge to be expressed in words and an awareness of body memory to develop. Whether spoken or not, every reaction to every significant event of life reflects this early learn-ing, this body knowledge.

In relation to sex and self-respect, there are four basic polarities of expe-rience which are influenced by the individual's body knowledge:

1. the capacity for love versus the inclination for ambivalence and hate;
2. the capacity to be alone versus the experience of loneliness;
3. the capacity for sexuality, pleasure and good feeling versus the ten-dencies to anxiety, shame, guilt, pain, and shock; and
4. the capacity for self-respect and self-regulation versus self-hate and chaos.

These polarities are dimensions of the interpersonal realm and the realm of self-experience. I believe that each of these polarities functions as an ongoing dialectic within the individual for a lifetime. Each polarity reflects or is reflected in ongoing life issues throughout the life cycle. The individ-ual does not land at one end or the other of the polarity and remain there at any point in life. The polarity always remains alive and dynamic.

The schematic analysis of the facilitating environment indicates the kinds of experiences contributing to the formation of body knowledge. Experiences may be regarded in light of the period of development within which they occur and in light of the dimension of the facilitating environ-ment which best describes them. Finally, the experience can be seen in terms of its effects on the organization in the individual of one of the four polarities of basic experience of self and others.

The analytic schema I am using is an extension of what Daniel N. Stern calls "the clinical child."[5] The clinical child I have in mind and use in practice is one that gradually evolved in my mind through my years as a therapist and undoubtedly out of my own childhood.

In my work, as I see the endless variations of the violations of sexuality and the disturbances in self-respect, I create, with my patient, his or her clinical child. This involves seeking an understanding of the particular and specific violations of sexuality and the particular and specific forms of disrespect of the facilitating environment. The schema I am using here is a distillation of those creations. I do not consider it a finalized theoretical construction.

BABY PERIOD

In the first eighteen months of life a neonatal organism becomes a child with a basic kind of mastery of his or her body and a beginning use of language.

Contact

- Eye contact; mouth to nipple; touch and skin contact with the baby's whole body

The basic meaning of contact is to touch, as in two surfaces touching. A baby's survival and development depends on touch and bodily contact. The respectful response to the baby lies in the provision of the contact it needs and wants. The attribution to an infant of the potential to be "spoiled," or whatever, through parental contact is a distortion and disrespectful.

The baby's first aggressive movement in relation to the world is drawing the first breath. In relation to the mother the first two aggressive movements are reaching for the nipple with lips and whole body and reaching for eye contact with the eyes. "Aggressive" means to move toward the world in the service of meeting needs. Thus looking and nursing are emotionally of enormous significance to the baby as the first expressions of its own aggressive efficacy. For the breast to be there and for mother's eyes to be there is the world for the baby. A baby left without contact in either of these ways is deeply deprived.

A great deal can be observed about the well-being of a baby by observing its eyes. A baby will generally have clear eyes when it has a contactful mother who has open and clear eyes herself. Its feelings and comfort or discomfort will clearly be reflected in its eyes, just as each cloud and breeze can be seen reflected or riffling across the clear surface of a small mountain lake. Most people have observed a baby seeking out its mother's eyes as it nurses and have felt the baby's total absorption in eyes and breast. Some classic paintings of the Madonna with the Christ child reflect this experience.

The baby seeks contact with the world with its eyes and mouth. The mother's response with her eyes and breasts is a parenting response in beautiful congruence with the unfolding maturational process. Mother also responds with her hands and arms, touching and holding the whole body of the baby. This contact is not a mechanical meeting of two surfaces; it is meaning, feeling, and communication. It is love. Good, respectful contact means that the mother is responding to Baby as Person, from herself as person. There is a self responding to emergent self.[6] In this good contact, the mother is supporting the baby's pulsatory process with that of her own body, an energetic connection which provides a continuity for the baby with its womb experience. It allows the baby to develop with a deep sense of relaxation and security in being.

Mechanical contact is disrespectful and disturbs the baby's experiences of looking and seeing, sucking, eating, breathing, and being close to. A rubber nipple is "mechanical" in comparison with a human nipple, whether or not it is necessary or preferred, and it provides a different experience to the baby. A baby can be nursed without eye contact and even holding, as well, and this too is a different experience. A baby also can be looked at as if it were not seen, not really looked at, or looked at with eyes showing irritation, pain, sadness, or anger or with eyes that are blank. The contact is effected in each case, and in each case the baby is effected in the depths of its being. Some warm, feelingful contact is essential for the infant's survival.

Holding

- Actual holding; the mother or caretaker holds the baby entirely in her arms

Winnicott's description of holding is apt. "Holding includes especially the physical holding of the infant, which is a form of loving. It is perhaps the only way in which a mother can show the infant her love. There are those who can hold an infant and those who cannot; the latter quickly produce in the infant a sense of insecurity, and distressed crying."[7] In being held the baby is in close body contact with the mother, immersed in her energetic field, which supports and fosters its growth and development.

Liedloff carries this kind of observation further and gives it a much broader perspective in her description of the "in arms phase" of the child-rearing practices she observed in South American Indians.[8] The mothers she observed consistently carry their infants from the moment of their birth until the time they can crawl. This means not only some months of constant body contact, it also means participation in a constant variety of exciting, active, daily experiences. To this experience, Liedloff attributes the equanimity and good feeling she observed in the older children and the adults, as well.

Support

- Love that is total and unconditional

The meaning of "support" is "to carry or bear the weight of; keep from falling, slipping, or sinking; hold up." I believe that it is the mother's love that supports the baby. Without that it slips, sinks, and falls. Such sinking is real, not metaphorical. It is often seen in the depression of unattended and unloved babies. Their energy rapidly falls, and they become more or less listless. If they survive, they may be left, not only with depression, but with a deep inner feeling of falling forever, which may be experienced consciously as dread and a chronic insecurity.

Love surrounds the baby as an energetic field. The mother's pleasure in the good feeling of love is one expression of her emotional responsiveness to the baby. This enlivens the baby too, creating pleasure, and supporting the full range of pulsatory functions of the baby. Love supports the baby in another way too. The mother and father with a strong capacity for love more easily find the energy for the demands of caring for a baby. When caretaking is experienced with more pleasure, it is more fulfilling, and this in turn supports the baby and its sense of well-being.

Nurture

• Nursing at the breast

Nurturing and feeding are one. Babies need the breast for the first two or even more years of life. The disrespectful response is to view the infant's cries for the breast as a threat to the parent, as prototypical egocentrism, as something to thwart so as not to "spoil," and other punitive responses. These attitudes are adult projections of despised aspects of the self into the infant. The effect of depriving a baby of contact, holding, support, and nurture is to create in it an almost inconceivable pain, and, if the deprivation is prolonged, to create harm that lasts a lifetime.[9]

Sexual Response

• Naming

Is it surprising to say there is a sexual response to a baby? Well, through the ages, what has been the first response to a healthy newborn? Hasn't it always been, "It's a boy!" or "It's a girl!"? Of course, this is naming (or identifying). Those attending the child's birth respond immediately to its gender, and I consider that a sexual response. The response is to name the child on the basis of the gender: Boy Philip, Girl Velma. So our life outside the womb begins with a sexual act as does our life in the womb. Nowadays, when ultrasound is available, this response may be modified, but it cannot be altogether abrogated. A person is a sexual organism at birth, and the naming response reflects that simple reality.

There are three aspects of parents' sexual response to the newborn and the child of any age: they respond to its gender and its genital, they respond to its sexuality, and they respond, themselves, sexually. The positive, respectful sexual response to the baby is simply to name the child. In truth, marked differences in parental response to male and female newborn are the rule rather than the exception, but the respectful response is nothing other than matter-of-fact acceptance and naming.

Baby Period: Body Knowledge Acquired

The baby period of life establishes the foundations for the experiences of loving and being loved and of the absence of love. Each person's deepest knowledge of what it is to love and be loved is formed by the love he or she experienced as a baby. This, of course, is a body experience. The baby, when it is loved, is immersed in love much as one is immersed in sunshine or soothing waters, and the body is bathed throughout. It is in his or her body as body knowledge.

A baby well breast-fed through its second year and beyond can have a robustness, fullness, and genuine happiness that many babies never have and most adults never know. A baby who has a mother capable of sharing her body and breasts with him or her, may grow up to be a wonderful lover, if other things go well, because he or she knows in their body what it is like to give and receive love and pleasure.

When the baby is coldly deprived of love, contact, and regular nursing, the adult's experience of love will be very different. The longing for love usually arises from longing for the love never received as a baby. A baby can be unconditionally loved for its total being. As adults our relationships are very different, as are our bodies, and we can only grieve for the love we did not receive as babies. A person who has been unloved may not always be so easy to love; that person may find that love, when offered, is difficult to accept. In addition, without knowing what love is from having been loved as a baby, the adult must learn to love through a painful process which includes learning that, as an adult, fulfillment comes, not from *being loved* but rather from having the capacity *to love*.

This period also establishes the capacity to be alone, or alternatively, it can leave an enduring, profound loneliness and a fear of being alone forever. The lonely outcome of the cumulative effects of early deprivation, is described in poignant detail by the poet, Kathleen Spivack.

All day in the crib the sunlit bars
slatted from left wall to right wall;
the angles grew sharper but no one came:
I played with the shadows of my fingers.

All night in the darkness, suffocating,
I breathed my sour terror in and out;
by morning I slept again, listless:
whichever prism day came next I lay through.

No footstep on the stair, no hurry, no comfort;
no larger body in sun-smelling clothes
to honey me to her softness: nothing moved
but my heartbeat, its cavernous persistence

training itself not to want.
Watchful, I stared at the corners
of things; the whole room flowering awake—
I am fading into my own absence.[10]

There is no exaggeration here. The timeless agony, the terror, the growing listlessness, the growing relinquishment of life itself as all wanting is
given up, the slow fading of the self and its replacement with watching and
autistic illusions—all are accurate. Abandonment and deprivation that
evoke these experiences and leave this kind of body knowledge are profound forms of disrespect of the baby.

The facilitating environment provides the basis for other deep layers of
body knowledge pertaining to sexuality and self-respect. Regarding sexuality, I hold a fundamental guideline: From birth onward, respectful treatment of the child requires that he or she be perceived as a sexual being;
otherwise the treatment will be disrespectful.

Not infrequently, parental response recognizes the newborn's sexuality
and denies it at the same time. It is remarkable how often people say that
one or both parents wanted them to be of the other sex. This confused sentiment suggests that the parent harbors an inner conviction that this particular child will be a disappointment, burden, or problem. There are
endless variations on these confused parental sentiments that enter children's lives literally from day one.

Not uncommonly, such burdensome disappointments fall on the girl
children. "My father wanted a boy" or "I was supposed to be a boy" are
commonly heard. The patriarchal joy attending the birth of a boy has its
unspoken corollary in the rejection of the female child as of inherently less
worth. The girl is denigrated, and the boy is burdened with idealized, premature, and exaggerated expectations. Each is marked for life; and it is the
same as if the genital were marked for life as soon as the baby emerges from
the womb. There is little wonder that our "primitive" ancestors devised rit-
uals of circumcision, clitoroidectomy, and other genital mutilations. The
genital is marked from birth in any case. Nor is there any wonder that most
of these practices continue today.[11]

A highly educated man who was expecting the birth of his first child,
whom he knew was to be a son, discussed with me his feelings and
thoughts about having the son circumcised. He wanted his son to identify
with and respect his religious tradition, and he felt that would happen only
if the son were circumcised, as he himself had been. I offered the observation that if he respected himself as a man and his son as a man, the son
would be likely to respect him, his own father, and his father's tradition,
and it is not circumcision that creates those respectful relationships and
attitudes. However, such attitudes leave no physical mark on the genital;
they only preserve its good feeling. And this man was not convinced. A
question to be asked in this situation, I feel, is not only whether the son will
identify with the father's tradition, but, How would the father react to his

son were the son not traumatized and mutilated in the same way as the father? Could the father "identify with" a whole son?

Confusions multiply in this domain. One also hears from men who say their mothers wanted them to be girls, or that their fathers were not as excited about them as about the little girls. Excitements and angers that parents express "unconsciously" can be in direct opposition to the overt pronouncements. An example of this is the family where the father's most intense relationship is not with the mother or daughter, but the conflicted, often overtly embattled one, with a son.

In addition to the above distortions, there is a common proclivity to desexualize baby altogether, to treat him or her as if, for this brief angelic period, it were neither. Thus baby becomes sexless, giving mother, and father too, a brief respite from any unwelcome review or preview of their own sexual troubles. This may sound acceptable in the case of a baby, but it is not; it is based on an actual perceptual distortion of the baby. One cannot look at a naked body of any age and fail to see it as male or female. To do so involves a distortion in the way one relates to that body, even when the body is a small one.

It might be thought that responding sexually to a baby's sexuality makes no sense in any case. However, babies have a very powerful energy and energetic effect in their own right. Parents respond variously to it. They can enjoy its softness and beauty, or they may need, unconsciously, to block it out of awareness. They can also exploit it for their own needs, for example, by constantly overstimulating the baby. This is usually followed by the need to "discipline" the baby in order to break the excitement and force the baby to discharge the excess tension through crying. A torturous pattern of excitation and pain is established in this way.

Self-respect is also a bodily process having a development beginning at birth in the context of the early vital connections. The baby's regulation is the first task of new parents. As Daniel Stern says, "When the baby first comes home from the hospital, the new parents live from minute to minute, attempting to regulate the newborn."[12] As that task is taken care of, the baby's regulation is intertwined with the parents' self-regulation.

This kind of regulation goes on for quite a long time, progressively maturing and developing through each of the three periods of childhood. The quality of the regulation the baby experiences begins to establish the baby's own quality of self-regulation and self-respect, as well as the child's future capacity for mutual regulation with a partner. When the mother responds in a timely, empathic way to the baby's needs, the baby learns the bodily feeling of an easy self-regulation.

What might happen, for example, when a baby is put on a feeding schedule very early, and is left to "cry himself out" at other times? The prolonged crying is not only painful, it depletes the baby's energy, and the deprivation undermines the infant's building of a trust in its own bodily experience. The next time the baby is left to cry alone, it will be with less energy. Eventually it will give up. The baby has "learned." What is learned is the body knowledge of depletion, lowered energy, and pain; what is learned is that bodily needs must be controlled by the will; what is learned is that the body is not to be trusted. What in fact happens is that the very foundation of the basic capacity for self-regulation and hence self-respect is undermined.

INTERMEDIATE PERIOD

This intermediate period is so named because the child is between the time of babyhood and the time of being one whose identity as a boy or girl has coalesced in the identification with the genital. In this period, the child develops prowess in autonomous mobility, and language and cognitive skills develop. A strong "social presence and feel," as Stern[13] calls it, develops. From the point of view of the facilitating environment, what is essential is the response to the child's developments in learning to negotiate its presence and its needs in an increasingly complex interpersonal world.

Everything, from putting on clothes in the morning to going to bed at night, involves a relationship with another person, and the child needs a place for him- or herself in the process. The needs that a child is learning to negotiate in the interpersonal arena revolve around all the major facets of life and self-regulation: food and eating, play, contact and being with, seeking comfort, having and discharging excitement, and learning a myriad of cognitive, social, and physical skills. Above all, a child has a heightened awareness of his or her bodily self and bodily functions in relation to others. These bodily functions include feelings, excitement, aggression, and pleasure, as well as bowel functions. The responses by others begin to define the meanings of these bodily functions.

Contact

* Emotionally contactful care and caring in relation to bodily needs, feelings, use of language, and developments in the sense of self

Respectful contact is emotionally contactful care and caring in relation to bodily movements, needs, and feelings. Physical contact shifts to emotional contact. The caregiver's awareness of the child's bodily needs, feelings, and movements is aligned with and attuned to that child's physical, cognitive, and emotional realities with the attitude that those realities matter just as much as the adult's. In this way the situation becomes truly interpersonal and collaborative rather than a relationship of power or control. The equality implied by this does not mean there is no difference between child and adult and no exercise of authority by the adult. It means that differences of role and maturation are guided by recognition of the personhood of the child and are not used in the service of power.

Holding

- A safe holding environment in which the child can move

Holding becomes the creation of a holding space. From the small, womblike circle of cradling arms, the holding environment becomes an interpersonal, emotional space in the familiar home environment. Here the developing child can learn and practice self-regulation of its needs in the context of the vital connections. The boundaries of this space are physical and emotional, and they include the firm limits of safety, tolerance, and acceptable behavior that protective and empathic parents must provide.

Support

- Respect

The support offered by the facilitating environment at these ages is the attitude most aptly characterized by this one word: respect. Without respect *for his or her very being,* it is impossible for the child to develop and establish self-respect.

New experiences in every arena abound for the child. Respect for developmental ups and downs supports development and the child's acquisition of a lifelong realistic sense of the ups and downs of all growth and development. As the child develops his or her own mind and perceptions, these need to be respected.

Above all, the child's bodily self must be respected. The child's efforts to meet its own needs must be respected if the child is to learn to respect the efforts of others to meet their needs. The child's vulnerability to shame needs to be respected without being exploited. The learning and accomplishing of tasks needs to be respected without overblown parental excitement and praise seducing the child into a sense of specialness. The child's beauty and aliveness needs to be respected too, without being made into something special for parents to exploit for their own narcissism. The child's needs for contact, soothing, and emotional expression need to be supported by being respected. All this means that the child's body belongs to him or her; it is not the parents', and it is not for the parents.

There is another aspect to this. The child needs time: time to be a child, and not more than a child. Respecting a child means allowing the child to be a child. One way well-meaning parents have of owning a child is precociously preparing him or her for adult roles. Another way is to use the child for their own emotional needs for companionship, stimulation, bodily contact, and comfort. All of this is extraordinarily disrespectful.

Nurture

- Soothing

Children, as everyone knows, have the capacity for becoming extraordinarily upset. The nurturing that the facilitating environment can provide at these ages is soothing.[14]

When upsets occur, the child needs the chance to have its own feelings, and they need to be soothed. They can become upset from disappointment, punishment, their own failures at learning, being the object of the anger of the parent, their own failures at self-regulation, stress, and fatigue. It is cruel and painful for the child to be left alone in a state of upset without comfort.

Soothing allows the autonomic nervous system to calm down and to reestablish homeostasis. Being left alone in a state of upset leads to the development of chronic hyperactivation of the autonomic nervous system and deep muscular tensions. Soothing reestablishes the vital connection and the goodness of relationships, which means, basically, their pleasurableness. Being repeatedly left in upset and tension establishes the feeling that relationships are basically hell and should be regarded with suspicion. Soothing supports the return to development along positive and pleasurable lines, and the learning of a self-regulatory style that will ensure harmony and good feeling in relationships, allowing the establishment of self-respect.

Sexual Response

• Seeing, enjoying, and allowing

In the intermediate period, the respectful facilitative response to the child's sexuality is to see it, enjoy it, and allow the boy or girl his or her own sexual movement without interference within the holding environment. This includes masturbatory activity, curiosity, playing at sexual roles, asking questions, looking, testing boundaries, and playing sexually with children of the same age. It does not include allowing the child to intrude into or participate in the sexual life of adults.

Intermediate Period: Body Knowledge Acquired

Respectful or disrespectful responses to the child's efforts at learning to regulate its needs in relations with others determine how it feels bodily to have needs of any kind. As the child's expression of needs lead to successful, manageable, and relatively pleasurable experiences in the context of the vital connections, the enjoyable capacity to be with others is enhanced. In addition, good experiences enhance the bodily knowledge of self-respect and self-regulation. For the child to be met and regulated in usually reasonable, usually pleasurable and nonpunitive ways, the body learning will be of pleasure in companionship.

The capacity for love can continue to develop in this period, and so, too, the tendency toward hate and ambivalence may arise clearly. Love is a bodily experience, and it will naturally arise in the child's feelings when relationships are relatively pleasurable and allow for the regular discharge of tension. Love is a natural outgrowth of the pleasure of being with the other person.

Just as the origins of love lie in pleasurable experiences, the origins of hate lie in painful ones. When the child's needs are treated disrespectfully or fulfilled painfully, begrudgingly, or indifferently, then the child learns that it is painful to have needs with another person and, therefore, painful to be with another person. The tendency toward hate and ambivalence is thus enhanced, and the bodily functions of self-respect and self-regulation are undermined, and self-hate enters. The child is left not only with the pain or frustration of unmet need but also with the loneliness that results from the disruption of the vital connection, which is even worse.

The vulnerability to shame and humiliation of children during this period can be exploited, resulting in a chronic sense of shame, humiliation, and self-hate. Self-regulation is disrupted, too great a stress is placed on the adaptive capacity, and efforts to deal with the world become more chaotic and stressful. With the basic conditions for establishing self-respect undermined, it is very difficult, if not impossible, for it to be established, and the task has to be undertaken in later life when it is even more difficult.

Humiliation is the alternative to respect in this period. The use of humiliation, shaming, criticism, and discipline quickly conditions the child to sense shame in relation to his or her own genital. In this way, the child learns to feel humiliated in the most basic way: as a male or as a female. Every movement that comes from masculinity or femininity will then carry a burden of humiliation.

Shame and humiliation thus established in relation to the genital permeate every other developmental function, including those on the ego and intellectual level. Shame deeply associated with the genital leaves a bodily feeling of badness which is understood very simply as "I am bad," "I am worthless," or "I am dirty." A bodily feeling on this level of conditioning is unbearably painful and is usually buried under many levels of characterological defensive behavior and distortion. It nonetheless permeates a lifetime.

Actual sexual abuse by adults or older children becomes more of a physical possibility as the child grows. Any exposure to adult sexuality will be disturbing and shocking. Unnecessary and harsh punishment for masturbation or sexual curiosity is extremely disturbing and can be damaging. Hate and conflicted attitudes about sex on the part of parents distort the child's attitudes toward his or her own genital feelings. Exposure to adult borderline and psychotic behavior, including alcoholic behavior, within the confines of the home disturbs the child's conception of adult sexuality, as does an atmosphere of secrecy and betrayal.

Children at this age are subject to exploitation and abuse on the emotional and energetic level without overt sexual violation. Children of this age are often very beautiful as small males and females. Their sexual beauty and innocence can stir strong feelings and yearning in adults, whose own innocence has long since been lost and fondest dreams dashed. The appearance of some good-looking adults reveals that they were looked at too much as children. Their faces take on a kind of movie-star patina that can be quite unreal, and they can become identified with that persona or dissociated from it, but confused in either case, as to their real sexuality.

Seduction of children at this age is so common as to probably appear normal. The child, whose heart is still open, and who wants to love its parents and be loved, is seduced into becoming the little man or woman, or the cute little boy or girl, for one or the other parent, compensating the parent for his or her own deficits in self-regard and self-respect. Many women speak of how they were trained to be Daddy's cute little girl. Similarly, many little boys are trained to be Mother's white knight.

These precocious seductions prematurely cast the child into a sexual role. However, there is more to it than a social behavior. In these family flirtations, the children are exposed to an adult level of excitation which their bodies are not ready to handle, and the result is a profound disturbance in their own capacity for sexual arousal and expression in later life. At the same time, there is always betrayal and heartbreak for the child in these relationships, and their hearts become closed and armored so they will not have to suffer another, possibly final and fatal, heartbreak. The legacy, in body knowledge, of such seductions is that a quest for an illusory sense of specialness is the only imaginable path to fulfillment.

PERIOD OF SEXUAL IDENTITY FORMATION

During the sexual identity formation period, the child's identification with his or her genital coalesces. It is arbitrarily conceived as from three and a half to five and a half years and on. It has begun before this time, but development allows it to coalesce. The child's interpersonal world expands during this time to reach beyond immediate family life into institutions of the wider society.

Contact

- Acceptance of genitality

Respectful contact at this time is typified by the acceptance of the sexuality—the femininity or masculinity—of the child in all the phases of its daily activities. The acceptance lies in the perception of the child's sexuality, allowing the child his or her expressions of masculinity or femininity, and allowing actual sexual expression appropriate to a child, including masturbation and sexual play with other children when that can be protected. Perception of the child's sexuality also means that physical contact is respectful of sexuality, just as physical contact with an adult should reflect awareness of and respect for masculinity or femininity.

Holding

- Freedom to love

The respectful holding environment permits the child the freedom to love. This means there is a recognition that children have passions of their own. Permitting the child to love means permitting them to love in their own way, with their own passion, not as a demonstration of routine affection for the reassurance of the parent. It further means that they may express angry feelings of competition, jealousy, and disappointment. Freedom means that, while parents or other adults take the children's feelings seriously, they are not taken as serious threats to the parents' own freedom to love. It is incredibly disrespectful when a parent takes a child's love of a spouse as a threat or a real competition and deprives the child of their freedom to love. All of these Oedipal rivalries are expressions of parental disrespect. Inflamed sibling rivalries[15] or eroticized sibling relationships are usually efforts to work out the disrespect and sexual violations inflicted in a variety of ways by the older generation.

Support

• Appreciative encouragement and education

It is tremendously supportive to appreciate and enjoy children for their sexuality, and that means for their sexuality in the form it takes as a child, without it being drawn into the arena of adult sexuality. It is respectful to enjoy children in this way because they are in fact so enjoyable *as boys and girls*. Not to appreciate them in this way is to deny their essence. The child is supported *as a child,* not by being "promoted" to a special kind of small lover of either parent. The appreciation is nonpossessive, and free of the adult's developmental needs.

In this period the child is also supported in a direct way by encouragement and education in relation to the expression of masculinity and femininity. Support of this sort was perfectly expressed by the father of a six-year-old boy when the father said, "We can go downstairs to the shop, put our feet up, and be men." The shop was their—the men's domain— away from older sisters and Mother. This father was enjoying and appreciating his son and his son's situation; he was encouraging the son in his masculinity; and he was educating his son in his own, the father's, way of being a man. The support was relaxed, pleasure oriented, nondemanding. Being a man in the shop did not mean high-stress, competitive performance; it meant freedom from certain kinds of demands and the freedom to be one's self. At the same time, this shop is a place of real productivity.

Nurture

• Maintenance of generational boundary

The boy or girl is respectfully nurtured in sexual development through the maintenance of the generational boundary. The child is allowed to continue to be a child and is not exposed to adult excitation or adult sexual life, any more than circumstances and living arrangements of the family might make inevitable.

Sexual Response

• Open-heartedness

The positive, respectful sexual response is to enjoy the aliveness and beauty of children with an open heart. The child is loved and met with an open heart as a boy or girl. The child has the opportunity then to experience on a bodily level what it is to be liked, enjoyed, and loved as a sexual being. The boy is liked for himself, and the girl for herself. It is disrespectful to disavow the child's sexuality; it is disrespectful to resent the child for its sexual potential, innocence, improved circumstances, or the opportunities or life that in adult fantasy lies ahead for the child but is supposedly denied the adult. To be met with an open heart allows the child's heart to stay open and to move into life with a good feeling. It allows the child to maintain, on a body level, the deep connection between the heart and genitals. The respectful response of parenting is to respond from the heart, with genital love being associated with another adult.

Period of Sexual Identity Formation: Body Knowledge Acquired

From the period of sexual identity formation, the man or woman has the body knowledge which is the foundation for appreciating the excitement and pleasure that are possible in relation to the opposite sex. Adolescence builds on this foundation. If the child was turned against, rejected, treated punitively, or shamed for excitement, there will be some hatred of the opposite sex. If the child is left feeling that sexuality is bad, wrong, taboo, dirty, shameful, or degrading in any way, the adult is left with a terrible loneliness and desperation based on a deep conviction that sexual love is never to be attained or that it must be avoided to escape terrible punishment.

If the child's sexuality is allowed, the adult will be able to bring it into the world in such a way as to allow an effective self-regulation and a well-organized, appropriately aggressive ego functioning in the world of work. If sexuality is violated, to that degree the individual's efforts in the world will be chaotic and self-respect will be undermined.

Genital injury is the fundamental outcome of disrespect and the violation of sexuality in this period. There are a variety of ways in which this occurs. Children of this age are vulnerable to sexual abuse by adults and older children around them and not infrequent victims of it. They are vulnerable to being sexually exploited by being seduced into a precociously adult role with one or another parent, by being the special little boy or little girl, as a kind of lover of one or another parent. Parents choose both opposite- and same-sexed children for these "favors." These roles will inevitably involve a mixture of debasement and inflation, contempt and exploitation. When the parent is psychotic, borderline, or alcoholic, induction into such roles includes a range of abuse from outright violence to more subtle versions of sadomasochism. The common occurrence of overtly psychotic behavior on the part of parents in the privacy of their own homes should not be underestimated. Alcohol induced psychosis is only one of its more common forms. Parents and others may also exploit a child as an object for competition, jealousy, moralistic condemnation, envy, and hate.

Physical punishments and the threats of it are always disrespectful. The fear they create becomes the basis for sexual guilt, whether or not the punishment is focused directly on the child's sexuality or sexual behavior. Sexual guilt is induced by fears of punishment, castration, and injury. I do not believe such fear and guilt is the basis of morality. I believe that the person suffering with guilty fears who does become a good, moral person, does so in spite of such guilt, not because of it.

BODY KNOWLEDGE, FULFILLMENT, AND SELF-RESPECT

Body Knowledge and the Dream of Love

Each period of development, with its many experiences in the relationships of the vital connections, leaves in the body a knowledge of love, and all these impressions are synthesized in the young adult in a "dream of love." In seeking love in the world, the man or woman seeks to realize this dream. The less the child is interfered with, allowed his or her own movement, and met as an alive organism, the more the dream of love will be based in sexuality and the identification with the genital. The dream will then be realistic, and it will be that much more likely it will serve the individual as a guide to fulfillment. If there is too much violation, hate, loneliness, and pain, the dream becomes divorced from reality, and the individual is left chasing rainbows on the one hand and unconsciously avoiding something miserable on the other, while the warm-bodied men and women of real life pass on by.

Body Knowledge Transformed to Body Memory

Body knowledge is often not "known" in a way that can be articulated. It is the "knowledge" that guides behavior. In the following vignette, we see the process of body knowledge coming into awareness and being transformed into body memory. As that happens, the individual becomes aware of attitudes, behaviors, and reactions that stem from early conditioning.

Paula writes about the emerging awareness of old body knowledge that pleasure is to be feared and the emergence and development of new body knowledge.

Fear isn't the enemy. . . . It's the key. My therapist says, "You're afraid right now." I say, "You mean a few minutes ago." "No," she says, "right now. Always. It colors everything, but you don't feel it, the fear." She suggests I try looking around the room and seeing what bodywork I want to do. I lie on the bed. I am afraid immediately. She asks if I'd like her to work with my neck. I'm confused because I'm busy being afraid. She touches my face very gently and tenderly. I love this and want it very much but it's very frightening. I'm afraid that the fear will drive her away but she stays and I get to have my fear and my awareness and enjoyment of her tenderness. She works with my neck which feels lovely and the fear goes away. She asks where—I don't know—she says good feelings can make it go away. I have no knowledge if this is true. I suspect she's wrong but who knows. Then she works on my back, shoulders, then hips. She asks how that feels. I say good, but I suspect I'm only willing to feel a little bit of the hip pleasure. "That's where the fear went," she says. It's starting to get clear. Fear isn't just the screaming terror. It can subtly cut down on the feeling of pleasure. She asks if I'd like to try again—being aware of wanting and of the fear. This is hard to do—to keep them both present for myself—but I can sort of do it. . . . She goes back to touching my face. I was surprised . . . I thought she would rock my hips again. After awhile I notice that the sense of tenderness is not so strong and it's awful . . . that must mean that I have that all confused with fear. She says no, the dampened fear has again cut off the pleasure. And I see. She's right. Allowing fear allows my experience of pleasure. Fear is no longer an enemy, to be locked away. Allowing it is my key to pleasure. It's not bad.

In this complex interweaving of experience, self-respect is being established as Paula is able to allow herself to experience her bodily sensations and the actual experience of fear. "Fear is no longer an enemy" expresses the transformation. The experience is not only accepted, it is respected as her own bodily experience, and it reflects the reestablishment of a degree of trust in her own bodily regulatory processes. It is seen that in giving in to the body, pleasure can follow, rather than something fearful, within the context of a trusted vital connection. In this way the capacity to form other vital connections is also established.

What is the body knowledge in this case? Paula "knew" that pleasure leads to something fearful and is therefore to be feared. This was a deep truth, not "contained" in her body but rather that her body had become. As such body knowledge comes into awareness, one can become aware that it represents a set of attitudes guiding behavior. Paula "knew," on the body level, that it would not be a good thing to feel that fear, and therefore, her attitude was that it was necessary to control it by suppression. She also had attitudes that were cautious, distancing, and supporting the suppression of pleasure and other feelings, all of which were appropriate to the world as she "knew" it.

Body knowledge, identified in this way, allows for the emergence and identification of body memory. As body knowledge, Paula's fear influences the present, dampening and cutting down on pleasurable feeling. As Paula again becomes aware of and can tolerate the experience of fear, it becomes body memory. It is associated with past events, separated from the present, and understood as conditioning from the past. New body knowledge begins to develop: that she can feel fear without her survival being threatened, that pleasure can follow fear, that her body can be trusted for its self-regulatory processes. This is the actual process of the establishment and deepening of self-respect.

THE INDIVIDUAL IN THE COUPLE

THE INDIVIDUAL'S FATE IN THE COUPLE

The quintessential movement of the human male is to desire, seek out, and penetrate the female, and the quintessential movement of the female is to desire, seek out, elicit the penetration, and actively receive the male; and for both it is to continue the movement in the union to orgastic climax. Union and the drive toward it are our core. Identification with the genital, the basis of the identity of the self, is lived out in this way; this is its fundamental expression. Once a union is realized, and the partners choose to remain together, a shift in perspective is needed. Now, to understand the individual's sexuality, we need to look at his or her experience within the union. We need to look at the fate of the individual in the couple.

The word *couple* here, is limited to referring to those dyads established by a man and woman out of a sexual motivation. Such a couple may have existed for twenty minutes or twenty years. A man and woman who are married form a couple, by definition; of course, not all couples are married. Obviously there are other twosomes who form pleasurable, interesting, and problematic dyads in other, closely similar ways, in particular, gay and lesbian couples, and even close friends. For present purposes I am restricting my examination to the couple as defined. In limiting myself to the exploration of the heterosexual couple I imply neither superiority for that form of coupling nor denigration for the coupling of partners of the same sex. I am limiting myself to what I know from my own experience, even as I hope these explorations will be useful to the homosexual—gay or lesbian—reader as well. The dyadic relationship, overall, has a very large scope in the psychology and sociology of human life, and it could hardly be encompassed in one chapter.

To speak of the "individual *in* the couple" might seem odd, because it seems to connote an entity having its own existence, apart from or in addition to the two people who comprise the couple, an entity which each could be *in*, as if it were a larger container of some kind. People sometimes speak as if this were the case, as when someone speaks of "my marriage," or "my relationship," or even "the relationship," as if they were referring to an entity outside of and larger than themselves, and as if they were speaking of something other than simply the way they are getting along with their partner. On hearing this kind of talk, I usually request the person to speak of their experience and their behavior with the other person, and leave out mythic entities. Nonetheless, there is a certain emotional reality to this kind of language, because a couple creates a new interpersonal milieu within which each partner operates. The fate[1] of the individual as one partner of a couple unfolds within this milieu.

To speak of the *fate* of the individual in the couple has an ominous ring, but fate is indeed the issue. The formation of the sexual union is hardly a matter of chance, whim, or, for that matter, deliberative choice. Many millions of years of evolution have ensured that it will happen. Nature has ensured that male and female *Homo sapiens* will not only come together but that they will stay together.[2] Desire, of course, brings men and women together; sexual excitement creates the union of the two; and the discharge of that excitement in the genital embrace and the fulfillment therefrom establishes the bonding, the basis for the continuation of the couple.

Another reason, too, supports the appropriateness of judging the individual's history in the couple as fate. Each individual brings not only him- or herself to the couple relationship, each brings his and her *injured* self and, specifically, the genital injury. Within the couple, the effects of the genital injuries inevitably, fatefully unfold. So it is that the excitements of the man and woman flowing together in mutual passion unifies the fulfillment of personal histories—loves existing for only the briefest flicker of time—with the fulfillment of millions of years of evolution. No wonder the fulfillment of sexual love can feel cosmic! Perhaps this is the reward for submitting to our fate.

As to the general pattern of that fate, that which common wisdom might suggest to us is not altogether irrelevant: That by falling in love, one is not guaranteed to live happily ever after; that in seeking a safe harbor, one might find oneself on stormy waters; that in pursuing desire and delight, one might discover disappointment and heartbreak; that in seeking to ensure excitement, fulfillment, and pleasure, one might run headlong into frustration, conflict, pain and suffering; and finally, and most dumbfounding, that in moving to enhance life, one might find oneself literally fighting for one's life. So it is—in some of the words of the traditional wedding ceremony—"to hold for better and worse."

THE MILIEU OF THE COUPLE

Each partner brings to the other him- or herself. Here is a reminder of the fundamental, determinative factor that is easily overlooked in discussions of couples: There are two *bodily* selves. The significance of this fact is that the milieu of the couple is energetically enriched. The two energy systems of the two people interact with each other, add to each other, excite each other, warm each other, and effect the bodies of each.

In the case of a partnership that starts off with some measure of excitement and happiness, each partner probably finds bodily contact of an intensity, pleasurableness, and gratification which is unlike anything he or she has experienced since infancy. Physical contact tapers off for most people very rapidly after early childhood. For the many years of life, say between three and twenty-one (an early marriage), there are many years in which the individual experiences very minimal touch, holding, close skin contact and—probably—sexual contact with another. I imagine something like a skin hunger grows during this time, out of the need for touch, contact, stimulation, and sexual pleasure.

The energetic intensity, physical contact, and need gratification focused with the partner in the couple, has specific effects on the individual at an organismic level. Once again the individual has a vital connection effecting him and her on the deepest bodily levels. The sexual organs are stimulated and excited, but other organs are stimulated as well: the heart, gastrointestinal tract, the breathing apparatus, the autonomic nervous system, and the brain. The whole body adapts to the energetic, pulsatory, and emotional milieu of the couple with its different levels of excitation and stress.

The new level of excitation in the context of the vital connection of the couple has specific and significant effects. It awakens a biological expectation of further developmental potential, and it awakens body memories and specific characterological reactions.

The organism retains throughout its life span the need for vital connection. *Homo sapiens* not only has a long period of developmental dependence, our species maintains a measure of developmental immaturity throughout its life span.[3] The energetically enriched milieu of the couple provides the conditions for the activation of a developmental drive. It is as if the individual had been waiting for a new, and possibly more propitious, vital connection to provide the matrix for continuing developmental potentials, or finding more satisfactory outcomes for conflicted and unsatisfactory developments which already took place. This is operative, I would say, whether the individuals are eighteen or eighty.

The focus of the activated developmental drive is not random, nor is it randomly distributed amongst the various developmental conflicts or deficits encountered by the individual in earlier years. It always finds its focus in the individual's masculinity or femininity, in sexuality. Further, since the individual's developmental conflicts and deficits are summed up and integrated into the genital injury, the repair of genital injury becomes the specific focus of the developmental drive activated in the couple. In fact, this same developmental trend, toward the repair of genital injury, already exists within the individual and is therefore a source of the movement toward union in the first place. It is also a source of the motivation for making the selection of the specific partner, the one who, according to some preconception, will be the one to fulfill one's needs.[4]

The awakening of the developmental drive is an energetic, or organismic, process. It happens on a bodily and emotional level outside of ego controls and conscious considerations. The intense conflicts that arise in couples and the enormous efforts made in coming to terms with them are direct manifestations of the power of this developmental drive. The conflicts and the partners' efforts to come to terms with them derive from the underlying genital injury and contain the biologically activated drive to repair it.

I believe there to be a single core nucleus at the heart of every conflict within couples, and it can be understood in the light of this description of the milieu of the couple. In earlier discussions, I described how excitatory movement and sexual excitement can be stopped. The particular timing, manner, and sources of their being stopped become structured bodily in the person. This is the essence of genital injury, and I believe that some degree of genital injury is virtually universal. The heightened energetic milieu of the couple activates and heightens sexual blocking, recreating the pain involved in the way movement was originally stopped. The pain of the stopped movement is always the core of the conflict for the couple, just as it is the core of the individual's pain.

Just as each partner brings the self to the couple, each imports into the couple his and her character structure. So it is that terrible conflicts are imported into the couple by the vehicle of the conflictful and desperately evolved character structures. Just as character is structured into the body, and has a biological basis, so too there is a biological inevitability to much of the pain and suffering lovers experience.

The milieu of the couple provides a heightened excitation which challenges and eventually activates the character reactions, because the function of character is to manage excitation and expression within determined limits. To the degree that his or her energetic, sexual movement was stopped and blocked in development, he or she is fated to reexperience such stopping in relation to the partner. These experiences inevitably are body memories. The individual experiences pain and the same kind of pain as he or she was subjected to in the course of development, experiences that are often embedded in shame, guilt, humiliation, self-hate, and other negative self states.

Conflict arises because the blocks stopping sexual movement are rarely experienced for what they are, that is actual energetic blocks in the body based on muscular tensions. The pain is very real, of course, but that is the least of the problem. The conflict is engendered by a failure: the failure to understand that the pain, anger, fear, humiliation, or somatic symptoms are derived from the past. Typically the pain is (characterologically) perceived as being caused by the difficulties inherent in the relationship with the partner. In reality, the pain, usually, is not caused by the partner or even any admitted difficulties of the relationship but rather is imported from the past into the relationship along with the character. The range of unhappy experiences implicated in all this—anger, fear, humiliation, betrayal, and somatic symptoms—runs the gamut of human unhappiness. As often as not, then, the milieu of the couple lies not in the Garden of Eden but instead, as the sad story goes, in those lands of toil, sorrow, and tears to which humans were exiled following their expulsion from Eden.

There are two contrasting characterological styles seen in couples in which all such unhappinesses are manifested: actively painful, actively expressive; and deadened, inexpressive. In the deadened style, the individual essentially loses his or her good feeling for the other, and a low level negativity pervades his or her attitude toward the other. This leads to a chronic coldness and low-level insidious hatred. The conflicts here are not hot and "out in the open," although they may flare up occasionally, only to be quickly put down, as if out of fear that the long smoldering conflagration could not be put out if it burst into flames. The deadening between the partners in cases like this reflects the terrible, long-standing armoring of their bodies and the killing of their sexual feeling.

The more active style is more alive and contains the greater possibility for love, healing, and pleasure. At the same time, the emotional aspects of the experience can become unbearable and lead to passionate conflict. The emotional suffering runs the gamut of ways in which suffering is possible: frustration, shame, guilt, humiliation, a sense of dirtiness, badness, evilness, whorishness, or defect; betrayal, abandonment, and abuse; rage, sadomasochistic fighting, and endless quarreling; and depression and despair.

The pain and suffering in these experiences are, for the most part, body memories originating in childhood, although they are experienced as a here-and-now reality; either the partner is blamed or the pain is attributed to the inherent difficulties of the contemporary relationship. When the pain is a result of actual abuse by the partner, the effects of the childhood pain, abuse, and guilt may interfere with the victim responding realistically and appropriately to what is happening, in particular by leaving the abusive partner.

Therapeutically, the basic step in resolving couple stresses and conflicts is taken when each partner can experience and accept his and her own genital injury for what it is. Essentially, this is the basis for establishing self-respect. The genital injury is inevitably experienced as some form of inadequacy or defect of masculinity or femininity, and therefore it is painful to acknowledge and bear. For example, an impotent or castrated feeling, can often be experienced and expressed in such simple terms as, "I'm not enough, I'm not adequate," or as a defensive stance through expressions of contempt, denial, or dismissal. Deepened capacity for sexual love is attained through a stronger grounding in the lower half of the body, a stronger identification with one's own genital, and a stronger sense of one's own sexual movement as a man or woman. These are bodily changes and developments.

Resolving conflicts may mean, in part, to fight it out with the partner, because each partner has to take up a fight for sexual freedom and expression he or she was unable to pursue as a child. The commitment to take on such a fight derives from a combination of real excitement and love for the partner and the developmental drive to repair genital injury and reestablish one's masculinity or femininity on more solid ground. The conflicts can be complicated and difficult for a number of reasons: the depth of the anger, the fact that there is an interlocking of the two character structures, and because each partner has the tendency to use the couple as an equivalent to his or her own character, that is, in plain terms, to blame the other or the circumstance.

I have written here about the potential of the milieu of the couple for fueling the fires of conflict, stress, and pain. However, I do not want to leave the impression that I believe the milieu of the couple is nothing but a source of pain. On the contrary, the whole point is that in the very depths of all the sources of pain and conflict lie the seeds for growth, health, and fulfillment.

The more deeply it is possible to reach into the real source of pain and conflict, the stronger will be the potential for growth. To work toward the resolution of pain and conflict through the mutual enhancement and facilitation of the development of each partner is a most desirable goal. I trust presenting this material will foster the realization of that goal.

It is my belief that an enduring sexual union provides the greatest opportunity available to work through problems of sexuality and to find the deep fulfillment in life that love can bring, even when it means facing pain and conflict. The basic tool for facing pain and conflict is self-respect. A mutual facilitation exists between respect for self and respect for other. Respecting one's partner fosters self-respect, because it is impossible to find self-respect if there is the least disrespect for the one with whom one sleeps. Similarly, learning self-respect enhances the capacity for respecting the other.

My argument in this section centers on the view that when two people come together in a couple, there is created a uniquely heightened energetic milieu. This heightened energetic milieu is created by the mutually interacting excitations, love, focused sexual desires, sexual excitement, sexual arousal, and orgastic fulfillment of the two partners. While the partners' excitement with each other is focused in their sexuality, it rests on the broader and deeper sea of excitation which effects the body throughout and effects the partners in their other movements in the world.

The heightened energetic milieu, directly effecting the bodies of the partners, has the specific effects of awakening body memories and a developmental drive for the repair and restitution of genital injury. The movement toward repair of genital injury is guided by the goal of a fuller sense of the self as male or female and the realization of that sense in the genital embrace and orgasm.

There is usually some image—template might be a better word in this case—that the individual carries of a fully realized masculinity or femininity.

The portrayal of these templates of ideal masculinity and femininity are favorite and common themes of myth, folklore, and popular culture media. It seems as if we all have some inner sense of what we might be as man or woman, were we not injured, were we the way we were meant to be. This template, like an archetype, is activated in the couple relationship. I believe a body feeling or body sense underlies this image. The body sense derives from a sense in the individual of what it is to feel freer in the body, to feel more energy more fully charged into the pelvis, and to feel more deeply identified with one's own genital movement. This sense of the body's potential can be distorted into exaggerated proportions and form the basis for an unreal image, or it can serve as a guide toward health. In either case, it enters into the dream of love.

CHARACTER AND THE DREAM OF LOVE

Desire, more often than not, I believe, is guided by a dream of love, a dream that holds powerful sway over our lives and often enough remains, over time, uninfluenced by reality. And why should it be otherwise? Without a dream of love, the soul is an impoverished realm indeed! The heart's desire and the loin's yearning—do they not meet in a dream of sexual love? And is this not where fulfillment lies? I guess everyone at one time or another has dreamt such a dream.

However, sometimes dreams guide and sometimes they delude, interfering with the realization of the very goals they purport to represent. Since the reality of loving another real, warm person is—by far—better than any dream, we will not betray our dreams by learning more about them and how they work. To do so we first must see the characterological context of the dream of love, that is, how it emerges out of and is a function of the individual's personal adaptation. (It has sources in evolutionary adaptation as well.)

Larry

That Larry has a dream of love can be spotted a mile away. He is a tall youth, barely twenty, with good looks, sensitivity, and intelligence. He is definitely dreamy. He likes and needs intimate closeness, is empathic and understanding, and precociously mature in his self understanding. With these qualities and his good looks, he has no difficulty attracting girlfriends. Once he has the girl, however, he finds himself troubled with inner preoccupations.

His present girl, S, is a "beautiful person," but he feels separated from her by his preoccupations. He is all too conscious of his dream of love—his vision of love, desire, and sex. The problem is, somehow, the here-and-now real girl never fits it, so he does not enjoy himself very much with S, despite her beauty and their common interests. He expressed his dilemma very poignantly saying, "I have this big vision of love that takes me off into space, and then there is the practical love, what I actually do and feel with S. What I want is to have the practical love."

Larry's actual love is nearly obliterated by his dream of love. He is like one bewitched, and it does not take much exploration to find out that he was bewitched by his mother. His parents are exceptionally attractive people who were in constant conflict during Larry's childhood. His mother is an earthy, statuesque beauty, while his father, who is brilliant and accomplished in his work world, was never able to share an emotional life with his wife or children. While Larry's brother was absorbed in conflicts with his father, Larry gave himself sympathetically, body, heart, and soul to his mother.

"What's a boy supposed to do?" he asks, remembering his love and excitement for his mother. He summed up his character in this nutshell: Not only was it out of the question for him to "stick it out at her," she needed his tenderness, sweetness, and softness—and not his aggression.

Being that sweet, sensitive boy appeals to him. It means he is not an "asshole" like his brother and father, with their angry, dominating positions about everything and, even better, "It gets you in with the girls, I'll tell you." He also sensed that being sweet and good was a way of dealing with his fear: his fear of not being loved by his mother and his fear about his situation with his father.

Larry says, "I don't want to just jump in the sack with S. I want intimacy." She, on the other hand, seems to have no problem with "jumping in the sack." He is, after all, her chosen boyfriend at the moment, and she is an active, independent person in her own right. His reluctance and holding back reveal his conflict about moving beyond the sweet boy role he learned with his mother, giving up that comfortable, reassuring way of being with the woman. Sooner or later, S is going to feel, bodily if not consciously, the effects on her of his slowing things down, and will experience it as a stopping of her excitement. In his sweet boy role, his own sexual excitement is stopped. Sooner or later conflict will erupt as the strong movement arises in both to overcome their blocked excitement.

Underlying Larry's hesitancy to "jump in the sack" is the guilt, shame, fear, and self-hate originating in his passionate love for his beautiful mother, his great excitement about her, and his competition with his brother and father. Larry's uncertainty about moving strongly with his excitement about S will eventually activate whatever guilt *she* has about *her* sexuality, and, again, they will both have to deal with the conflict to resolve their guilts and to become freer with one another. The readiness for the engagement of the systems of self-hate, shame, and guilt is apparent.

Larry's movement toward healing his genital injury is disguised in his characterological way of dealing with sex with S. There is intense fear, and he has not yet been able to come to terms with his old dilemma. "I don't just want to jump in the sack. I want intimacy." The effort to establish "intimacy" is also an effort to establish a relationship of the sort he is used to, that is, one where he can be the good boy he once was. At the same time, it is an effort to free his desire, free a stronger sexual movement, and free a stronger masculine position with the woman, a movement now quite held back even with an affectionate and desiring partner. It is as if one strives to do over again the first love relationship, but this time make it turn out "right"—that is, to match the dream of love.

Larry's interesting idea of "practical" love points to his quandary as well as to something more universal. Love is not general; it is specific. It means choosing one person, one woman or one man. When the individual is dominated by a dream of love that is not based in a capacity for sexual love with a real person, he or she is unable to choose. The dream of love and, in fact, the drive to heal genital injury, helps in choosing a partner only when it is grounded in the basic movement toward sexual union.

Carl

Carl was a man in his mid-forties who had been very successful in his work world. For him the dream of love functioned as a profound disguise for the deeply troubling effects of severe violations of sexuality that had prevented him from marrying and establishing a family. The dream of love also took troubling forms. For example, one night, feeling severe distress, he had been unable to sleep. He would start to drift off to sleep, and then his thoughts would send him into a "convulsion, like epilepsy." His thoughts had to do with wanting a woman to love and hold him, wanting a family, and yearning for the woman, Dorie, with whom he had lived for six years, but had been reluctant to marry. He called these episodes of anguish "Dorie attacks." He worried himself frantic and filled himself with remorse about not having been able to make the commitment and have a family with her. When the terrible preoccupation about Dorie was put aside, he experienced painful feelings of loss and of being alone.

Part of what had happened to him was that his mother had "gotten her claws into him." She seductively involved him with herself, solicited his affection and sympathy, and at the same time undermined his sexuality. He realized that, in his feeling, he had stayed with her for many years, and that his lingering attachment to her made him sick. He expressed a great deal of rage and cried deeply. He recognized his guilt about his movement toward freedom and pleasure.

Carl's use of his dream of love—fantasies about having a marriage and family—hid his recognition of the reality of his situation with his mother. Had he not played his mother's game, so to speak, he would have been "lost," a "nothing." He would have been an "outcast," as he said, and he had the image of himself as a little boy shouldering his belongings on a stick and marching out into the world all on his own. In a profound way he actually had been alone as a child. The night he felt so convulsively anguished he had been close to feeling that aloneness. His aloneness and the terrible reality of his childhood precipitated his "Dorie attack."

In the following two stories, the dream of love takes on still other qualities and functions.

David

David, a precociously successful young man, not yet thirty, has a constant preoccupation with the various women he dates. While he has a deep misery and frequent underlying thoughts about suicide, he seems to understand his pain only in terms of the longing for one or another companion, but rarely in terms of what is within himself. At one point, he was particularly obsessed with a woman, how cold she was to him, rejecting of him, how much he loved her, how beautiful she was, and so on. These morose monologues were almost unbearable, and I wanted to interrupt him to say, "Please. I can't bear to hear any more about Miss N. Tell me about your mother." Or at other times, I asked him to stop talking for a moment, ground himself and breathe.

In reality, his mother was a borderline personality (according to the psychiatrist who knew her), nearly psychotic at times, who dragged him around like a small narcissistic extension of herself, took him into her bath until he was thirteen, and while actually neglecting him, seduced him into a profound sympathy and alignment with her. She committed suicide when he was sixteen, and he found her dying. He was numb at the funeral, has been in shock since, handles his feelings about his life with her and his father's rejection of him with denial, and is tormented with guilt.

David is rather undernourished and immature looking. Overall, his appearance is "cute" and boyish. He can sustain very little energetic charge while working with his body, gritting his teeth and bouncing uncontrollably after bending forward in a grounding position for only a few moments. Sadness then fills his eyes, and he finds a lump in his throat, although he cannot cry.

In his dream of love, he pins all his hopes on finding a woman to love him, and she will save him. He once told me how it works. He has to get through so many dates with the woman, performing, being the witty, urbane, successful man, and then he will *have* her. Then he won't have to perform, he will be able to be himself, and she will love and accept him. Then he will be saved—saved from his aloneness, his guilt, and his terrible feelings about himself, "someone as despicable as me," as he once said.

David's feelings in all this, while perhaps intense, are hardly uncommon. The individual often approaches courtship with the hidden (or not-so-hidden) agenda that by "finding the right person," he or she will be—in essence—saved and a damaged sexuality made whole. David expected that in being in a couple he would be restored to a happy life, and he will not have to bear his own pain and his own aloneness. The partner is sought as a way to heal an injured self, meet developmental needs that were unmet, make restitution for past pain, initiate energetic expansion and sexual aliveness, and in short, to provide salvation; and even in the seeking, the self is relinquished all the more. This is one example of a characterological use of the couple.

Originally character is formed, and subsequently maintained, for the purpose of managing unbearable pain. In David's case this is exactly the function "being in a relationship" is expected to serve. While a good relationship does offer a certain kind of protection in life, when it functions as a character formation, it conflicts with the possible development toward greater freedom and sexual aliveness and actually reinforces the sexual injury and loss of self.

When David allows himself to be pried away from the dream or his preoccupation about one or another woman, then unbearable feelings, memories, and images emerge, all that which the character is meant to suppress. He feels "a degraded image of myself" and recalls the horrifying memories of his mother's suicide. A terrible feeling of aloneness also emerges. David was alone as a child. The character is a desperate effort to reestablish, preserve, or maintain the vital connection, and so the adult's dream of love contains in it that desperate quest as well. The threat of losing the vital connection as a child is the threat of death.

The biological need for the vital connection can drive a relationship toward something that looks like fusion or symbiosis between the two partners. This is particularly true when the vital connections of childhood have been infused with anxiety by threat of loss, disruption, or violation. David's obsessions about his various women often had all the symptoms of a yearning for a fantasized symbiosis.

When two people are characterologically interlocked, there does seem to be an invisible, strong glue keeping them stuck together.[5] No sooner have the partners been pried apart at one point, then they are stuck back together at another. Where there appears to be this symbiosis-like stickiness, I attribute it to the factors I am describing: the lifelong biological need for vital connection, the developmental drive toward repair of genital injury, and the characterological use of the couple—all three of which are activated in the energetic milieu of the couple.

The need for vital connection is at all times a reality in the life of the individual. Similarly, on the organismic level, the drive to repair genital injury and resume the development and expression of movement once stopped is a drive which can at any time in the individual's life be directed toward health and integrated in a positive way. As the individual emerges from the embrace of his or her character, there is an individuation and differentiation that occurs, and in this process there may be also a kind of separation from a partner.

Carlotta

Carlotta seemed unable, at one point in her life, to sustain a sense of herself as a separate person and be in a couple too. She complained constantly that her lover did not respond to her expression of feeling. She wanted to be "understood" in a very special way. She wanted her lover's response always to reassure her—support her in *having* feelings, reinforce the *reality* of her feelings, and affirm her basic *right* to feel. Otherwise, she felt she was in a "battle" with her lover. She felt she had to separate herself entirely from him to save herself, or she had to submit entirely to him, relinquishing any sense of herself in order to retain the relationship with him.

Carlotta was striving to recreate the possibility of a vital connection in which she could have the experience of becoming and being a self. At the same time, she wanted the vital connection to serve as the context for her very strong developmental drive toward repair of genital injury and the opportunity for a fuller and more pleasurable genital realization. Her lover's understanding demonstrated the safe presence ensuring the sure reality of the vital connection. Her dream of love was a feelingful and comprehensive expression of her developmental needs, and through it she could begin to reestablish self-respect.

HOW CHARACTERS INTERLOCK

The interlocking of character structures refers to the ways in which the various facets of the characters and individual histories of the partners engage with and activate each other. The activation and engagement of the character structures allows each partner to use the couple as an equivalent to his or her *own* character structure. A schematic example may clarify this concept.

Consider two people, Dick and Jane, let's say in their late twenties, who found they were very excited about each other and fell in love, and now they are a couple. I am inclined to suppose that sooner or later there will be a fall from grace for this young couple and that the fall will take the form of painful conflict and ensuing unhappiness. "The honeymoon," as the old saying goes, "is over." The once-beloved will have turned, for a time—possibly a long time—into an object of hatred, fear, or loathing. Where once was a promise of paradise, now is a foreboding of the worst kind of pain. In any case, Dick and Jane are going to have to find some way of resolving the conflicts that now lie between them. All their dealings must be on a new ground. If they are able to get to know themselves and each other on a deeper level, however, their happiness might be restored and their fulfillment deepened, and they will have the added satisfaction of the process of maturation, development, and the gaining of wisdom.

Dick and Jane will no doubt each have their own individual dream of love, and while those dreams may have led them to one another, they will also be one source of the painful interlocking of their characters. A dream is still a dream, and the clash with reality can be a painful awakening. Each time the other is experienced as a source of pain, those dreams are sorely tried, and the experience is one of disappointment of more or less depth, maybe bordering on despair.

In their dreams of love, each will have an idealized image (based on their template of genital wholeness) of themselves and of their ideal partner. Similarly, hidden in the dream of love, or disguised by it, each will have a degraded, negative image of themselves and any possible partner.

The various facets of these images complement, engage, augment, and reflect each other like so many facing mirrors. Dick, for example, has hopes that Jane will be his (fantasized) ideal woman; he dreams, her sexual desirability will dissolve his own genital injury, and he will be more the man he would like to be. Such dreams on his part are more than likely to mesh with a wish, more or less delusional, on Jane's part to be perceived in just such a way. Not only would Dick then not have to recognize his painfully negative view of women (reflecting his difficulties with his mother), he would also not have to acknowledge to Jane that his deepest fear (and maybe his suspicious thought) is that *she is just like that*. Adding particular fuel to these potential fires is the likelihood that Jane's efforts to live up to the sexy image that Dick (and maybe she) hold out is driven by her fear of being just the opposite, a fear informed not only by her own negative images of herself and women but by Dick's negative images of women as well.

A complementary but converse process goes on at the same time, in the same breath. At times, it can seem that it is to Dick's emotional advantage (in a neurotic sense) to be fully convinced that Jane is as bad—that is, lives up to his negative image of women—as he wants to claim she is. Why? "If she's that bad, I'm okay," is the peculiar emotional logic involved here. If Jane is the sick, bad, crazy, nonsexual one, Dick can attribute his troubles to her, and he is saved the painful process of looking at what is wrong with him. Unfortunately, in our times, it is still not uncommon for Jane to be the accomplice in these negative attributions, since they may fit all too well with what she has already learned about women's inadequacies.

In fact, Dick can spare himself the trouble of self examination, with either a positive or negative image of Jane. If Jane is strong and sexy in his eyes, that could prove his manliness. On the other hand, if she is weak and dependent, that too could be used to "prove" that by supporting her, he is the strong one. The possibilities, it is easy to see, are exhaustingly endless for both Dick and Jane.

The fact of the matter is that the individual does not want to feel or look at his or her own deepest pain, nor in fact is he or she usually able to do so without help, and certainly not without some experience of life, often painful. The function of the character is to protect the individual from pain and to allow him or her to function in the world. It is very commonly assumed that "having a relationship" will do just that. In addition, the individual does not want to see the pain in the partner. He no more wants to look at hers than his own, and she no more wants to look at his than her own. There is, then, a certain barrier in each to a clear perception of the other. Working things out will have to include attaining a clearer perception of the other, just as surely as attaining a clearer perception of the self.

While all these possibilities have a potentially painful side, they can also have a positive impact on each of the partners. The couple then becomes an experiential, developmental laboratory in which the individuals find out more about who they are, face their bad sides and characterological distortions, become better people, and become more loving of the other person and less invested in making the couple function to meet self-protective, egocentric needs in a destructive way. This entails establishing self-respect in the service of respecting the other.

THE DEVELOPMENTAL LABORATORY OF THE COUPLE

When we choose a partner and a couple is created, we find ourselves in a developmental laboratory whether we will it or not. In fact, the milieu of the couple offers an enormous opportunity for maturation. The self-regulatory systems of both organisms evolve in the new milieu. The sexuality and sexual relations of the couple energize and focus changes and developments. The capacity for self-respect is developed and deepened as the necessity of learning the actual daily meaning of respecting the other deepens. When children enter the scene, and the couple becomes a family, the milieu changes again, and new developmental demands are placed on the partners. For now, I am going to keep the focus on the simpler situation of the couple, exciting enough and demanding enough just as it is.

Norma and Jim

The story of one couple's "laboratory," Jim and Norma, two attractive people in their early thirties, illustrates many of the findings discussed above. They were a characterologically entwined couple who were compelled to go through a number of painful separations before they were enough at peace with themselves and each other to make a home together.

Jim and Norma had been together for thirteen years. They had married and had chosen not to have children. They had experienced a great deal of misery together, yet each had a fear of leaving the other and being alone. Each had the feeling that the other, this *specific* other, was necessary to survival, and each had a deeply feelingful loyalty and love for the other.

Norma looked to Jim's response to her to provide her with a sense of self and a sense of aliveness. His withdrawal, passivity, and depression, especially on weekends, would devastate her, and she, too, would then go into a bitter, depressive withdrawal. She attributed her own lack of aliveness, her own deadness and lack of self to Jim's depressions. She thus avoided perceiving those states as inherent in herself, and she kept herself entwined with Jim. In her self-blaming way, she assumed it was all her fault, that Jim was sick and depressed because of the way she was, that she was "a cold-assed bitch." Then she would "try even harder": to do her therapy better, to attend to Jim better, and so on. She assumed responsibility for his depression. All this served to drive Jim deeper into his depression. Only after she finally managed to separate herself from Jim could she see in perspective this masochistic surrender of herself, supposedly in the service of trying to make someone else happy.

In Jim's physical appearance, there was much of the baby, of the infantile, but it was of an infant grown massive in the size and strength of its musculature. "There are no outs," was an expression he used that characterized his energetic distress. He had very little capacity for discharge or emotional expression. All his "outs," or outlets, were blocked. The pelvis was extremely tight, the throat was blocked, and the torso tended to blow up with undischarged energy. He was a writer, and writing was the best outlet he had, when he felt free to pursue it. His writing has an incredibly stark, sometimes horrifying impact, reflecting the horror, emptiness, and contactlessness of his characters' lives. In much of his free time, however, he sank into apathy, "vegging out" in front of the television set and eating. In contrast, Norma could hardly cease from activity, working, dancing, housecleaning.

One week she reported going home excitedly and saying, "Jim, I found out that we are alone, and I have to leave you alone." Her genuine discovery of such a feeling indicated the depth of her body sense that some kind of entwinement with a partner was the natural order of things, as if she had never developed a separate sense of self.

Norma's expression of feeling was much freer than Jim's. Her sobbing evoked Jim's hatred. To him she sounded like an abandoned baby crying (i.e., himself), and it drove him mad. He simply could not stand it. Jim not only rejected any needs for contact, warmth, closeness, or dependence, but he also had a grossly distorted view of such needs as monstrous and infantile. Since he was unable to experience the monster in himself, he saw it in Norma anytime she cried or expressed her needs. Jim's longings for a vital connection evoked in him an unbearably raw sense of abandonment and primary deprivation. In his withdrawal from the world, he surrounded himself with a bitter shell, countering every opportunity to receive what he needed most, a nurturing contact. Jim maintained himself in his shell of bitterness and rejected Norma's efforts to reach him.

Over time, Norma moved toward a sense of personhood. At one point she said that perhaps her dream of "having myself, radiating that and having something with other people, too—that may be for me too." As her sense of self developed, a crisis with Jim evolved. She felt more and more strongly that something had to change; she could no longer tolerate their conjoint deadness. Where before, any stance, even any separate feeling in itself, carried the threat of the loss of Jim, she now had more and more of her own ground to stand on.

Jim had reached the point where he was afraid he would break down, where he would finally feel how destroyed he was. Now his experience of Norma was that she was coming at him and coming at him, until he felt as if he were ready to kill himself or her. Allowing any closeness would have meant "giving in to someone who was going to subjugate me," someone who would have used and exploited him. Jim was at the end of his rope, but this was only an exaggeration of what he often experienced with Norma, and the reality and depth of his difficulty in being with her was finally on the surface.

A long separation grew out of the deepening crisis. Typically, following a weekend in which Jim had dropped into his depressive morass, they

would both be in intense pain, feeling hopeless and suffering from the contactlessness and sexual stasis that characterized their lives. The situation
came to a head in one dramatic moment.

One weekend, while swimming together, Norma affectionately reached
out her arms to Jim. To his own horror, Jim found himself reacting with
total revulsion. Instantly, they both felt that their marriage was ended. Jim
was appalled by his own reaction which, as he described it, was his revulsion at "this needy, sniveling woman (reaching out) to strangle me." Jim
moved out almost immediately following this incident. For both, their first
reaction was relief.

Both Norma and Jim had hateful mothers, mothers who actually hated
their child, expressed a lot of hatred in their lives, and evoked the child's
hatred of them. For Jim and Norma, each would again and again become a
hateful mother in the eyes of the other. For Norma, Jim's angry depression
represented her mother's depression and misery, for which she always felt
guilty and responsible as a child. Similarly, for Jim, Norma's compulsive
efforts, sadness and "dependence" roused him to guilt, rage, and a feeling
of being entrapped, since he felt he would have to sacrifice himself to her—
just as he had with his mother. With his hatred, guilt, and conflict about his
own needs, giving in to his need for Norma was a total threat, one that
could kill him. The mutual evocation of hateful mothers instigates one of the
deepest and most difficult forms of characterological entwinement.

Three or four months after this separation, they began again, very ten-
tatively, to see each other. For over two years they maintained separate
domiciles. During this time they managed a degree of pleasurable companionship; and at the same time they continued to work on their own problems. Toward the end of this period, through hard work, Jim improved his
professional and work situation, and they bought a house and began living
together—in earnest. The work in their developmental laboratory will continue, probably all their lives. The self-respect of each had evolved through
their dedication, and their deep feeling and love for each other won out
over very high odds.

THE BIOENERGETIC FUNCTIONS OF THE COUPLE

The bioenergetic functions of the couple are twofold: the realization of the
genital embrace and provision of the "developmental laboratory" for the
restitution of genital injury and the facilitation of adult development. These
functions are inherent in the biology of the person, and it is through them
that human life is fulfilled. The evolutionary, genetic function of the couple, reproduction and care of the young, is fulfilled as a result of the workings of the bioenergetic functions.

Reviewing some of the material seen in Jim and Norma's developmental
laboratory will clarify these concepts. For them, in the course of time and
with very hard work, their strengths triumphed over their adversities, even

though they walked along the edge of disaster many times. Through their trials they retained a good feeling for each other, in spite of everything, and each gradually gave up the conviction that the other was responsible for his or her own misery. They shared a genuine recognition, acceptance, and liking for the other, and a genuine sexual excitement about the other, the two conditions which permit but do not guarantee a positive outcome. They knew their own parents had not been able to find much pleasure in life or peace in their marriages, and Jim and Norma kept seeking the clues that would allow them to escape their parents' fate. Through all this, their self-respect developed. Theirs is a triumph of the human spirit, to be admired and learned from. How did they do it?

They eventually emerged—individually and as a couple—from years of pain and suffering. It is their endurance and triumph that make their story exceptional. At the same time, we must be sobered by the sheer suffering they lived through, even as such suffering is the fate of many. How do we understand and make sense of their pain and suffering? I embarked on this book to answer just this kind of question. Everything to this point is addressed to it, but here I wish to raise the question directly and review, from the perspective of the bioenergetic functions of the couple, some further aspects of the answers emerging from their experience.

We know this: their suffering is *in* them, and it *is* them. It is *their* suffering and it is *their* fate. Its origins lie in their personal histories. Their relationship, their "forming a couple," provided them with a "laboratory," as I like to call it, in which to do the "research" required to become free of their pain. This kind of research consists in the accumulation of consistently examined experiences. The milieu of their couplehood generated the experiences which informed them about their sexual selves, and these experiences are the basis for establishing self-respect, the repair of genital injury, and the development of the capacity for love.

Two elements of their suffering deserve to be singled out: the amount of destructive feeling contained by both and the repeated separation and reunion.

How are we to understand the inordinate destructive feeling each carried? Where does it come from? How did they manage it? There were moments when Jim's destructiveness seemed on the edge of becoming dangerous. Norma contained a great deal of destructiveness in her own, feminine, way in her unrelenting efforts to get things *right*.

Their destructiveness is a function of their entrapment in their character. As adults they are trapped in their character, just as children they were trapped in their relationships with their parents; they are "prisoners of childhood," in Alice Miller's felicitous phrase.[6] Character blocks the movement toward genital fulfillment creating frustration and tension and substituting destructive movement. The child is trapped in the conflict between his or her own movement and surviving in the face of familial realities. These traps of adulthood and childhood are very real and very destructive.[7]

Jim's torturous trap is completely revealed in the horrible swimming pool incident where he experienced Norma as coming at him as if she were going to strangle him by sheer virtue of her misery and needs. This experience had to reflect his childhood trap. He is the man with "no outs," and that meant, for one thing, that it was intolerable for him to experience his own longings for contact. Jim had been entrapped with his depressed parents in such a way that both his longings and his aggression had to be relinquished in the service of accommodating their impoverished and tragic situation. Norma was trapped between her mother and father, their sexual confusions, competitions, and hatreds.

The destructiveness that arises in adulthood is the result of these traps, and it is also a source of the aggressive energy needed to break out of the trap and move toward the goals of adult relations. The drive toward genital repair and genital realization takes destructive forms when that drive is entrapped and stopped.

The developmental drive toward genital realization and genital repair takes another distorted form that is very common but is not well illustrated in the story of Jim and Norma. Since this distortion involves egocentric and infantile behaviors, it is usually referred to as a *sense of entitlement*. (I sometimes use the term *baby prerogatives* to describe these behaviors.) The individual will act as if he "had the right"—had the right to whatever it might be that could make up for any childhood deprivation, conflict, trauma, or loss. Jim, for example, sensed he had the "right" to more or less completely disregard Norma's presence if and when he chose, in order to secure his own sense of freedom; Norma had the "right" to clamor endlessly for his presence.

Once the vital connection is established in adulthood, the individual tends to lay claim to his entitlements, often in no uncertain terms. These claims may have a certain validity, both historically and in the present, but their mode of expression is derived from a childhood form of self-regulation which is not functionally connected in any real way to the present. The conflicts generated by a sense of entitlement typically involve a good deal of sulking, spite, and various forms of temper tantrums.

Sometimes the partners' baby prerogatives conflict; sometimes partners take turns being baby; and sometimes one partner will successfully lay claim to all the entitlements, while the other acquiesces in a pseudoparenting role in relation to the entitled one. Needless to say, such claims can not be met in any real way, even when intimidated partners offer all sorts of substitutes for what the other one never received as a child. As with other forms of conflict, they have the potential to become the vehicles for establishing new forms of mutual respect and self-respect.

Repeated separation and reunion was the other striking element of the suffering in Norma and Jim's story. How should we understand these painful separations, and what was their function? They must be seen in the light of an effort to disentangle the characterological entwinement. The separations required of the adult partners reflect childhood separations needed but never completed, as from a mother or father. Paradoxically, separation is the opportunity to experience the pain, grief, loss, failure, and despair the person had always been unable to bear alone.

The laboratory of the couple provides the milieu in which adult self-respect can develop in the context of deepening respect for the other. This is an organismic process. Two bodies are learning to live and function together in a system of mutual regulation. Whole systems of self regulation are stressed and challenged, and new forms and modalities need to be developed.

The positive, desirable outcome of this process points toward the other bioenergetic function of the couple: The new milieu will eventuate in each partner having a heartfelt appreciation for themselves as well as for the other, allowing for the ebb and flow of excitement about the uniqueness and differentness of the other, so that, in the milieu they create, the never-ending delight, mystery, pleasure, and gratification of the genital embrace, will be ever present to return to again and again for its endless sources of renewal, joy, and love.

LIVING ONE'S SEXUALITY

Sexual repression and reproductive restrictions help explain why modern
human societies have become the most deadly organisms on the planet.

—Lynn Margulis and Dorion Sagan

THE LONG ROAD TO PERSONHOOD

The idea of "living one's sexuality" has two components, one inevitable, one
more guided by self-respectful choice. In reality, I live my sexuality, whether
I will it or not. More accurately, my sexuality lives me, just as life is lived
through my particular body. As I am born, breath, feel, act, decline, and die,
the underlying organismic processes of life proceed. My sexual being, with
its history of health and violation, rests on this broader organismic base, and
its state can be more or less alive, more or less expanded with more or less
feeling, and my sense of myself can be more or less informed by it.

The issue here is not whether sexuality exists and lives itself through me;
the issue is, What do I make of it? What do I make of my sexuality? What
do I make of my fate? What do I do about who I am? What do I do about
my desires, frustrations, pains? What do I do with my potential for passion, excitement, orgasm, and love? What do I do with my quest for fulfillment? What do I do in relation to the partners with whom I make love?
What do I do with myself when I encounter the effects of the violations of
my sexuality and I find myself trapped in painful, destructive repetitions?
The issue of living my sexuality has to do with how I answer these and
other questions.

These answers are not mental. They are lived answers, a way of life. In
the language of psychology, the answers have to do with the relations
between my ego and my body and sexuality. Every life contains answers to
these questions, and there are as many answers as there are lives.

The second component of the idea of living one's sexuality refers to a deliberate orientation to life in which my sexuality plays a central and guiding role, and often it will be *the* guiding role. In this orientation, I live in ways that foster the centrality of my sexual being, I strengthen my identification with my sexuality, and I make the commitment to dealing with the effects of childhood violations of sexuality. In making this commitment to my sexuality, I am making the commitment to the bodily process of establishing, strengthening, and maintaining self-respect.

Sexuality can remain central throughout life, not just in the years of early adulthood when sexual drive and urgency are at their height. Daniel J. Levinson, pioneering researcher and theoretician of adult development, has pointed out how little attention there has been to middle adulthood, as well as to late middle adulthood. The early work on sexuality by Freud and Reich was mostly based on young adults. We know little of the development of sexuality in middle adulthood and later, but these eras of life are increasingly important. As Levinson points out, the eras after forty are the time for individuation and personal development.[1] I believe that during those eras, living one's sexuality can be the fulcrum and the guide, and it can provide the enormous energy needed to advance the potentials of individuation in the middle and later years.

Carl

Carl's story illustrates the unfolding of personhood in middle adulthood through focusing on the living of his sexuality and the exploration of effects of the violations of his sexuality. It is no exaggeration to say that some of his road lay through the valley of the shadow of death, making it a long road to personhood. The brief encapsulation possible here hardly does justice to his story.

When I first met him, he had a way of presenting himself that looked very good. He was a handsome man with dark lively eyes, an extremely energetic and strong manner, a well-formed, strong body, and he was appealing to women. He had completed a Ph.D. very young and was established as a senior research scientist in a large corporation. He'd had many sexual relationships but had not married or had children.

He'd had periods even in the past few years when he felt he was going to go crazy. He felt terribly driven in his work, terribly tense, and often had sleepless nights. His facial expression was haunted, brooding, melancholic, and horrified. His body was extremely tight all over, the lower body seemed boyish, the pelvis in particular, and there was a peculiar prominence to the buttocks which I did not understand but felt sure was significant. Without being able to say exactly what it was, he conveyed that he had a deep sense that something was wrong, something sexual.

A sad, and quite tragic, episode from his youthful years in graduate school illustrates the struggle, pain, and suffering he experienced in his sexual life. He had met a woman, a fellow graduate student, who was obviously in love with him, and they had much sexual pleasure. This pleased him but also disturbed and frightened him terribly; it made him feel so dirty and ashamed that he was tormented and could not tolerate the tension. On one occasion, when they went to the movies, he felt as if everyone, maybe including his faculty, were looking at him, knowing what he was doing, and, nearly in a panic, he wanted to run out of the theater.

I raised the possibility that had any of his friends or faculty known that he had such a wonderful lover and companion they might have been pleased for him. He realized that at that time he could never in a thousand years have thought such a thing. He was unable to establish a relationship with her, and spent those years very alone. Yet he was obsessed with sex, masturbated compulsively, made furtive trips to massage parlors, and indulged in dealings with prostitutes which he had no intention of consummating. It was a sad life, and he immersed himself in his work.

Only over the course of several years of therapy did the traumas and horrors behind this sad story emerge. His discovery of masturbation illustrates what life was like for him in his teen years as well as his underlying sexual fear. He had always been peculiarly uninformed about sex. One day, while bathing just before dinner, he discovered masturbation quite by accident. His feelings and the ejaculation frightened him a great deal. When he sat down at the dinner table in the presence of his father, Carl began to cry out of sheer fear. Father, in his typical rageful and hateful way, said to Carl's mother, "The boy must have done something wrong."

A secret came out after four years of therapy. In his adolescence he had spied on his mother to see her naked in her bath and had been terribly excited and frightened. This was strictly the culmination of his mother's seduction begun when Carl was small. It was two more years before the memories of his sexual excitement about his mother finally broke through. During one summer he stayed with her in their summer cottage while his father remained in the city. He was absorbed in a tremendous excitement about her. Probably in a near-delusional state, he felt he could have slept with her and that she was on the verge of it.

The excitement was fused with a feeling that this was bad. He was aware of his father; he was a bomb that could go off at any moment, annihilating Carl and everybody else. We could now well understand the depth of his fear of his father, for whom he had a profound terror and rage. A feeling of poison in his pubic area he experienced so often could be understood in light of the intense conflict between his incestuous genital desires and his terror, guilt, and actual frustration.

The catharsis of these body memories emerged with deep crying, intense fear, and remembered excitement. Then deeper feelings in his body and about himself emerged. "I feel dirty. So dirty that I feel a grotesque horror, associated with a painful helplessness—that is what it is like to feel that dirty. I feel like a smelly, stinky vegetable, and that's what I do to women. A wretched puky disgusting kid." Even with these terrible feelings, he was able to feel, "It's wonderful and painful and very scary to have such a deep awareness of [pointing to his genital] right down here."

Self-respect is built with experiences such as this and the identification with the genital is strengthened and cleared of bad feeling. This development continued over the next few years, into the seventh and eighth year of therapy. He then said,

[When I touched my genitals] I felt a very old feeling that was so shameful. My genitals are me. They haven't been me. They've been this thing I've had to deal with—something that was an embarrassment to my family. Genitals didn't exist in my family. I associate my chest with a more tender, soft, loving part of me. Maybe my genitals could be loving too. For somebody who had a family where genitals are shameful, where they don't exist, it's a step to feel they could not only be a part but a loving part. This feels very new.

As Carl confronted these and many more aspects to the violation of his sexuality, his tensions, depression, and anxieties gradually subsided. He was able to establish a lasting relationship with a woman. The effects of his therapy, while it focused on his sexuality, spread into the rest of his life, particularly his work life. With the diminution of his terror of his father, he was able to establish a "parity," as he called it, with the men he worked with and reap more of the fruits of his excellent work and productivity. All of this took dedication and hard work, and I can hardly convey in so brief a section the courage and integrity with which Carl walked the long road to his personhood.

SEXUAL LOVE

Sexual love is the fruition of the development of a self-respecting sexuality. The hallmark of sexual love is an irresistible imperative for sexual, genital union with the object of one's love. When that is denied, there is a deep and painful disappointment and frustration. When such love is—or even seems—unavailable, there is a deep yearning, sometimes very painful and a feeling of loneliness. Sexual love involves the heart, and its passion arises when the heart is informed by the genital and the blood from the heart fills the genital.

Sexual love encompasses the whole body and the whole being. Opening the eyes to the sight of the beloved initiates sexual passion, opening the pathway to the heart. As the heart stirs, there is a yearning that moves up from the heart to the eyes and the arms in a movement to reach out for contact. At the same time, the excitement of the sight of the beloved and the promise of remembered pleasure and gratification stir the genitals whose movements are energized by the downward pulsation of the heart's energies and blood. Tenderness, care, and continued association are consequences of our responses to sexual pleasures given and received, and are usually enough to balance the natural inclinations to promiscuous mating in both male and female. Tenderness depends on open-heartedness and a feelingful appreciation of the other.

Self-respect is the basis for respect of the other. Personal fulfillment is impossible without respect for the other. Without the respect for the other, and the love for the other, sexual gratification will not develop into an ongoing sense of sexual fulfillment. With the acknowledgment of the other, gratification and pleasure are a foundation for choice, commitment, love, and a *wish* for the other to be there always.

Personal fulfillment depends on addressing those violations of sexuality in one's history that remain as body memories. We are all, even those raised by the most loving and caring of parents, at least partly like the biblical Jacob. "Jacob was left alone. And a man wrestled with him until the break of dawn. When he saw that he had not prevailed against him, he wrenched Jacob's hip at its socket, so that the socket of his hip was strained as he wrestled with him. . . . The sun rose upon him as he passed Penuel, limping on his hip." We are only partly like Jacob because, while he is told that he has "striven with beings divine and human, and have prevailed,"[2] we have by no means prevailed, in fact none have, yet everyone *is* still left limping with the mark of an archetypal struggle in the expression of their sexuality.

There are those who are presented to the populace—and those who present themselves—as having prevailed and as having no limp. While this is the worst sort of deception, there are those who wish to believe it. These self-delusions and illusions of specialness, fame, and whatever replace a communally shared vision of the nature of humankind which combines humility and self-respect, dignity and ordinariness. Love and self-respect arise out of natural movement and facing the deep struggles of one's existence, not illusions of specialness.

The capacity for sexual love requires living in the simple reality that the essential nature of adult human beings is sexual, the basis of human identity is sexual, and that sexual identity is organized around the genital. Living in this simple reality carries self-respect with it because it is based on nothing more nor less than a profound and respectful recognition by the individual of his or her own body and sexuality. Self-respect is not, then, a separate dimension from sexuality. For the individual, the realization of sexuality is through self-respect, and self-respect is realized through sexuality.

Human identity is not founded in philosophical, religious, ethnic, or nationalistic abstractions, be they of the highest order, nor, ultimately, is life's meaning to be found there for those whose genital being is curtailed. If these "higher" abstractions are not in the service of the sexual self-respect of humanity, they lead—as today is everywhere apparent—to war, massacre, and destruction.

The violations of sexuality violate the individual's capability for sexual love. Violations of sexuality arise when the adult generation refuses or is unable to acknowledge and respect a child's inherent developmental imperative toward their own adult sexuality. For each person, the recognition of the violations of sexuality in one's own history are the first and most basic step in taking responsibility for one's own pain, for one's own body, for one's self, for one's life—and often for the respectful care of children. This form of responsibility is self-respect. Self-respecting sexuality minimizes adult destructiveness and emphasizes devotion to mutual respect and sexual love—the most ordinary and natural of positive human movements.

Loving a child is obviously different from the love that occurs between adults. Heartfelt love for a child does not become genital passion. When the two—love for the child and love between adults—are confused, even in fantasy, the child is in jeopardy. It is necessary to love the child separately enough to see the boy or girl as the sexually matured man or woman he or she will one day hopefully become—if nature is allowed to take her course. The same respect we offer to adults for the privacy and privilege of their own sexual life, is also, within developmental realities of care and protection, due to any child. This is not an argument urging "permissiveness." It is a recognition of the nature of the organism and a description of what it means to respect the development of self-respecting sexuality from the moment of birth.

REFLECTIONS ON PERSONAL FULFILLMENT

Sex and self-respect are the ground of personal fulfillment. A fulfillment is an effect, an outcome, whether it be the effect of the activity of an hour or a lifetime. People find fulfillment in many significant ways. A woman finds it in bearing her child. Fulfillment may be found in the carrying out and completion of any task, large or small. Dedication to a cause, common enterprise, or group whose goals represent desired ends; to a profession dedicated to the realization of desired ends; to one's work, marriage, and children are all sources of fulfillment. There are those whose fulfillment comes from devotion to the holy or to the carrying out of sacred duty. The place of love in a fulfilled life has been long recognized.[3]

Fulfillment is found in virtually every aspect of human activity and in virtually every way of life. The fulfillment does not come about from a particular activity, way of life, outcome, practice, or end result. It comes from the devotion to the process, itself, the effect on the self of being devoted and the carrying out of the devotion. Fulfillment is a lingering effect on the self; it represents a change in the self; it carries a positive affective state, perhaps similar to joy. People have been known to say that having been fulfilled in certain ways, death is easier to accept.

Lack of fulfillment signifies frustration or disappointment, and something deeper as well. The opposite of personal fulfillment is to be found in the experiences of despair, loneliness, and meaninglessness; it is to be found in a feeling that life has passed one by, that one is or has been forever outside of life, that one has missed the essence of life. Seen in this light, personal fulfillment is no small matter. It represents the measure of a life, a summing up in a whole state of being all of a life's meanings, experiences, and activities. This is the context for understanding the place of sex and self-respect in an individual life.

There is ancient wisdom which suggests that fulfillment of the self can be realized only through devotion to that which is outside of the self, or through a relinquishment of the self. Knowledge of this paradox is ancient.[4]

The position that sex and self-respect are the ground of fulfillment forces that paradox into sharp focus. It would seem as if sex and self-respect point only in toward the self, not out to that which is beyond and outside the self. The resolution of this paradox is seen in the capability for sexual love which develops out of a self-respecting sexuality. Love is the paradigm for that which both takes one beyond oneself and allows the fulfillment of self. Sex and self-respect, as the basis of personal fulfillment, provides no exception to the rule that fulfillment entails a movement toward that which is beyond the self.

There is a certain form of objectivity to the path of following one's own body and sexual nature. It is objective in the sense that the body has its own life and to be fully followed, the ego and egocentric motivations must be set aside to allow the body its own life and movement. In this sense "objective" contrasts not with "subjective" but rather with "egocentric." Each person's body is an object in nature and has its own existence, just as any other animal's body. Out of the ego's management of the body in its environment, we develop the illusion that our own ego is somehow the sun around which life orbits. Nothing could be further from reality.

It is a beautiful and joyful experience to be able to give in to the body, to the body as the self, in a nonegocentric way. To do so is a source of joy and fulfillment. Such experiences are always very close to those of sexual love, and are also available to those who have no one immediately in their life for sexual love. In orgasm, to the extent that it approaches a deep surrender and giving in, there is also a degree of loss of consciousness or self-consciousness, that is, loss of ego.

The path, or approach, to personal fulfillment described here is not that different from descriptions found in the context of some religious and spiritual teachings. Sex and sexuality are not usually considered an essential feature of religious or spiritual life, and the discussions I presented are biological and psychological, not religious or spiritual. However, if humans have acquired any wisdom through the ages, there must be a correspondence between the deeper meaning of religion and the biological, including the sexual.[5]

Spiritual qualities do not exist apart from the sexual person. The holy qualities of life and the spiritual approaches to life are not lost in a life lived out of sexuality. Without sexuality, spirituality may become arid[6] or even reduced to its emotional opposite, as when the individual blocked and deprived of a fulfilled sexuality is left in a state of frustration, despair, and emptiness.

SOCIALITY

Just as sexuality is the foundation of self-respect, so it is the foundation of the individual's sociality. Our sociality is a natural function of our biology. Our inclination to participate in group, social life and to regulate our behavior in accordance with the mores of our social group is inherent in our behavior.[7] The self, in some of its functions, is an outcome of our evolution as a group animal.

In saying that we have a natural sociality, I am not saying that we are naturally "good" in some way; we are evil just as naturally as we are good, but evil is also expressed socially. Humans are group participants.

A life path grounded in sex and self-respect is the most basic way of taking responsibility for one's self—personally and socially. With that grounding, the inclination to be involved with one's own kind in positive ways will emerge more freely, less begrudgingly, and less distorted by envy, rage, rebellion, and revenge. The quest for beauty, participation, and contribution is more freely pursued along with the quest for fulfillment in sexual love than with frustration, loneliness, and despair. If we violate children's sexuality and sexual development from the beginning of their lives through their adolescence, their social participation will eventually be another kind of violation. There is no difference between social and sexual development. A person living the life of the body and sexuality is more relaxed and social and also in tune with common human joys and sorrows.

Sex, on the surface, seems in opposition to that which is social. Sex takes one away from the social group to the gratification of one's own bodily desires. Indeed the needs of the group, or even one's own social needs, might be in conflict with sexual needs. There is a polarity involved, yet self-respecting sexuality and self-respecting (and other respecting) sociality rest on the same underlying structure.

The implications of the polarity between love and work[8] are clearer if "work" is replaced with "sociality." Each individual participates in some way in his or her social group, regardless of whether the participation is called work or something else. Consider an old fashioned example, but one still pertinent to the issue of sexuality, that of the woman who "stays home" as a wife, mother, and "homemaker" (and was not, in the past, considered to have been "working"). The man, the husband, "went out and worked." The real issue is that her "homemaking" and his "work" are both forms of sociality. The diminishing of the woman's sociality in comparison with the man's and setting work off against sex and love in such stark fashion are both distortions and ones that have been typical to our society.

SEX AND SEXUALITY IN TODAY'S WORLD

Humankind will be sexual as long as the species exists. What we make of it is what in the end determines the extent to which sexuality is the underpinning and basis of individual life, its source of vitality, and its source of self-respect. What we make of it determines whether or not children are raised in respect and allowed a self-respect based in their sexuality. The studies of the violations of sexuality discussed in Part II reveal some share—and not a small share—of what present society does in fact make of sex and sexuality.

My approach to sex and sexuality fits in to today's world in a fashion that parallels the efforts and concerns of the conservation and environmental movements and their efforts at preservation of the earth's habitat. The most seriously destructive side in this debate takes the form of dismissing environmental concerns as the freakish preoccupations of a few misguided conservationists. There are also the few who are capable of holding the vision of life on earth as a unitary biological system and the wisdom to know that all human enterprise lives only in that system. Sex and ecology— toward both there is a peculiar ambivalence and both hold a peculiar centrality for human life. In the case of sexuality, too, the most destructive form of belief and behavior is that which dismisses the issues or tries to assign some form of immorality to any positive approach to sexuality.

The parallels with environmental concerns are by no means coincidental. Sex and sexuality are the final and ultimate inner preserves of wildness, freedom, and natural being of the human species. Our survival as a species is tied as surely to our sexuality, this inner biological basis of our being, as the survival of any species is tied to their external habitat. Individually and collectively, we can further our well-being by recognizing this biological foundation and incorporating that recognition into our way of life.

It is from this perspective, in any case, that I look out into the society at large to consider in it the place and role of sex and sexuality. It is from this perspective that I raise questions whose purpose is to discover those aspects of the society which support and those antithetical to this perspective. I am accustomed to hearing the same questions from those with whom I work. As people move to free themselves from old constraints, to find in themselves a fuller movement and expression of their bodily being, I hear them begin to think aloud about where they might find support for that kind of movement in their world at large.

How do things stand? As things stand, in the popular culture, sexuality is used very much as one more resource to be exploited much in the same way as other natural resources are, water, timber, minerals, soil, and so on. Sexual imagery floods the media and every form of popular entertainment. It is used to sell products of every sort. Erotic life is so much in the service of economic life, that the realities of love and sex are lost in the profusion of activity and imagery arising from the market.[9]

In addition, and more subtly and perhaps more destructively, the complex of genital attitudes used in many areas of social life to support egoistic ambitions and goals results in the extremely selfish and asexual use of sexuality.[10] The life of the body is often at odds with the life of the ego. Ego drivenness demands endless work; and, where it does not exploit the energies that might go to love and companionship, it just as often demands putting one's sexuality into the market place as one more commodity or one more ego-enhancing attribute. The life of the body demands relaxation, sexual fulfillment, pleasure; and it requires that productivity and social involvement are commensurate with the person's energies and these other needs. Today, the person is often trapped in a conflict between self-aggrandizement and ordinariness, between egocentric specialness and healthy commonness.[11]

In comparison, there are a few who care and who wish to devote their resources—time and money—to develop the capacity for sexual love and the true sense of self that can only be found through sexuality. These are the conservationists of sexuality, the builders of a sexual ethic, and, while there are some few respected social avenues for their efforts, I believe that for the most part they must build on their own.

The widespread state of sexual confusion and misery leaves many people with an underlying, hidden hatred of sex , of all that is genuine in sexual life, and of all that is genuine in sexuality. I take the common diminution of women (or their idealization) as the most obvious and widespread indication and symptom of that state, a widespread misogyny. The profusion of sexual imagery in the popular culture actually exacerbates this hatred by inducing a feeling of personal failure and lack through the insidious comparison with pop culture icons.

What of the hatred of sex and sexuality? Metaphorically the hatred goes up and it goes down, as the up and down pertain to the human body. Some of the objects at which the hatred is directed represent functions of the upper end of the body (ego and father), and some the lower end (sexuality and mother).

The upwardly directed hate is directed to all that represents the father in the culture, a widespread ambivalence that can become loathing directed at social institutions. On the other side, as a way of handling the ambivalence, is the slavish devotion and submission to such representations which become fixed in harmful rigidities, violent loyalties, discriminatory righteousness, and inner enslavement.

The hatred directed downward is derived from the hatred of the mother, and is directed at all that represents woman. It is directed toward the softer feelings, tender love, sexual love, the body and the genitals, and the earth. It comes out in greed, environmental destructiveness, and the hatred of women.

At the same time, people become more removed from their own bodies in their daily work lives as their work becomes more engaged with technology. The incredible management of digitized information through computational technologies creates a Peer Gynt world of wizardry with which the vulnerable, naked, sexually uncertain self is a miserable contrast. The gap between bodily reality and the imagery supported by technology, which also drives the imagery of popular culture, widens and has arrived at the point where, in the minds of many, it is the body that is unreal.

A SEXUAL ETHIC

Something is clearly lacking. The same thing is lacking in regard to sexuality as is lacking in regards to the attitudes toward the natural world. In *The Diversity of Life*,[12] Edward O. Wilson seeks the basis for an environmental ethic, an attitude based in appreciation—love, really—for the natural world. This same kind of ethic is needed in the case of sex and sexuality, and the basis for them both—sexuality and environment—is the same. They both begin with a recognition of our own bodily, biological, natural reality and our place in the natural world. In a sexual ethic, the capacity for sexual love is to be seen as the biological heritage and inner wilderness of every human being. From the beginning of life to its end, sexual life would be recognized, preserved, and supported. The sexual ethic cultivated in this way would be based first and foremost on respect for sex and human sexuality.

A sexual ethic would promote a practice in which the daily familiarity of sex and sexuality evokes appreciation, warmth, reverence, and humility. The attitude which I have in mind would lead to wholehearted, joyful appreciation of sexual life as adults and a respect for that capability in the future for children. This attitude leads to a way of living in which the inner wilderness of sexuality is nourished and preserved and in which sexual life and experiences are received with gratitude. Living in this way means that sex is experienced not as a resource to be exploited but as something like the refreshing spring that runs through life. In short, it means respect for life.[13]

I believe there is a natural proclivity toward a sexual ethic; at the same time that proclivity is eroded by deep sources in our social life and traditions. The long-standing ambivalence about sex and sexuality is greater even than the ambivalence toward the natural world. Respect is usually reserved for idealized objects representing something "elevated" in relation to daily life and from which we therefore feel removed. Sexuality, associated with the lower realms of the body, does not usually carry such claims.

An ethical approach to sexuality requires that we look at and experience the pain associated with the violations of sexuality in our own development. It requires that we see and experience our own and our partners' sexual, genital injury and even the injury we may have inflicted on our own children. The images of the self that may emerge from these examinations often contrast miserably with the idealized fantasies offered by the wider culture. Many factors contribute to an ever widening gap between individual personal reality and culturally proffered fantastical images.

Wilson writes:

[H]uman advance is determined not by reason alone but by emotions peculiar to our species, aided and tempered by reason. What makes us people and not computers is emotion. We have little grasp of our true nature, of what it is to be human. . . . Humanity is part of nature, a species that evolved among other species. The more closely we identify ourselves with the rest of life, the more quickly we will be able to discover the sources of human sensibility and acquire the knowledge on which an enduring ethic, a sense of preferred direction, can be built.[14]

As a biologist, Wilson identifies certain characteristics, all of which point, I believe, to the sexual nature of our species: our emotional life, our evolution, and our close tie with the rest of life. A "grasp of our true nature" is close at hand by first recognizing the essential sexual nature of the human being. Without this recognition our understanding flounders endlessly. With a grasp of sexuality, we know a great deal of what it is to be human. We can understand the deepest core of our emotions, we can recognize our evolutionary heritage, and we can identify closely with nature.

Our failure to recognize ourselves in our sexuality is a result of the degree to which our minds have been clouded by the ambivalence that has long surrounded sex and sexuality in our civilization. It is time to relinquish the cloud that has surrounded this matter and to once again rejoin our intellect with our simple bodily realities. In the biblical story, Jacob struggled with "beings divine and human," and so do we all. We gather strength thereby. In each individual's very personal experience of their own sexuality, nothing is more important than to come to terms with the reality of the tension, ambiguity, ambivalence, guilt, and shame that so commonly infuses sexuality. This is done by freeing the body, learning and developing self-respect, and a recognition of the body as self. Long-held beliefs and dreams will inevitably be overturned, but they will be supplanted with a deeper contact with life which can only be the basis for a firmer faith in life, respect for one's self, and a deeper capacity for sexual love.

NOTES

ABBREVIATIONS

Char. An.: Wilhelm Reich, *Character Analysis.*
CP: Sigmund Freud, *Collected Papers,* Vol. 1–5.
Function: Wilhelm Reich, *The Function of the Orgasm.*
IIBA Journal: Bioenergetic Analysis: *The Clinical Journal of the International Institute for Bioenergetic Analysis,* (IIBA, 144 E. 36th St., New York, NY 10016).
SE: Sigmund Freud, *Standard Edition of the Complete Psychological Works.*

INTRODUCTION

1. I am heterosexual. I believe that in sexual matters I can write honestly only about what I know bodily. I sincerely hope that what I say is applicable, and certainly not in any way inimical, to those who choose same-sex partners.

CHAPTER 1: SEX AND SELF-RESPECT IN PERSONAL FULFILLMENT

1. *Function,* Chap. 7, p. 237. (Note: Since the pagination of various editions of *Function* and *Char. An.* differ, I have included chapter numbers in the references to facilitate location of extracts.)

2. Ibid., Chap. 7, pp. 234–238. Further discussion of this concept is found in *Function,* Chap. 2, 3.

3. The historian Peter Gay utilizes this view in his series, *The Bourgeois Experience: Victoria to Freud.* See Vol. 2, *The Tender Passion,* p. 4.

4. Erik H. Erikson wrote in 1950, "The study of identity, then, becomes as strategic in our time as the study of sexuality was in Freud's time" (as if the study of sexuality were no longer "strategic"). He went on to acknowledge the continued relevance of sexuality and concluded, "Different periods thus permit us to see in temporary exaggeration different aspects of essentially inseparable parts of personality." *Childhood and Society,* 2d ed. pp. 282–283. His acknowledgment of the

"strategic" significance of the study of sexuality is ambivalent at best, and I see this as an indication of a turning away from sexuality.

5. A remarkable account of such a conspiracy of silence is to be found in "Town Secret," *Boston Globe Magazine,* August 29, 1993. A whole town managed for years to deny the widespread sexual abuse of children by a priest of one of the town's churches.

6. I first noted this distinction in the writings of C. G. Jung.

7. Reich's first publication on these matters was in 1934 in a theoretically and clinically brilliant and original paper called "Psychic Contact and Vegetative Current," which is published as Chap. 13 in *Char. An.* Capturing the kind of beautiful insights this work opened up are the lines, "Man's vegetative life is only part of the universal process of nature. In his vegetative currents, man also experiences a part of nature" (p. 354). Between 1934 and 1938, Reich produced a body of experimental and theoretical studies on vegetative currents, published in *The Bioelectrical Investigation of Sexuality and Anxiety.* This work predates the kind of sex research which Masters and Johnson would develop decades later. Reich summarized his thought on vegetative currents in *Function.*

8. The epistemological complexities of a concept such as "the self" were deeply explored by Ludwig Wittgenstein, the acknowledged genius of twentieth-century philosophy. An accurate and accessible interpretation of Wittgenstein is provided by Ray Monk in *Ludwig Wittgenstein: The Duty of Genius.* See the discussion of William James's conception of the self, pp. 477–478. As to the relationship between the body and the self, a glimmer of what Wittgenstein's thought offers can be seen in a remark like, "It is like the relation: physical object—sense impressions. Here we have two different language-games and a complicated relation between them. — If you try to reduce their relations to a *simple* formula you go wrong." Ludwig Wittgenstein, *Philosophical Investigations,* Pt., IIv p. 180. From Wittgenstein we also have the well-known, brilliant apothegm, "The human body is the best picture of the human soul" (*Philosophical Investigations,* Pt. IIiv, p. 178).

9. Marjorie Taggart White, "Self Relations, Object Relations, and Pathological Narcissism," in *Essential Papers on Narcissism,* Andrew P. Morrison, ed.

10. See Fred Pine, *Drive, Ego, Object, & Self.*

11. On self-acceptance see Alexander Lowen, *Narcissism: Denial of the True Self,* p. 31. On self-expression, self-assertion, and self-possession, see *Pleasure: A Creative Approach to Life,* pp. 103–110, 147–165.

12. White, "Self Relations, Object Relations, and Pathological Narcissism."

13. Sydney E. Pulver, "Narcissism: The Term and the Concept," in *Essential Papers on Narcissism,* Andrew P. Morrison, ed., pp. 103–111.

14. White, "Self Relations, Object Relations, and Pathological Narcissism," pp. 160–16l.

CHAPTER 2: IDENTIFICATION WITH THE GENITAL

1. Thomas Gregor, an anthropologist, discusses "sex-negative" and "sex-positive" cultural orientations in *Anxious Pleasures: The Sexual Lives of an Amazonian People,* p. 4.

2. See Gregor, *Anxious Pleasures,* pp. 40–43, where he describes the Mehinaku's identification of gender and self with primary sexual characteristics.

3. Myron R. Sharaf, *Fury on Earth: A Biography of Wilhelm Reich,* pp. 56, 58.

4. See Wilhelm Reich, *Passion of Youth, An Autobiography, 1897–1922.* Reich's youthful anguish finds poignant expression in this autobiographical fragment. In *Fury on Earth,* Sharaf discusses Reich's own awareness of his childhood sexual development on pp. 41–46, 68–70. Philip M. Helfaer remarks on effects of his developmental experiences of which Reich seemed unaware in Review of *Passion of Youth,* in *IIBA Journal,* Vol. 4, No. 1 (spring 1990), p. 164.

5. See *Function,* Chap. 4. Two collections of Reich's earlier papers contain his first papers on this subject. *Genitality: In the Theory and Therapy of Neurosis* and *The Bioelectrical Investigation of Sexuality and Anxiety.*

6. *Function,* Chap. 4, p. 87.

7. Wilhelm Reich, "Orgastic Potency," Chap. 1, *Genitality,* pp. 30–31.

8. Humor, derision, and envy all find expression in Woody Allen's movie *Sleeper.* A recent novel offers an example of how otherwise intelligent people cannot seem to stop making jokes about Reich: *The Mind Body Problem.* In *Childhood and Society,* 2d ed., Erikson's description of genitality (p. 265) is right out of Reich with no citation. Sharaf points out this unacknowledged borrowing of Erikson's in *Fury on Earth,* p. 102.

9. *Char. An.,* Chap. 7, p. 155.

10. Ibid., Chap. 4, p. 51.

11. Ibid., Chap. 7, p. 155.

12. Ibid., Chap. 4, p. 46.

13. Ibid., Chap. 7.

14. Ibid., Chap. 4, p. 42.

15. Ibid.

16. In his biography, *Freud: A Life for Our Time,* Peter Gay characterizes Freud precisely in these terms—bourgeois, Victorian. In his extensive three-volume history, *The Bourgeois Experience: Victoria to Freud,* he is at pains to place Freud and Freud's intellectual development in this context.

17. *Function,* Chap. 5, pp. 109–110.

18. Ibid., p. 110.

19. *The Bioelectrical Investigation of Sexuality and Anxiety,* p. 67. The concepts of core and periphery are developed in this text, especially Chap. 2. For example, see pp. 33, 67–68. See *Char. An.,* Chap. 13, p. 313, where Reich graphically depicts anxiety as "the tendency to escape into oneself," or p. 316 where anxiety is described as "the expression of crawling into oneself." This material is summarized in *Function,* Chap. 7.

20. *The Bioelectrical Investigation of Sexuality and Anxiety,* p. 69.

21. Ibid., p. 68.

22. By a biologist, William E. Seifriz, whose observational style was similar to Reich's. Filmed lecture and demonstrations. 1954. I do not know if this film is any longer available. The International Institute for Bioenergetic Analysis in New York has copies of it.

23. This paper is published as Chap. 13 in *Char. An.*

24. Ibid., p. 313.

25. This is in *The Bioelectrical Investigation of Sexuality and Anxiety,* Chap. 1, "The Orgasm as an Electrophysiological Discharge."

26. Ibid., pp. 4–5.

27. Ibid., p. 4.

28. *Function,* Chap. 9, p. 338.

29. Ibid., p. 336.

30. Ibid.

31. Ibid.

32. Reich's formulations regarding neurosis here meet Freud's idea of the "actual neurosis." See Sharaf, *Fury on Earth,* pp. 88–90.

33. *Char. An.,* Chap. 14, p. 394.

34. *Function,* Chap. 9, p. 337.

35. "Psychic Contact and Vegetative Current," *Char. An.,* Chap. 13.

36. *Char. An.,* Chap. 13, p. 321.

37. Ibid.

38. Ibid., p. 326. He gives two pages of such descriptions.

39. *Function,* Chap. 7, pp. 241–242.

40. Ibid., p. 242.

41. *Char. An.,* Chap. 13, p. 345.

42. Ibid., Chap. 9, pp. 368–372.

43. ". . . involuntary trembling, jerking of muscles, sensations of hot and cold, itching, crawling, prickling sensations, goose flesh, and the somatic perception of anxiety, anger and pleasure." *Function,* Chap. 7, p. 242.

44. *Char. An.,* Chap. 9, Chap. 8, p. 365.

45. See *Function,* Chap. 8, p. 275.

46. *Char. An.,* Chap. 14, p. 365.

47. The orgasm reflex is discussed in Chap. 14 of *Char. An.* and in Chap. 8 of *Function.*

48. *Char. An.,* Chap. 9, p. 361.

49. Ibid., Chap. 14, p. 358.

50. Ibid., p. 356.

51. See *Function,* Chap. 8, pp. 264, 310–311, 320 ff., Chap. 9, p. 337. Also see Wilhelm Reich, *Cancer Biopathy.* Also, Alexander Lowen, *Love, Sex and Your Heart.*

52. Such as that found in Robert M. Sapolsky, *Why Zebras Don't Get Ulcers, A Guide to Stress, Stress-Related Diseases, and Coping.*

53. *Char. An.,* Chap. 14, p. 359.

54. Many observers consider the rate of depression, for example, to be epidemic. See G. L. Klerman, and M. M. Weissman, "Increasing Rates of Depression," *Journal of the American Medical Association,* Vol. 261 (1989), pp. 2229–2235.

55. *Char. An.,* Chap. 13, p. 304.

56. Reich, *Passion of Youth,* pp. 144–145.

57. *Char. An.,* Chap. 14, p. 392.

58. Lynn Margulis and Dorion Sagan, *Mystery Dance: On the Evolution of Human Sexuality,* p. 41.

59. "[I]f orgasm in women evolved any role in evolution, it is still relatively minor compared with that of . . . ejaculation of sperm." Ibid., p. 85.

CHAPTER 3: SEEING THE PERSON

Parts of this chapter were adapted from "Finding Your Movement," *Bioenergetic Analysis,* Vol. 6, No. 1 (1995).

1. Alexander Lowen offers autobiographical accounts of his work with Reich and his development of bioenergetics in *Bioenergetics* and *Joy.*

2. Alexander Lowen, *Bioenergetics*, p. 40. For a description of the use of the stool, see Alexander Lowen, *Pleasure: A Creative Approach to Life*, p. 45. The use of the breathing stool and many other bioenergetic exercises are fully described in Alexander Lowen, and Leslie Lowen, *The Way to Vibrant Health: A Manual of Bioenergetic Exercises*.

3. Some of Lowen's views and opinions about orgastic potency and Reich are expressed in an interview conducted on the occasion of his eightieth birthday. *IIBA Journal*, Vol. 4, No. 1 (spring 1990), pp. 1–11. His position on orgastic potency is also clearly stated in *IIBA Journal*, Vol. 5, No. 2 (spring 1993), pp. 3–8.

4. *IIBA Journal*, Vol. 5, No. 2 (spring 1993), p. 6.

5. Ibid., p. 5.

6. Lowen, *Bioenergetics*, p. 30.

7. *IIBA Journal*, Vol. 5, No. 2 (spring 1993), p. 6.

8. Lowen, *Bioenergetics*, p. 43.

9. Lowen's discussion of pleasure in *Pleasure: A Creative Approach to Life*, is one of his most creative, enjoyable, and inspiring contributions.

10. Ibid., p. 44.

11. Alexander Lowen, *The Spirituality of the Body: Bioenergetics for Grace and Harmony*, p. 187.

12. Alexander Lowen, *The Spirituality of the Body*, pp. 114, 115, 188–198.

13. *IIBA Journal*, Vol. 5, No. 2 (spring 1993), p. 7.

14. At least since Descartes the philosophical problem of the duality of mind and body has been embedded in European thinking. The tool that Reich had at hand to deal with this problem was dialectical materialism, an analytic method he had absorbed from Marx, but which derived from the nineteenth-century German philosopher Hegel (1770–1831). From this background, Reich derived his concept of functional unity in identity and antithesis. This provides the philosophical underpinning for declaring mind and body to be both the same and different, an "antithetical unity," two expressions of a functional unity. For a good discussion of Reich's use of dialectical materialism see Boadella, *Wilhelm Reich, The Evolution of His Work*, pp. 240–242.

15. Alexander Lowen wrote an interesting essay on the bioenergetics of this sense of seeing. "Seeing is Understanding (Some Thoughts on the Subject)," in the *Newsletter* of the IIBA ,Vol. 8, No. 1 (winter 1988), pp. 1–2.

16. Lowen, *Joy*, p. 309.

17. Jane Goodal describes the agonizing apathy induced in chimpanzees kept in laboratory cages with little stimulation and with no contact and companionship with people or other chimpanzees in *Through A Window, My Thirty Years with the Chimpanzees of Gombe*, pp. 225–234.

18. *Char. An.*, Chap. 7, p. 156. This was written in 1930. Further discussion of this remarkable statement will be found in this volume, Chap. 5, "Genital Incest Desires."

19. *Function*, Chap. 8, p. 267.

20. *Millennium: Tribal Wisdom and the Modern World*, by David Maybury-Lewis, offers a pleasurable panorama of this plasticity. Thomas Gregor comments, "The anthropology of sexual behavior has established that sexuality is astonishingly plastic and variable in its expression from culture to culture." *Anxious Pleasures*, p. 3.

21. See Joseph E. LeDoux, "Emotion, Memory, and the Brain," *Scientific American*, Vol. 270, No. 6 (June 1994), pp. 50–57.

22. Contemporary stress research and theory substantiates this assertion through a number of programs of research. One summary is found in Sapolsky, *Why Zebras Don't Get Ulcers*, Chaps. 10, 11.

23. A much-used term, *burnout*, refers to this deep biological process.

24. Lowen, *Bioenergetics*, pp. 193–198, contains an introduction to grounding.

25. Lowen introduced the conception of the "pendular swing" in *Language of the Body*, e.g., pp. 66, 93.

26. This colloquialism was always a favorite of Alexander Lowen's, and it also usually fit him. "We describe a person who is vibrantly alive with feeling as being 'bright-eyed and bushy-tailed.'" *Narcissism*, p. 218.

27. Lowen, *Language of the Body*, p. 72

28. *Char. An.*, Chap. 13, section entitled, "The Intellect as Defense Function."

29. Lowen, *Language of the Body*, p. 78. A question seems to be raised by this analysis. Why aren't the feet considered to be the lower end of the grounding wave? The feet and legs support the energy swing, and in one way they are its lower end. If we consider a four-legged animal again, however, the two ends can only be seen as head and tail. The head and pelvis function as containers and reservoirs of energy in a way that the legs do not. The pelvis also functions in discharge; and while the legs discharge energy during locomotion, they do not function in a charge-discharge capacity as does the pelvis.

30. Lowen, *Language of the Body*, pp. 65–67.

31. Lowen, *Language of the Body*, p. 92. Lowen does not use the term, *pulsatory grounding wave*. My discussion of this aspect of grounding rests primarily on Part 1 of this book.

32. Susana Kaysen, *Girl, Interrupted*, p. 167.

33. The first, and perhaps the greatest teacher of psychotherapy I ever encountered said, "The most important task of a human being is to make up his mind—what's for him and what's not for him." In *Semrad: The Heart of a Therapist*, edited by Susan Rako and Harvey Mazer, p. 76.

34. See Lowen and Lowen, *The Way to Vibrant Health: A Manual of Bioenergetic Exercises*.

CHAPTER 4: THE SEXUAL MISERY OF OUR TIME

1. This is Wilhelm Reich's phrase. See, for example, *Function*, Chap. 6, pp. 177, 199. The closest to a definition is: "A humanity which has been forced for millennia to act contrary to its fundamental biological law and has, therefore, acquired a second nature which is actually a *counter*-nature, must needs get into an irrational frenzy when it tries to restore the fundamental biological function *and at the same time is afraid of it*." Ibid. p. 204.

2. With remarkable frequency patients say they became substitute husband, wife, or lover for a parent. This is a basis for later misery.

3. Alice Miller, in *Prisoners of Childhood, For Your Own Good*, and later works, has done magnificent service in tearing the hypocritical facade from parental brutality and punitive child rearing.

4. See Sigmund Freud's description of this "complete Oedipus complex which is twofold," in *The Ego and the Id*. Norton Library Edition, p. 23 (*SE* Vol. 19, p. 33).

5. For a similar conception, see: Stephen Sinatra, *Heartbreak and Heart Disease*, and Alexander Lowen, *Love, Sex, and Your Heart*, with an *Introduction* by Stephen Sinatra.

6. David S. Bell, *The Doctor's Guide to Chronic Fatigue Syndrome: Understanding, Treating, and Living with CFIDS.*

7. When someone uses this dreaded name from the Holocaust, I do not take it lightly. Often it is the correct word to depict a childhood.

8. Sigmund Freud, "Screen Memories" *CP* Vol. 5, pp. 47 ff. (*SE* Vol. 3, pp. 301ff.)

9. Female genital mutilation, however, is still practiced. See, Marguerite Holloway, "Trends in Women's Health: A Global View," *Scientific American,* Vol. 271, No. 2 (August 1994), p. 83. Of course, circumcision is too, and in most circles, no one considers it genital mutilation. It is. For an interesting and disturbing historical perspective see Peter Gay, *The Bourgeois Experience: Victoria to Freud,* Vol. 1, *The Education of the Senses.* The section on masturbation titled, "A Profession of Anxiety," pp. 294–318, gives some idea of the anti-sexual societal forces, unleashed in families, churches, and physicians offices, and directed against children and young adults, alike, that could, and still can, result in the deprivation of a sexual life.

CHAPTER 5: GENITAL INCEST DESIRES

Parts of this chapter were adapted from "Genital Incest Desire and its Actual Frustration," *Bioenergetic Analysis,* Vol. 4, No. 2 (1991).

1. Myron R. Sharaf, *Fury on Earth: A Biography of Wilhelm Reich,* Chap. 14, gives the story of Reich's break with organized psychoanalysis. Sharaf also discusses Reich's relationship with Freud's death instinct theory. David Boadella, in *Wilhelm Reich, The Evolution of His Work,* provides discussions of Reich's rejection of the death instinct theory.

2. "Freud tasted the miseries of self-imposed sexual frustration, about which he was to theorize so authoritatively later, in his own faultlessly bourgeois life." Peter Gay, *The Bourgeois Experience: Victoria to Freud,* Vol. 2, *The Tender Passion,* p. 11.

3. Sharaf, *Fury on Earth,* p. 40 ff. I have relied extensively on Sharaf's biography.

4. Wilhelm Reich, *Passion of Youth: An Autobiography, 1897 to 1922.*

5. See Sharaf, *Fury on Earth,* Chap. 3, "Reich's Childhood and Youth: 1897–1917."

6. In *Freud,* Peter Gay goes over many important aspects of the controversies while remaining staunchly sympathetic, and he mentions a good deal of the literature. In Gay's *The Bourgeois Experience: Victoria to Freud,* Vol. 1, *The Education of the Senses,* some of the most interesting materials that he presents are the cultural manifestations of men's fear of and anxiety about women, especially, Chap. 2, "Offensive Women and Defensive Men." Gay points out here that Freud never questioned women's sexual drive, understood it to be suppressed by the culture, and more importantly developed the tools for revealing, understanding, and studying men's anxieties about women (pp. 165–167).

7. See Gay, *Freud,* section titled, "Woman, the Dark Continent." Freud's was not the first generation of men to consider the female genital a mutilation. See Josephine Lowndes Sevely, *Eve's Secrets: A New Theory of Female Sexuality.* She quotes (p. 7) Galen, a Greek physician (AD. 129–c. 199), who called it that too.

8. "The Passing of the Oedipus Complex" (1924), *CP,* p. 269 ff. (*SE* Vol. 19, p. 173ff).

9. *The Ego and the Id,* p. 23, Norton Library Edition. (*SE* Vol. 19, p. 33).

10. "The Passing of the Oedipus-Complex," *CP* Vol. 2, p. 271–273. (*SE* Vol. 19, pp. 175–177.)

11. The reader may believe this sensibility about the castration complex has been left behind by psychoanalysis. It has not. See Peter L. Giovacchini, *Narrative Textbook of Psychoanalysis*. See p. 106: "With the emergence of sexual feelings toward the mother, the father makes a thunderous, threatening, forbidding appearance."

12. Even as sensible a man as D. W. Winnicott failed in perceiving the horror of the idea of the castration complex. "Guilt implied that the boy could tolerate and hold the conflict, which is in fact an inherent conflict, one that belongs to healthy life." Winnicott, "The Sense of Guilt," in *The Maturational Process and the Facilitating Environment*, p. 17.

13. Gay, *Freud*, p. 89. "It matters to the history of psychoanalysis that Freud is very much his father's son, dreaming and worrying more about paternal than maternal relations." The title Gay gives to the last chapter of *Freud* is, "To Die in Freedom." On the surface he was referring to Freud's escape from Nazi held Vienna. I cannot but wonder if he means it at another level as well.

14. Genesis 22.

15. Alice Miller, *The Untouched Key*, Pt. Three, Chap. 1, "When Isaac Arises from the Sacrificial Altar," p. 141.

16. *Char. An.*, Chap. 7, pp. 153–158.

17. Ibid., p. 156.

18. Ibid.

19. Ibid.

20. *The Mass Psychology of Fascism*. Some of his discussion is summarized in *Function*, Chap. 6, pp. 203–220.

21. "Heredity and the Aetiology of the Neuroses," 1896. *CP* Vol. 1, pp. 148–149. (*SE* Vol. 3, p. 163).

CHAPTER 6: SEXUAL CRAZINESS VERSUS SEXUAL PASSION

Parts of this chapter were adapted from "Genital Incest Desire and its Actual Frustration," *Bioenergetic Analysis*, Vol. 4, No. 2 (1991).

1. See the stories of Nancy, Chap. 7, and Carl, Chap. 13.

2. Study of the sexual craziness of everyday life deserves more attention. A brief example must suffice: "It is about a socialist, antifamily political movement that encourages women to leave their husbands, kill their children, practice witchcraft, destroy capitalism and become lesbians." (*Time*, Sept. 7, 1992.) Psychotic discourse has a ring signally similar to this. The words are those of a politician of national stature ostensibly speaking about the equal rights amendment.

3. Sigmund Freud, *Three Essays on the Theory of Sexuality*, in *Freud on Women*, edited by Elizabeth Young-Bruehl, p. 117, n. 16. (*SE* Vol. 7, p. 189 n. 1.)

4. Sigmund Freud, *New Introductory Lectures*, Chap. 3, p. 112 (*SE* Vol. 22, p. 80.)

5. Ibid, Chap. 3, p. 104. (*SE* Vol. 22, p. 73.)

6. A recent movie, *Pretty Woman*, popular in the United States, captured, in simple, clear form, a significant version of these delusions. The theme is that a young woman, working as a street prostitute, is "saved" and turns into a "pretty

woman" (as pretty as the *prettiest* woman), once she is accepted, needed, and loved by an irresistible, phallically powerful man. Her line in the movie is, "I'll save you right back," supposedly by rescuing, with her "prettiness," his phallic potential (his capacity for sexual love) from his compulsive pursuit of money and power (actual impotence). The delusions given expression in this wish fulfilling fantasy are that the bodily and inner feelings associated with the degraded sexual images can be negated by the right lover, and the idealized delusions about the self and the other can become reality. Delusional images—"pretty woman"/phallic potency—are made real. Degraded, damaged senses of self—whore on her part, helplessly dependent, anxiously impotent, child-failure on his—vanish. This truly captures a nearly universal delusion about how love works.

7. Lynn Margulis and Dorion Sagan, *Mystery Dance: On the Evolution of Human Sexuality,* p. 102.

8. Ibid. p. 119.

9. Ibid. p. 123.

10. Ibid. p. 32.

CHAPTER 7: SHOCK, GENITAL INJURY, AND DISSOCIATION

1. Robert M. Sapolsky, *Why Zebras Don't Get Ulcers,* Chap. 9, "Stress Induced Analgesia."

2. Symbolic meanings of the foot fetish are not adequate explanations of a behavior. Meanings don't eventuate in behavior; the need to discharge excitation and find fulfillment do.

3. "Post-traumatic Stress Disorder—Part II," *The Harvard Mental Health Letter,* Vol. 13, No. 1 (July 1996), pp. 1–5.

4. For the use of kicking in bioenergetic analysis, see Alexander Lowen and Leslie Lowen, *The Way to Vibrant Health: A Manual of Bioenergetic Exercises,* p. 43; and Alexander Lowen, *Joy,* pp. 59, 129.

CHAPTER 8: THE HATED CHILD

This chapter was adapted from "The Hated Child," *Bioenergetic Analysis,* Vol. 3, No. 2 (1988/89).

1. Jean Liedloff, *The Continuum Concept,* Chap. 12.

2. For example, Richard Rhodes, *A Hole in the World, An American Boyhood.*

3. Alexander Lowen, *Pleasure,* p. 178.

4. Ibid.

5. In Lowen, *Pleasure*; Alexander Lowen, *Love, Sex, and Your Heart,* p. 14.

6. *Char. An.,* Chap. 13, p. 290.

7. "After all, 1995 will not be just another year. It will mark the 50th anniversary of the end of the cruelest of all wars in recorded history. But it should also remind us of our never-ending struggle for an even greater victory: good over evil, compassion over hatred—in effect, man's victory over himself." Elie Wiesel, *Boston Sunday Globe. Parade,* December 25, 1994.

8. Lowen, *Love, Sex, and Your Heart,* p. 14.

9. See Chap. 4, n. 1; also Alexander Lowen, *Bioenergetics,* p. 104. Reich introduced the concept of a second nature in this sense in *Function,* Chap. 6, p. 204.

10. I find hate a distressing topic, and I guess it must be to many others too. For example, I find no reference at all to hate in two important psychoanalytic works on the borderline personality: Gerald Adler, *Borderline Psychopathology and Its Treatment*; Otto Kernberg, *Borderline Conditions and Pathological Narcissism*. Kernberg uses the phrases "intolerable reality in the interpersonal realm" (p. 231) and "covert but intense aggression" (p. 234), which I understand as euphemisms for hate, in discussing the etiology of the narcissistic personality. He can't quite call hate by its name. Hate must also be understood on the larger cultural scale as Peter Gay attempted in *The Bourgeois Experience from Victoria to Freud*, Vol. 3, *The Cultivation of Hatred*.

CHAPTER 9: SHAME AND GUILT

1. I have heard other dreams of this sort: the penis being sliced up; the penis being chewed to pieces by the person himself.

2. Sigmund Freud, "On Narcissism: An Introduction." *CP* Vol. 4, p. 30 ff. (*SE* vol. 14, 167–175.)

3. Andrew P. Morrison, *Shame: The Underside of Narcissism*. Morrison discusses why shame had not received the clinical attention given to guilt, p. 5.

4. *Webster's New World Dictionary of the American Language, Second College Edition*. New York: Simon and Schuster, 1980.

5. Ibid.

6. Morrison, in *Shame*, repeatedly refers to the "searing" quality of shame. See for example, p. 36.

7. *Compact Edition of the Oxford English Dictionary*, New York: Oxford University Press, 1971.

8. Ibid.

9. Ibid.

10. Beautifully described in compassionate detail from a psychoanalytic perspective by Andrew Morrison in *Shame*.

11. I discuss the "institutionalization" of the private belief system in Philip M. Helfaer, *The Psychology of Religious Doubt*.

12. Morrison, *Shame*, p. 36. This selection is not meant to give a full picture of Morrison's views.

13. Ibid., p. 182.

CHAPTER 10: THE VITAL CONNECTION

1. The term is also used by Stephen Sinatra, "Heartbreak, Heartache, and Cardiac Pain: A Study of Coronary-Prone Behavior," *IIBA Journal*, Vol. 3, No. 1 (summer 1987); also *Heartbreak and Heart Disease*. Alexander Lowen also uses the term (e.g., *Joy*, p. 135). I don't know which of us originated the term in the way I am using it.

2. "Guilt implied that the boy could tolerate and hold the conflict, which is in fact an inherent conflict, one that belongs to healthy life." D. W. Winnicott, "The Sense of Guilt," in *The Maturational Process and the Facilitating Environment*, p. 17.

3. No one has said it more graphically and to the point than Wilhelm Reich. "Sex repression serves the function of keeping humans more easily in a state of submissiveness, just as the castration of stallions and bulls serves that of securing willing beasts of burden." *Function*, p. 195.

4. Cultural expressions of this complex exist. Cheerleaders are one form. A more interesting example is found in the American practice of sending attractive young women to entertain soldiers who are on the front lines of combat. The men have no opportunity for sex with these women; the women can only serve to stir up the men and frustrate them, supposedly reminding them of what they are fighting for. On a National Public Radio broadcast, I heard one woman describe her experience as a "Dolly Girl" during the Vietnam War. She and others were sent by the Red Cross to serve refreshments and entertain soldiers who had just come from terrible fire fights.

5. As early as 1908, Sigmund Freud described in excruciating detail the price of the tightrope walk he himself was depicting for modern people, in a paper titled "Civilized Sexual Morality and Modern Nervous Illness." Its poignant message is still relevant. (*SE* Vol. 9 pp. 179 ff.)

CHAPTER 11: A FACILITATING ENVIRONMENT FOR SELF-RESPECT

1. Reich used "the red thread" to refer to the main theme of a character analysis. See Elsworth Baker, *Man in the Trap,* pp. 62–63.

2. We owe to D. W. Winnicott the felicitous conception of the maturing organism in the good-enough facilitating environment. *The Maturational Process and the Facilitating Environment,* pp. 223, 239. Jean Liedloff's study, *The Continuum Concept,* adds a further dimension and broadens the conception of the facilitating environment. Her concept of the continuum describes the evolutionary significance of the congruence between inherent maturational capacity and parenting response. See pp. 21, 23, 25–26, 223, and 239.

3. I have deliberately avoided the word *phase.*

4. These periods may be compared with the phases in Margaret Mahler et al. *The Psychological Birth of the Human Infant: Symbiosis and Individuation.* Period 1 corresponds to the forerunners of the separation-individuation process, the first subphase, "differentiation and the development of the body image," and the second subphase, "practicing." Period 2 corresponds to the third subphase, "rapprochement," and to the fourth subphase of the separation-individuation process, "consolidation of individuality and the beginnings of emotional object constancy." Period 3 corresponds to the later part of the fourth subphase and "beyond."

5. Daniel N. Stern, *The Interpersonal World of the Infant: A View from Psychoanalysis and Developmental Psychology,* p. 14.

6. Ibid., p. 28.

7. Winnicott, *The Maturational Processes and the Facilitating Environment,* p. 49.

8. Liedloff, *The Continuum Concept,* p. 49ff.

9. Liedloff describes the horror of this kind of pain in full and appropriate detail. *The Continuum Concept,* pp. 62–63.

10. Kathleen Spivack, "The Abandoned Baby," in *Swimmer in the Spreading Dawn.*

11. An article in the August 1994 issue of *Scientific American,* "Trends in Women's Health: A Global View," offers disturbing evidence of the profound world-wide impact of the reaction to female children as the less valued sex. The widespread practice of female genital mutilation is discussed in the same article.

12. D. W. Stern, *The Interpersonal World of the Infant,* pp. 42–43.

13. Ibid., p. 8.

14. One theory of borderline personality disorder is that it represents a failure to acquire the "holding soothing introject." Gerald Adler, *Borderline Psychopathology and Its Treatment.*

15. Vernon R. Wiehe with T. Herring, *Perilous Rivalry: When Siblings Become Abusive.*

CHAPTER 12: THE INDIVIDUAL IN THE COUPLE

This chapter was adapted from "The Individual in the Couple," *Bioenergetic Analysis,* Vol. 1, No. 1 (1984).

1. Alexander Lowen introduced the concept of fate into bioenergetics. See *Fear of Life,* p. 38, and in the same book, Lowen notes (p. 46) that Freud also spoke of fate in connection with neurosis. Lowen also discusses "the fate of love" (p. 64).

2. See Lynn Margulis and Dorion Sagan, *Mystery Dance: On the Evolution of Human Sexuality,* pp. 51–58. They stay together not only for the sake of their long-dependent children but also because of the peculiarities of male competition and paternity.

3. This characteristic is termed "neotony," the retention of such juvenile characteristics as hairlessness, throughout life. Our sensitive skin makes possible the benefits of, and need for, contactful and nurturing touch throughout life. See Margulis and Sagan, *Mystery Dance,* "Our neotenous heritage surfaces in the response not only of parents but of lovers . . ." (pp. 110–111).

4. The position I am developing here is different from the one taken by Alexander Lowen. He says, in *Fear of Life,* "In effect . . . each boy marries his mother and each girl marries her father" (p. 37). The shift I am making is important. Neither in reality, nor "in effect," does one—as a man or woman—marry one's parent. There will, however, be awakened in each man the drive to resolve with his wife, the sexual issues (genital injury) that originated in his relations with his mother *and father*; and conversely each woman will be driven to resolve her sexual issues (genital injury) with her husband as those originated in her relation with her father *and mother.* This formulation puts an important developmental process directly into the realm of adulthood where it actually occurs, rather than viewing it simply as a neurotic, regressive, infantile matter. With whom other should one resolve one's sexual conflicts if not one's wife or husband? With whom else does one have such an opportunity? The therapeutic relationship activates the same developmental drive. Peculiarities, confusions, and abuse can arise in therapy, because, while the focus of the drive remains the repair of genital injury, a central core of that repair cannot be realized in the therapeutic relationship; it can only ultimately be realized in the sexual relationship.

5. At one time I thought this underlying "glue" was a trend toward actual symbiosis or fusion which lay within everybody. In this view, I was following Margaret Mahler and her associates: "This creates an everlasting longing for the actual or coenesthetically fantasized, wish-fulfilled . . . state (of fusion) . . . for which deep down in the original primal unconscious . . . every human being strives." Margaret S. Mahler, Fred Pine, and Anni Bergman, *The Psychological Birth of the Human Infant. Symbiosis and Individuation,* p. 227. I no longer believe this explains the enmeshed condition in a couple.

6. Alice Miller, *Prisoners of Childhood* (published in paperback as *The Drama of the Gifted Child*).

7. Wilhelm Reich referred to character as a trap. *"The trap is man's emotional structure, his character structure."* From *The Murder of Christ,* quoted by Elseworth Baker in the epigraph to *Man in the Trap.*

CHAPTER 13: LIVING ONE'S SEXUALITY

This chapter was adapted from "The Long Road to Personhood," *Bioenergetic Analysis,* Vol. 4, No. 1 (1990).

1. Daniel J. Levinson et al., *The Seasons of a Man's Life.* An "era" in the life-span is about 25 years (p. 18), and there are a series of overlapping eras (pp. 18–39). Regarding little attention to middle adulthood and beyond, see pp. 328–330. Regarding the definition of individuation and its development after forty, see pp. 195–196.

2. Genesis 32: 25–26, 32, 29. *The Torah. The Five Books of Moses.* A new translation of The Holy Scriptures according to the Masoretic text. First Section. Philadelphia/Jerusalem: The Jewish Publication Society, 1962.

3. Bertrand Russell, dedicating his autobiography to the woman he loved, wrote:

> Now, old & near my end,
> > I have known you,
> And, knowing you,
> I have found both ecstasy & peace,
> > I have known rest.
> After so many lonely years,
> I know what life & love may be.
> Now, if I sleep,
> I shall sleep fulfilled.

The Autobiography of Bertrand Russell, Boston: Bantam edition/Little Brown, 1951, Epigraph.

4. "For whoever would save his life will lose it . . ." Mark 8:35. Hillel, a Pharisaic teacher of the generation before Jesus of Nazareth, said, "If I am not for myself, who will be for me? And if I am only for myself, what am I . . . ?" Quoted in Abba Eban, *Heritage: Civilization and the Jews.*

5. A concept of fulfillment appears in the writings of Martin Buber, one of the twentieth-century giants of moral and religious thinking. "[T]hey have never tasted the fulfillment of existence, that their life does not participate in true, fulfilled existence, that, as it were, it passes true existence by." Buber, *The Way of Man According to the Teaching of Hasidism,* p. 37. In addition, fulfillment, according to Buber, has to do with the body. "[U]nification of the soul would be thoroughly misunderstood if 'soul' were taken to mean anything but the whole man, body and spirit together. The soul is not really united, unless all bodily energies, all the limbs of the body, are united." Ibid. p. 25.

6. Buber, *The Way of Man:* "The highest culture of the soul remains basically arid and barren unless, day by day, waters of life pour forth into the soul from those little encounters to which we give their due" (p. 39).

7. The natural quality of sociality is well described by Jean Liedloff in *The Continuum Concept.*

8. When asked what a normal person should be capable of, Freud said, "Love and work." Erik Erikson tells this story in *Childhood and Society* (pp. 264–265). In his telling of the story, Erikson reveals his ambivalence, even cynicism, towards sexuality and genitality.

9. The cover of *People Weekly*, a magazine, October 18, 1993, shows a middle-aged actor with his attractive-looking woman companion (in a revealing gown). The caption reads "The Sexiest Couple Alive!" What could this possibly mean? The briefest consideration of any possible real meaning makes a mockery of sexual love, and in fact leaves one slightly nauseous. See also Lewis H. Lapham, "Sex Is Merchandising, and the Product of Desire, like Kleenex, is Disposable," in *Harper's* (August 1997), p. 39.

Television commercials actually play little stories of romance in which the union of a couple occurs as the offshoot not of sexual excitement for each other but out of a shared erotic feeling for a food or some other product. One gathers that these little stories are offered with a sophisticated tongue in cheek, as droll irony. But what is the irony about if not sexual love itself?

Such is the plasticity of human erotic life, that in fact these commercials represent a degree of social reality: eroticism in the service not of pleasure, reproduction, or personal fulfillment—but of product sales. The confusion in this is horrifying if looked at for what it is, but does anyone really want to look at it?

My point here is not that such things are immoral or wrong. Whether they are or not, they reveal something deeper—the lack of a sexual ethic and a resulting exploitative approach to life. Sales, not respect.

10. Genital attitudes pervade everyday social life and organizational and institutional settings, and they deserve more attention than I give them. Some relevant discussions: A. H. Maslow, H. Rand, and S. Newman, "Some Parallels between Sexual and Dominance Behavior of Infra-human Primates and the Fantasies of Patients in Psychotherapy," (*Journal of Nervous and Mental Disease*, Vol. 131 (1960), pp. 202–212; also in *Interpersonal Dynamics*, 2d ed., W. Bennis et al., eds., Homewood, Ill: Dorsey. Philip E. Slater, *Microcosm: Structural, Psychological and Religious Evolution in Groups*, gives a lengthy discussion of the genital attitudes that appear in the evolution of small group life. There is also some reference in W. E. Bion, *Experiences in Groups*, especially the pairing group.

11. Alexander Lowen discusses the issue of "specialness" and "ordinariness" in *Fear of Life* and *Narcissism*.

12. Edward O. Wilson, *The Diversity of Life*.

13. "There flashed upon my mind, unforeseen and unsought, the phrase 'reverence for life.'" Albert Schweitzer, *Out of My Life and Thought*, p. 155.

14. *The Diversity of Life*, p. 348. Wilson's ideas about an environmental ethic were influenced by Aldo Leopold, one of the fathers of the American conservation movement. In Leopold's *A Sand County Almanac and Sketches Here and There*, he writes about "the land ethic" saying, "It is inconceivable to me that an ethical relation to land can exist without love, respect, and admiration for land, and a high regard for its value. . . . I mean value in the philosophic sense" (p. 223). Love, respect, and admiration would be the living of the ethical attitude.

REFERENCES

ABBREVIATION

IIBA Journal: *Bioenergetic Analysis: The Clinical Journal of the International Institute of Bioenergetic Analysis* (144 E. 36th St., New York, NY 10016)

Adler, Gerald. 1985. *Borderline Psychopathology and Its Treatment*. New York: Jason Aronson.

Baker, Elseworth. 1967. *Man in the Trap*. New York: Collier Books/Macmillan.

Bell, David S. 1994. *The Doctor's Guide to Chronic Fatigue Syndrome: Understanding, Treating, and Living with CFIDS*. Reading, MA: Addison-Wesley.

Bion, W.E. 1961. *Experiences in Groups*. New York: Basic Books.

Boadella, David. 1973. *Wilhelm Reich, The Evolution of His Work*. Chicago: Contemporary Books, Inc. Available in a Dell paperback.

Buber, Martin. 1966. *The Way of Man According to the Teaching of Hasidism*. New York: The Citadel Press.

Eban, Abba. 1984. *Heritage: Civilization and the Jews*. New York: Summit Books.

Erikson, Erik H. 1963. *Childhood and Society,* 2d ed. New York: Norton.

Freud, Sigmund. 1933. *New Introductory Lectures*. W. J. H. Sprott, tr. New York: Norton.

———. 1953–74. *Standard Edition of the Complete Psychological Works*. London: Hogarth Press

———. 1959. *Collected Papers,* Vol. 1–5. New York: Basic Books.

———. 1962. *The Ego and the Id*. Norton Library Edition.

———. 1990. *Freud on Women,* Edited and with an Introduction by Elizabeth Young-Bruehl. New York: Norton.

Gay, Peter. 1984. *The Bourgeois Experience: Victoria to Freud,* Vol. 1, *The Education of the Senses*. New York: Oxford University Press.

———. 1986. *The Bourgeois Experience: Victoria to Freud,* Vol. 2, *The Tender Passion*. New York: Oxford University Press.

———. 1988. *Freud: A Life for Our Time*. New York: Norton.

————.1993. *The Bourgeois Experience: Victoria to Freud,* Vol. 3, *The Cultivation of Hatred.* New York: Norton.

Giovacchini, Peter L. 1987. *Narrative Textbook of Psychoanalysis.* New York: Jason Aronson.

Goldstein, Rebecca. 1983. *The Mind Body Problem.* New York: Penguin.

Goodal, Jane. 1990. *Through a Window: My Thirty Years with the Chimpanzees of Gombe.* Boston: Houghton Mifflin.

Gregor, Thomas. 1985. *Anxious Pleasures: The Sexual Lives of an Amazonian People.* Chicago: University of Chicago Press.

Helfaer, Philip M. 1972. *The Psychology of Religious Doubt.* Boston: Beacon Press.

————. 1990. Review of *Passion of Youth. IIBA Journal,* Vol. 4, No. 1, pp. 161–164.

Kaysen, Susana. 1993. *Girl, Interrupted.* New York: Turtle Bay Books, Random House.

Kernberg, Otto. 1975. *Borderline Conditions and Pathological Narcissism.* New York: Jason Aronson.

Klerman, G. L., and Weissman, M. M. 1989. "Increasing rates of depression." *Journal of the American Medical Association.* Vol. 261, pp. 2229–2235.

LeDoux, Joseph E. 1994. "Emotion, Memory, and the Brain." *Scientific American.* Vol. 270, No. 6 (June), pp. 50–57.

Leopold, Aldo. 1949. *A Sand County Almanac and Sketches Here and There.* New York: Oxford University Press.

Levinson, Daniel J. et al. 1978. *The Seasons of a Man's Life.* New York: Ballantine Books.

Liedloff, Jean. 1977. *The Continuum Concept.* Reading, Massachusetts: Addison-Wesley.

Lowen, Alexander. 1958. *The Language of the Body.* New York: Macmillan.

————. 1970. *Pleasure: A Creative Approach to Life.* New York: Coward McCann, Penguin Books, paperback. 1975.

————. 1975. *Bioenergetics.* New York: Coward, McCann, & Geoghegan. Penguin paperback edition.

————. 1977. With Leslie Lowen. *The Way to Vibrant Health: A Manual of Bioenergetic Exercises.* New York: Harper Colophon Books.

————. 1980. *Fear of Life.* New York: Macmillan. Collier paperback edition.

————. 1983. *Narcissism: Denial of the True Self.* New York: Macmillan. Collier paperback edition.

————. 1988a. *Love, Sex, and Your Heart.* New York: Macmillan.

————. 1988b. "Seeing Is Understanding (Some Thoughts on the Subject)," Newsletter of the *IIBA,* Vol. 8, No. 1, pp. 1–2.

————. 1990a. Interview. *IIBA Journal.* Vol. 4, No. 1, pp. 1–11.

————. 1990b. *The Spirituality of the Body.* New York: Macmillan.

————. 1993. "Sexuality: From Reich to the Present." *IIBA Journal.* Vol. 5, No. 2, pp. 3–8.

————. 1995. *Joy: The Surrender to the Body and to Life.* New York: Arkana/Penguin.

Mahler, Margaret, Fred Pine, and Anni Bergman. 1975. *The Psychological Birth of the Human Infant: Symbiosis and Individuation.* New York: Basic Books.

Margulis, Lynn, and Dorion Sagan. 1991. *Mystery Dance: On the Evolution of Human Sexuality.* New York: Summit Books.

Maslow, A. H., H. Rand, and S. Newman. 1960. "Some Parallels between Sexual and Dominance Behavior of Infra-human Primates and the Fantasies of Patients in Psychotherapy." *Journal of Nervous and Mental Disease*, Vol. 131, pp. 202–212. Also in *Interpersonal Dynamics*, 2d ed. W. Bennis et al., eds. Homewood, Il: Dorsey.

Maybury-Lewis, David. 1992. *Millennium: Tribal Wisdom and the Modern World*. New York: Viking.

Miller, Alice. 1981. *Prisoners of Childhood*. New York: Basic Books.

———. 1990a. *For Your Own Good*. New York: Noonday Press, Farrar Straus & Giroux.

———. 1990b. *The Untouched Key*. New York: Doubleday.

Monk, Ray. 1990. *Ludwig Wittgenstein: The Duty of Genius*. New York: the Free Press.

Morrison, Andrew P. 1989. *Shame: The Underside of Narcissism*. Hillsdale, NJ: Analytic Press.

Pine, Fred. 1990. *Drive, Ego, Object, & Self*. New York: Basic Books.

Pulver, Sydney E. 1986. "Narcissism: The Term and the Concept." In *Essential Papers on Narcissism*, edited by Andrew P. Morrison. New York: New York University Press.

Rako, Susan, and Harvey Mazer, eds. 1980. *Semrad: The Heart of a Therapist*. New York: Jason Aronson.

Reich, Wilhelm. 1961. *The Function of the Orgasm*. New York: Farrar, Straus, & Giroux.

———. 1970. *The Mass Psychology of Fascism*. New York: Farrar, Straus, & Giroux.

———. 1972. *Character Analysis*; Third, enlarged edition. New York: Farrar, Straus, & Giroux.

———. 1973. *The Cancer Biopathy*. New York: Farrar, Straus, & Giroux.

———. 1980. *Genitality: In the Theory and Therapy of Neurosis*. New York: Farrar, Straus, & Giroux.

———. 1982. *The Bioelectrical Investigation of Sexuality and Anxiety*. New York: Farrar, Straus, & Giroux.

———. 1983. *Children of the Future*. New York: Farrar, Straus, & Giroux.

———. 1988. *Passion of Youth, An Autobiography, 1897–1922*. Edited by Mary Boyd Higgins and Chester M. Raphael, M.D., with translations by Philip Schmitz and Jerri Tompkins.

Rhodes, Richard. 1990. *A Hole in the World, An American Boyhood*. New York: Simon and Schuster.

Sapolsky, Robert M. 1994. *Why Zebras Don't Get Ulcers, A Guide to Stress, Stress-Related Diseases, and Coping*. New York: W. H. Freeman and Co.

Schweitzer, Albert. 1990. *Out of My Life and Thought: An Autobiography*. (A. B. Lemke, tr.). New York: Henry Holt.

Seifriz, William E. 1954. Filmed lecture and demonstrations.

Sevely, Josephine Lowndes. 1987. *Eve's Secrets: A New Theory of Female Sexuality*. New York: Random House.

Sharaf, Myron R. 1983. *Fury on Earth: A Biography of Wilhelm Reich*. New York: St. Martin's Press/Marek.

Sinatra, Stephen. 1987. "Heartbreak, Heartache, and Cardiac Pain: A Study of Coronary-Prone Behavior." *IIBA Journal*. Vol. 3, No. 1, pp. 55–63.

————. 1996. *Heartbreak and Heart Disease*. New Canaan, CT: Keats Publishing.

Slater, Philip E. 1966. *Microcosm: Structural, Psychological and Religious Evolution in Groups*. New York: Wiley.

Spivack, Kathleen. 1981. *Swimmer in the Spreading Dawn*. Bedford, MA: Applewood Books.

Stern, Daniel N. 1985. *The Interpersonal World of the Infant: A View from Psychoanalysis and Developmental Psychology*. New York: Basic Books.

White, Marjorie Taggart. "Self Relations, Object Relations, and Pathological Narcissism." In *Essential Papers on Narcissism*, edited by Andrew P. Morrison. New York: New York University Press.

Wiehe, Vernon R., with T. Herring. 1991. *Perilous Rivalry: When Siblings Become Abusive*. Lexington, MA: Lexington Books.

Wilson, Edward O. 1992. *The Diversity of Life*. Cambridge, MA: Belknap Press of Harvard University.

Winnicott, D. W. 1965. *The Maturational Process and the Facilitating Environment*. New York: International University Press.

Wittgenstein, Ludwig. 1953. *Philosophical Investigations*. New York: Macmillan.

INDEX

About the Author

PHILIP M. HELFAER, Ph.D., maintains an independent psychological and bioenergetic practice. He is a member of the Faculty of the International Institute for Bioenergetic Analysis, and teaches in Israel and Norway, as well as the United States.